1001 ways to operate your business more profitably

Books by Mel Mandell

Being Safe (Saturday Review Press, 1972; Warner Paperback
  Library, 1973).

*The Handbook of Business & Industrial Security &
  Protection* (Prentice-Hall, Inc., 1973).

Mr. Mandell also contributed chapters to

Miniaturization, ed. by Horace D. Gilbert (Van
  Nostrand Reinhold Co., 1961).

The Encyclopedia of Management, ed. by Carl Heyel, 2d
  ed. (Van Nostrand Reinhold Co., 1973).

*Handbook of Modern Office Management &
  Administrative Services,* ed. by Carl Heyel
  (McGraw-Hill Book Co., 1972).

1001 ways to operate your business more profitably

MEL MANDELL

1975
Dow Jones-Irwin, Inc.
Homewood, Illinois 60430

First Printing, June 1975

ISBN 0-87094-097-X
Library of Congress Catalog Card No. 75–7278

Printed in the United States of America

To RUTH BURGER
My "super" editor at
The Research Institute of America

Acknowledgments

To my good friend Jack Lyndall, senior editor of *Fleet Owner,* for his many wise suggestions on cutting the cost of operating trucks; to Ira G. Corn, Jr., vice-chairman of Michigan General Corp., for providing some confidential information; to James T. Clark of International Business Machines Corp., for his careful review of Chapter 4; to my typist, Anita McCarthy, for her dedication and responsiveness; and, finally, to my son Matt for putting up with my lack of attention when I was immersed in creating this book.

May 1975   MEL MANDELL

Contents

chapter 1

Introduction

THE WORST RECESSION since the Great Depression is gripping the nation and much of the world as this is written. Adding to the burdens of the businessman are continued inflation, shortages of natural gas, the prospect of much higher prices for oil and the myriad products made out of petroleum, shutdowns of nuclear reactors and other threats to vital power supplies posed by major utilities approaching bankruptcy, deterioration of the financially strapped railroads, seemingly impossible standards imposed for the health and safety of workers, and the closing down of vital suppliers of raw materials because of pollution.

Taken altogether, these problems might well induce in businessmen the sense of "helplessness" that U.N. Secretary General Kurt Waldheim sees gripping so much of the world.

If you are the kind of businessman who has been or is likely to be overcome by helplessness, this book is not for you. First, because there are many, many ways—more than the 1,001 indicated in the title—to plug up all the drains on profits. Second, and this is the most significant single notion advanced here, the aggressive business executive should be taking advantage of current conditions to revitalize his company and make it emerge from hard times a much stronger organization–absolutely as well as relative to competition.

The revitalization process should begin with your employees. After decades of near-continuous prosperity, too many Americans have forgotten what it is to give a day's work for a day's pay. Aside from the question of exerting themselves, many employees just don't give a damn. Now, when their jobs may be at stake, is the time to reinspire and reenergize your employees—including executives.

Employees should be taking greater responsibility not just worrying about what they are doing. During the period of shortages one experienced production manager said that the best way to handle the situation "is to make the product right in the first place."

The need for greater responsibility does not apply only to production workers. Clerical workers have a responsibility to cut down on all the waste associated with creating and handling paperwork, as detailed in Chapter 9. Sales personnel need some remotivation too, particularly when business is declining or if yours is one of the rare companies still enjoying a seller's market. Instead of savoring the latter, businessmen should worry about what happens to salesmen when they deteriorate into mere order-takers. How to keep salesmen on their toes during seller's markets is detailed in Chapter 7. Greater responsiveness to the market is also one of the fringe benefits of installing the sophisticated inventory controls detailed in Chapter 4. The concept of instituting improvements with many fringe benefits beyond the initial and main objective cannot be stressed enough.

One of the best ways to remotivate employees is for your executives to set the example. What kind of an example? First, by driving to work in a small or compact car or, even better, as part of a car pool. Next, by using the company plane—if you still have one—only for business purposes. When you leave your office for lunch or any extended absence turn off the lights. To help all employees accommodate to higher temperatures in summer work in short sleeves without a jacket or tie. Conversely, in winter executives can set the style by wearing sweaters to work under their jackets. As a result of France's stringent efforts to hold down imports of oil, offices are much colder during winter working hours. President Giscard d'Estaing is setting the example by wearing a turtleneck sweater at the Elysee Palace. (It's much warmer than a red sash.)

Do you still need a private secretary? Why not reinforce the growing trend toward more executives per secretary by sharing your secretary with one or more executives. In many companies the ratio of secretaries to executives has declined from the now old-fashioned ratio of one-to-one to one-to-five.

Giving up your private secretary is suggested as much to downgrade the importance of executive perquisites as to as to raise clerical efficiency. In fact, there is a strong emphasis throughout this book on "asset conservation" as the new watchword to replace the "image building" of the affluent 60s.

DEADWOOD BEWARE

What a perfect time this is to eliminate all the supernumeraries in your company, the empire builders, the bumbling relatives, the time-servers, and especially the executive deadwood.

The general manager of a thriving job shop "whose profits were lagging behind sales" told me how current conditions provided the right situation for pulling a real thorn out of his side. The thorn was an elder brother of the company's founder, president, and majority stockholder. If this unproductive executive had merely been grossly overpaid, he would not have been such a problem. More importantly he was damaging the job shop because he was a real obstructionist and because he caused foul-ups. Moreover, his reputation as a foul-up was so widely accepted within the company that others used it as an excuse for failures with which he was only peripherally involved. He also was blocking the path of others to higher positions, with the result that some good people left the company while others of lesser talent stayed.

The general manager, who was neither a member of the family nor a stockholder, waited until the president took off for Europe on an extended vacation. Then he called the brother in and told him he was to be retired effective immediately. To his great relief and surprise, the brother did not protest his forced retirement and made no effort to reach his younger brother in Europe. As a result, when the president returned, he was presented with a fait accompli, which he made no effort to reverse and did not criticize. Naturally he was aware of his elder brother's deficiencies. Perhaps he was secretly pleased that he had not been forced to push out his own brother.

THE SPECTRE OF A NEW ENERGY CRISIS

In addition to all the other concerns of the businessman, there is always the possibility that the energy crisis will intensify.

When the Arab oil embargo was imposed, I realized immediately that ultimately it would have a beneficial effect on the United States. For years experts in government, industry, and private groups, such as the Ford Foundation, had been charting and deploring the profligate consumption of over one third of the world's annual output of raw materials by less than 6 percent of the world's burgeoning population—us.

How long would the rest of the world accept our waste and relative overconsumption? Before the embargo the less affluent had begun to show their growing intolerance of our conspicuous consumption. For example, during Fleet Week in June 1973 at the annual gathering of truck operators (complemented by an exhibition of new trucks and accessories) in Chicago, one technical session was devoted to the then current shortage of diesel fuel and what to do about it (this was four months before the Arab oil embargo was imposed). Operator after operator got up to complain about the problems of doing business while restricted to 95 percent of the previous year's consumption of diesel fuel.

This sequence of self-pitying statements was dramatically interrupted by a dark-skinned young man speaking the English of the Indian subcontinent. In scathing terms he denounced Americans for complaining about a "shortfall" of only five percent in diesel fuel allotments when his nation, India, with close to 20 percent of the world's population made do with only 5 percent as much diesel fuel as the entire United States.

There are a lot of people outside our borders who are very very angry with us. They won't let us continue to consume a grossly disproportionate share of the world's production of basic materials. We must learn to do with less and make the most of what is available to us.

You might ask, "What's all the shouting about? The scarcities of yesterday are the gluts of today." All the scarcities, however, have not evaporated, and we never know when and how quickly the others will fester again.

Electric power is limited in some parts of the nation and is sure to remain scarce because the power companies are cutting back sharply on new construction. The situation in electricity is quite unreal, resembling Alice's Wonderland. As the power companies raise their charges, consumption of power is declining. (Hooray! The Law of Supply and Demand has not been revoked.) This means that the power companies' total revenues are declining; so they can't afford to build needed new plants. To maintain their revenue base, they quickly return with a new round of rate hikes. So consumption drops some more.

How does this affect business and industry, which have already cut their consumption of power substantially? To merely remain in place in terms of costs, efforts are made to save even more power. So rates go up again. Merely to stay even in terms of cost, we have to run all the harder.

Natural gas is abundant in Oklahoma, but the suppliers of this clean-burning fuel are refusing to accept new customers in the East. Private and confidential communications indicate there are a lot of "capped" wells in the Southwest and in the Gulf of Mexico that are waiting for higher prices to start pumping.[1] If and when you obtain the natural gas you need, you will most likely pay a far higher price for it.

Worst of all, the underdeveloped nations that supply other necessary raw materials such as copper, are trying to apply the successful price-gouging techniques of the Organization of Petroleum Exporting Countries (O.P.E.C.) , the petroleum cartel. Even if they are not as successful in their efforts as the oil monopolists, prices of many basics are sure to rise. In other words, now you must conserve to beat the inflation.

Learning to do with less is not all that hard, as we found during the energy crisis. There are a thousand and one ways in which business and industry can cut down on its consumption of vital materials, starting with energy. I've detailed as many as I can in this book and indicated sources for others.

In particular a procedure for conserving is proposed here that provides a framework and reference for all efforts to make do. I call it the Waste Audit. The concept came out of a discussion with Bill Stocker of the McGraw-Hill Publishing Company. Now in management, Stocker was formerly an editor of *American Machinist* and has remained close to the situation in metalworking (the advocacy of numerical control in Chapter 4 is largely based on my conversations with Stocker) . He told of one manufacturer that made a care-

---

[1] These private communications contradict the very pessimistic government position on natural gas in "A Realistic View of the U.S. Natural Gas Supply," a report of the Bureau of Natural Gas, Federal Power Commission, Washington, D.C. This report, published in December, 1974, is available on request.

ful survey of opportunities to eliminate waste in all operations. After all the opportunities were exploited, under the direction of the president of this substantial company, the company's net after taxes actually doubled! Suddenly the phrase "Waste Audit" sprang to my lips.

The Waste Audit is applicable in any company, distributing and retailing as well as manufacturing. Each department, as suggested here, has a role to play in starting and maintaining a Waste Audit. And the concept really has no significance if it is not an ongoing activity. The objective is to beat each previous year's performance in curbing waste and increasing the return on scrap salvage.

Now a skeptic might reasonably ask, "Why maintain a Waste Audit if the company has set up profit centers that make a far more tangible and measurable contribution to company profits?" The answer is that the contribution to the Waste Audit reaches lower down than profitability. A lower-level employee may not be able to make a measurable contribution to profits, in fact there is a good chance he is not interested at all in company profits. But he can sense and be proud of his contribution to the reduction in waste, which appeals to his innate patriotism.

There is another significance to the Waste Audit in relation to the standard financial audit. A comparatively small improvement in the Waste Audit may make a contribution to the maintenance of company operations out of all proportion to the dollars involved. For instance, if your company is under allocation in natural gas, a $1,000 annual reduction in payments for this desirable fuel may have one hundred times the significance of the $1,000 saving in maintaining production at a critical stage in the process.

You don't have to call your program for conservation a Waste Audit. It could be called the Conservation Audit. What is important is that the company is making a conscious, organized, formal effort to eliminate waste, not only of energy but of all materials consumed in operations.

AGGRESSIVE AND PERVASIVE COST-CUTTING

The Waste Audit should be coupled with a program of aggressive and pervasive cost-cutting. Not thoughtless 10-percent-across-the-board cuts, but those usually commonsensical (but occasionally elegant) savings that achieve much without in any way lowering the ability of the company to compete.

For example, to cope with shortages of packaging materials, companies substituted materials and redesigned their packaging in ways that first saved on scarce materials, but also gained the following benefits: lower cost, less damage in transit, lower shipping charges, less space devoted to storing packaging prior to use, and even greater ease in disposal after use (see Chap. 12).

No business executive needs to be told that this is a time for pervasive and aggressive cost-cutting, including the collection and sale, where possible, of scrap materials such as:

Scrap paper and obsolete forms that can't be salvaged (see Chap. 9), not much in demand as this is written, but should be systematically collected with any upswing in demand for paper or if any commercial process is developed for converting paper into alcohol (for combination with gasoline).

Used crankcase oil, which can be burned as fuel in furnaces or in diesel trucks.

Scrap metals.

Plastics from "retired" products, such as old electrical motors, for recovery into new plastics or to be burned as fuel. Salvaging of previously unsalvagable plastics is now under study at the Bell Telephone Laboratories; in Japan the Sanyo Electric Company is converting scrap plastics into heating fuel.

Scraps from company cafeterias, which can be converted into food for livestock or burnable alcohol.

The money gained by selling scrap or saved by avoiding paying for its removal will not make any great contribution to your profit picture and may merely result in a breakeven operation. In fact, you may end up merely giving away these scrap materials. Nevertheless, scrap collection may still make sense for three reasons: (1) it helps reinforce in employees the desire to save materials—it provides constant and visible reminders that the company is very serious about conserving; (2) it demonstrates to the community that your company is a good corporate citizen; (3) it maintains the *machinery* of collection because shortages in many materials are bound to reoccur.

Some executives and employees may criticize such measures as going too far—"Nobody else is doing this!" This is a criticism that always riles me. Look at most of the great business successes in America and it's obvious that they got that way by *not* doing business in the manner of their competitors.

Others are sure to complain that some of these cost-cutters are petty. Perhaps, but Thomas Aquinas Murphy, the new top boss at General Motors, referred to cost-cutting as an "inch-by-inch, penny-by-penny proposition." To paraphrase a famous but less commendable remark by another top GMC executive: If penny-by-penny cost-cutting is good for General Motors, it's good for U.S. business.

An even more effective reply to critics is to point out that the cost-cutting measures can result in much more than petty savings. Applying one of the major measures advocated in Chapter 4, one company increased its pretax earnings by an estimated $1 million!

WHO SHOULD BE IN CHARGE?

The specific program that stimulated the term Waste Audit was instituted and supervised by the "activist" president of a company in the $100-million-annual-sales category. Does this example suggest that the president of your company should be in charge of your Waste Audit or whatever you call your program of conservation and cost-cutting? Obvious reasons why he should not come to mind. First of all, presidents of companies are supposed to delegate responsibility. Isn't the chairmanship of the Waste Audit Committee the kind of responsibility that should be delegated? Second, the Waste Audit implies immersion in some rather nitty-gritty details. Aren't these below the dignity of the boss?

The answer has to do with your concept of the role of the president of a company. Delegation, of course, but not to the extent that the president loses his feel for what's going on within his company.

My own concept of the role of a company president is much colored by my experience. The first real executives I had to work with were the captains of naval vessels during World War II and the Korean War. The captain of a ship receives and reads many reports on what's happening on board. He also goes out and looks around. In a sense, he's making an inspection of the operation every time he leaves his quarters. These informal inspections are supplemented by regular formal inspections of the entire ship. The captain sees for himself.

The president of a company should also see for himself. No report, no matter how detailed, matches an "eyeball" inspection.

NEW OPPORTUNITIES IN PRODUCTS AND SERVICES

Retrenchment is not the only response to tough times. Expansion is also possible. The marketplace is already seeing new products and services created especially to help cope with various disruptions. Some older products that have fallen into disuse are suddenly given a new lease on life by current conditions.

An example of an old product that was revived is the metal coil that one twists into one's gas tank to prevent syphoning. These coils, which were revived under such trade names as Gas Guard, were first offered during the Great Depression, when they sold for as little as 25 cents. When they were first reintroduced at the height of the energy crisis, they were priced at $5. However, this outrageous price was not sustained for long, and by the time the Arabs lifted their oil embargo the coils were selling for as little as 79 cents. Even at that price, they were still a profitable item, since a manufacturer of hardware told me that he estimates it can't cost more than ten cents each to mass produce these coils, including labor.

To stress that services as well as new products should be considered as new sources of sales and profits, consider the American Loan Plan. A service of the Ryder System, American Loan Plan matches tractors with no loads to haul back with loaded trailers waiting to go someplace (see Chap. 11). What's so inspiring about this example is that the service required a small initial investment (computer time is rented from a service bureau), it has low operating expenses, and it became profitable only a few months after it was introduced early in 1974. That's the way to go!

By now the appeal of this book should be obvious. This is a book for activists, for competitors, for pluggers who don't give up easily. Conversely, if you're a standpatter or one who is ready to throw in the towel when the going gets rough, put this book aside.

Egomaniacs should also set this book aside because it stresses over and over again the need to suppress executive ego in favor of measures that not only save money but even more importantly set a good, conservative example for fellow employees. In other words, this book is devoted to managerial substance rather than managerial style.

It may be that my fears of the imminence of even greater disruptions is much exaggerated and that the crisis is really decades not years away. I hope I'm overly pessimistic for the sake of all of us. However, even if I'm way off you have nothing to lose by creating a leaner, tougher, more flexible, more efficient organization. It's a lot easier to keep an organization in fighting trim than to turn around a flabby organization. And in the meanwhile, you may very well become the leader in your field and put yourself in a position to take over profitable, well-established companies that are choking for lack of working capital. There's no downside risk in a program of conservation and cost-cutting.

ADDITIONAL READING

A Time To Chose: America's Energy Future. Final report by Energy Policy Project of the Ford Foundation. Cambridge, Mass.: Ballinger Publishing Co., 1974.

chapter 2

Who's responsible for cutting costs?

IN AN ERA of disruptions, every department and executive in a company must participate in the big, coordinated effort to not only cope but also come out ahead:

Marketing comes first because accurate, up-to-the-minute information on what the customer really wants and buys is essential if the company is to obtain the best and most efficient return on its efforts. In addition, if yours is the now rare company that is forced to put its customers on allocation, the marketing department must develop and implement plans and policies for fair and honest treatment of customers. Salesmen must take on more of the character of consultants, advising customers on how to get the most out of the company's products. And if supplies of gasoline are curtailed once more, which also means restrictions on air travel, companies have to show their salesmen how to maintain the most mobility and customer contact.

Purchasing has the tough job of finding alternate sources of supply and getting the most out of present suppliers. Purchasing agents have to learn how to anticipate disruptions and react accordingly. In addition, they must be especially wary should shortages reoccur: some suppliers may offer scarce goods under demanding conditions, such as cash in advance, and the purchasing agent must learn how to reject the shoddy and suspicious.

Financial management has to come up with the cash to pay inflated prices without straining the company's capital resources too much. Much more effort will have to be devoted to forecasting cash needs while complementary efforts are made to speed up payments from customers, without antagonizing them too much.

In manufacturing companies, the production department has the tough job of maintaining an even level of work when key materials, parts, or ingredients are missing or arrive late. Quality may go down or may be erratic, which means that more time and money must be spent on incoming inspection and quality control.

Product designers and formulators must develop quick reaction capabilities to such anguished requests from production or purchasing as "Can we use grade B instead of the usual grade A in this product because we can't find any grade A?" Instead of the highly creative act of developing new products, designers must adapt more to the less prestigious but highly essential function of specifying substitutes. Yet the marketability of the finished goods must not diminish.

Shipping must learn how to cope with lower grades of packaging materials, yet somehow avoid undue product damage in shipment. In addition, traffic managers must keep much closer tabs on the performance of common carriers hampered by fuel shortages, lower speed limits, and strikes. Warehouse personnel must figure out how to store more incoming and work-in-progress inventory than ever before, without calling for big capital investments in space and equipment.

Maintenance is responsible for effecting many lesser but highly visible measures, such as curtailing lighting, heating, and air conditioning and rearranging cleaning schedules. If the company operates vehicles and maintains them, the maintenance department has the tough job of keeping those machines running in the face of high prices for consumables and actual shortages in such essential fluids as antifreeze.

Personnel managers must cope with layoffs induced by declining business or other disruptions and may also be put in charge of car pooling and arranging for more public transportation.

Security managers must increase surveillance of any facilities storing scarce and increasingly costly materials, including the company gas pump. Unfortunately, keeping a careful watch may be hampered by the requirement to cut nighttime lighting. In addition, the security department may have to aid the purchasing department in checking out fraudulent products that supposedly save energy. The security department may also be required to check for compliance with the requirements of insurance carriers.

The public-relations department may have to rearrange its priorities and devote more efforts to maintaining the morale of company employees who are fearful of layoffs and to marshalling community support for company efforts to cope with disruptions.

The main burden of disruptions must, of course, fall on top management. If a company falters or fails, the chief executive can't blame any of his subordinates. He and he alone has to face the music. This means that top management has to shift its emphases too. Most top executives came out of sales, finance, or—in manufacturing organizations—engineering. Very few come out of production or distribution. In these days, especially in manufacturing, but in wholesaling and retailing as well, much closer attention must be paid to inventory and how it is controlled. With interest rates still so high, companies can't afford to tie up too much of their limited capital in inventory.

This is why it is not too surprising to learn that top management is asking for much more detailed and frequent reports from subordinates, such as which incoming shipments are late or short and why inventories are out of balance. One giant conglomerate is keeping very close tabs on the ratios of inventories-to-sales of its many subsidiaries. Whenever the ratios climb too high, someone from headquarters is on his way to find out why—and rectify the imbalance if possible.

One simple way to cut costs is the Waste Audit, as outlined in the previous chapter. The boss, of course, must see the Waste Audit—and make sure that all other executives are aware that the boss is paying very close attention to the Waste Audit and expects the same of those who can improve on company performance by lowering waste.

If the company is unionized, the top executive may find himself spending far more time with the heads of the local unions. First, the unions should be enlisted in any effort to conserve natural gas or electric power. If an honest effort is made to explain the company's predicament, the union and its leaders will join in the effort to make scarce essentials last. They will understand that their jobs are at stake.

A great example of cooperation between business and its employees, plus the entire local population as well, took place in Danville, Virginia, over the winter of 1974–75. The town was confronted with an announced cut of over half its allocation of natural gas. When such cuts occur, the usual response is to favor residences over factories, which in this instance would have shut down most of the town's industry, which depended on natural gas for processing. To avoid such a disastrous loss of employment, the local government launched a heating conservation campaign for all homes and shops, coupled with pressure on the supplier of natural gas to raise its allocation. In addition, one local company, Dan River Fabrics, purchased about 1.4 million gallons of propane, which was delivered to the city for conversion into gas for distribution to all local industry. This community rejected "helplessness."

The company may also be forced to lay off production people if declining sales or other disruptions curtail full production. To maintain the best possible relations with the union and production personnel, the chief executive should personally explain all such moves to the head of the union and the shop stewards. If a layoff is required, it should be obvious that all extravagances of the top executives must be curbed.

Unfortunately, some bosses have such enormous egos that they can't subordinate their personal needs to the good of the company. Some years ago the president of a company experiencing its first sales decline and subsequent losses asked me what to do. Along with some highly specific technical suggestions I urged him to put his costly red Mercedes-Benz in the garage and drive his wife's old station wagon to work. But his delight in his new toy outweighed his good judgment. So he continued to race about in his roadster to the chagrin of the townspeople, many of whose relatives had been laid off. Not too surprisingly, he earned a very bad press that plagued him for years.

Reporters and townspeople alike were ready to believe any un-
favorable rumor about the man and his company, few of which had
any basis in fact.

To help overcome disruptions top management will also have to
develop one other quality that it may lack at present—anticipating
trouble. Big companies, that is the successful big companies, have
practiced long-range planning for many years, if not decades. In fact,
that's one of their advantages—the longer you practice prophesying,
the better you get at it.

Now smaller companies have to emulate big outfits in anticipating
problems. Anticipation is essential because many of the most effective measures in countering disruptions must be put into effect before the shortage develops. Once the disruption is felt, it's too late.
For example, it should be obvious that modular design in a line of
products makes it easier to cope with parts shortages. If there are
many parts in common in a line of products, it's obviously simpler
to maintain adequate safety stocks for both the common and unique
parts. Thus, if a part unique to one item in the line is short, most of
the rest of your inventory of parts can still be used to assemble other
items in the line.

Once a shortage develops, however, it's too late to institute
modularization. When shortages develop, the only sensible course is
to stick with established sources of supply.

Time and time again in succeeding chapters there will be re-
ferrals to situations in which anticipation played a key role in enabling companies to counter disruptions.

For some small companies, developing the quality of anticipation
is difficult because there is no staff to which that this important function can be assigned. In giant companies, where so many of the big
decisions are made in committee, there are usually "questioners"
available. In smaller companies, where nearly all authority is often
concentrated in one man, there may be no executive with sufficient
stature to tell the boss he's wrong.

What is the small businessman to do? He needs to find some outsider who can play the role of devil's advocate, someone who can
throw cold water on silly ideas and punch holes in poorly thought out
plans. This could be a consultant or another businessman with good
judgment—and the time to listen to your problems. (Because so
many smaller companies are ill-equipped to cope with crises, their

management may decide to sell out to a larger outfit with greater resources. However, before selling out, management should put its organization in the best possible posture.)

One more injunction. If the company is hampered or hurt by disruptions, top management must keep its bankers fully informed. Disruptions strain financial resources, and local bankers may be the only source of needed working capital. If they know and trust top management, they are far more likely to meet emergency cash requirements. Finding alternate sources of capital is time-consuming and costly and makes you vulnerable to unscrupulous individuals masquerading as sources of capital.

chapter 3

Financing, the keystone function

IN AN ERA in which conservation of assets is paramount, the financial officer has a leadership role to play. More than any other executive, he should provide the chief executive of the company with not only an absolutely current report on the company's assets, but also be able to indicate many months, if not years, in advance if and when capital will be required—and what to do if that critical capital is not forthcoming.

In addition, the financial officer has these mostly obvious responsibilities:

Possible modification of accounting methods to reflect a conservative financial position.

Tightening of credit policies.

Clamping down on all expenditures for show and image.

Setting careful priorities for capital expenditures and reviewing them frequently.

Sharing in review of insurance policies for adequate protection in an era of rapidly shifting values.

Constant reviewing of inventory position.

NEW PRIORITIES FOR FINANCIAL OFFICERS

All of these new or enhanced responsibilities obviously place great demands on the time of financial officers. Fortunately or not, the decline in the stock market and in acquisition activities should free financial officers from much that is time-consuming and usually not too productive. Most likely few financial officers—and chief executives, too—of public companies are pestered today the way they were at the end of the past decade when the stock market was booming. The population of security analysts, and "money managers" as well, has declined sharply. Individual investors are in a state of shock; so they are not likely to be calling up directly for information.

Nevertheless, the revival in the stock market might trigger a wave of inquiries. These must be kept in perspective. If they can't be fielded by simply mailing the inquirer the latest copy of your annual report (hopefully of a spartan nature—see Chap. 9), it may be necessary to set up a buffer in the form of a young assistant trained to handle all inquiries related to the company's stock and performance in an informative, diplomatic manner. The trained financial officer has much more productive efforts to which to devote his precious hours.

With the great decline in the stock market, acquisitions for stock are down sharply too—and acquisitions for cash are most likely to be avoided because the company has higher needs itself. So investigations of companies up for acquisition should be down too. They take a lot of time and represent a poor expenditure of time because so few come to fruition. (This does not doom all acquisitions, as detailed later in this chapter.)

One more cost-cutting recommendation for public companies: do what many, including some of the largest, are doing and drop plans to hold your next stockholder meeting in a fancy hotel; instead, convene the meeting in your company cafeteria or some other spartan setting.

CONSTANT REVIEW OF CAPITAL NEEDS

In these perilous times, the financial officer should be able to provide an instant report of a company's financial position. In case of trouble, top management should not be taken by surprise by an unanticipated decline in the company's cash position or current ratio. Furthermore, alternatives to help the company overcome whatever crisis has arisen should be offered along with the information on the company's asset position. This means that the financial officer should be running through mythical exercises to help him prepare for crises. For example, what to do if:

The XYZ Company, a major customer, cancels a contract for $500,000 worth of widgets, or asks that all deliveries be delayed for 90 days.

The ABC Company, one of the company's two suppliers of an essential raw material, suffers a disastrous fire that will put it out of production for six months.

Smith, Jones & Brown, Inc., a long-time customer which takes about 15 percent of the company's output, files for bankruptcy.

IMAGE EXPENDITURES

Expenditures with a high image content can take two forms: operational and capital. Examples of the former, and how to avoid them, are scattered throughout this book, especially in the pages dealing with the paper shortage and vehicle operation.

Capital expenditures with a high, if sometimes, well-concealed image aspect, must also be avoided. Most such expenditures involve the construction of new buildings, but could also go for renovation of offices or for the purchase of a prestigious new computer system.

No one needs to be reminded that these are hardly appropriate times for the construction of fancy company headquarters or other prestige buildings. For one, construction costs are horribly inflated, but not likely to ever decline. (Laboratories are another category of building with a high image content. A designer of R&D laboratories once revealed that company executives involved in a new lab construction project spend about 99 percent of their time in committee discussing the facade of the building, an aspect that represents about 1 percent of the cost.)

Countering proposals for a new headquarters may be demanding. In addition to all the usual arguments given for contracting for a new company office building, one supposedly powerful point is that it will permit efficient "consolidation" of employees now scattered about in many adjoining or even remote buildings. Is it in fact true that consolidation promotes efficiency? Consider as contrary evidence the fact that high esprit de corps is usually the result of strong relationships among the members of the group rather than great loyalty to a higher organization, such as one's university, company, the national leadership, or even one's country. This well-documented fact (based on reports from soldiers in World War II and Viet Nam) indicates that when a company is blessed with well-functioning department or subgroup, little is to be gained, and perhaps much is to be lost, by moving that group from some separate or isolated facility into the headquarters. All businessmen are aware of instances in which a large company acquired a small, highly profitable operation, moved the small division or subsidiary in with some larger operation—and then wondered where the magic went.

Because they can't afford to move to larger, more splendiferous quarters, some companies are compromising by making extensive renovations of present quarters. Frankly, costly renovations should be questioned as rigorously as a move to a more prestigious new building. Aside from the fact that a renovation is a major disruption, how essential is it under today's conditions? How about a good paint job, accomplished over a weekend or vacation period so that work is not disrupted? At the same time that the offices are being painted, badly worn or scratched desks could be refurbished, perhaps one or two at a time, with the refurbishing outfit providing substitute desks or tables while the company's own furniture is out.

PRIORITIES FOR CAPITAL EXPENDITURES

Over and over again in these pages alternatives are offered for refitting equipment or renovations of buildings that generate high payoffs in either saving energy or extending the life of the equipment or structure. Obviously, if your company was in a strong cash position and operated such equipment or occupied such structures, these might appear to be worthwhile investments.

But few companies are in a strong cash position these days. All investments in capital equipment must be examined with great care, and very thoughtful priorities must be set for all capital projects—with frequent reviews. Now the main criterion against which any capital project is matched is not about to change: fast payoff is and always will remain the first consideration. However, some other criteria must now be given strong consideration as a result of growing shortages and the steady rise in the price of energy.

For example, an investment in heavier insulation for either a process or a building is not likely to pay off as quickly as one in a new machine tool or materials-handling equipment. However, if the company has been warned by its local power company that natural gas is in short supply and will remain on allocation, then the investment in more insulation or a new more efficient boiler or some alternative process that does not depend on natural gas suddenly takes on a new dimension. The investment in insulation also meets another important criteria for a long investment life. While machine tools wear out, insulation does not. Added insulation or a new boiler also adds to the value of buildings, either for sale or mortgaging. Unfortunately, an energy-saving investment in a building is subject to much slower depreciation than an investment in a piece of equipment.

An investment in insulation for a building or a new boiler is also comparatively riskless. The return is less certain. In contrast, an investment in some new processing equipment is riskier because there is a greater chance that the process will be made obsolete by new technology—or the company may abandon the product line created by that process.

"Transferability" or "versatility" is another criterion that should be applied to capital investments. For example, the aluminum truck bodies discussed in Chapter 10 are characterized by long life. When the chassis on which they are initially mounted is worn out, say in five years, the body can be remounted on a new chassis. Since truck bodies are subject to the same depreciation rate as chassis, the aluminum bodies can be depreciated at the 5-year rate, after which they may still perform for another 10 to 15 years.

All those who submit requests for capital investments should also be required, where possible, to indicate alternate capital improvements with the same objective in mind. For example, thermally controlled cooling fans for big trucks are discussed in Chapter 10. By equipping a truck with these fans, savings in fuel consumption as high as 10 percent may be achieved, plus other secondary benefits. However, these fans cost several hundred dollars apiece, plus several hours installation time. "Self-feathering" fans made of lightweight material also save fuel, although not as much as the thermally controlled fans. However, they cost only $30 to $40 apiece and can be installed by company maintenance men in minutes. When submitting a request for authorization to equip the company's trucks with these fuel-saving devices, all alternatives and payoff rates should be included. For example, the thermally controlled fans, since they have moving parts, do wear out. But the self-feathering fans have a much longer life, unless they are subjected to material fatigue.

ECONOMIES IN EDP

The computer room is also subject to cost-cutting alternatives in capital expenditures. Since electronic data processing (EDP) is often under the direct control of the financial officer, some cost-cutting opportunities are suggested in this important aspect of business. (In Chap. 9 some ways to cut down on paper consumption in the computer room are also indicated.) These include used computers, leased computers, facilities management, a service bureau, and desktop "super" calculators.

Used computers are one of the great bargains in EDP. Fully debugged, well-maintained computers that cost $1 million six or seven years ago sometimes can be purchased for as little as $100,000 or less. Particularly where an EDP operation is still card-oriented, the older computers can do the job. Assuming that the original manufacturer or the company that took over its computer operations is still in existence, it is bound by law to maintain used computers of its own manufacture. In most instances, the original manufacturer will maintain the used machine on your premises. However, there are now organizations of trained computer service technicians who can maintain these computers. They charge about 10 percent less per hour than the computer manufacturers with whom they compete. More up-to-date peripheral equipment, such as tape drivers, can be attached to these older machines. Their only drawback is that they can usually only be used where they operate by themselves and not in conjunction with remote terminals. However, some of the earlier machines with communications capability are now available on the used market.

LEASING COMPUTERS

Most of the smaller companies that I visit rent their computers. Year in and year out they continue to pay the generally high monthly rate when they could save from 10 percent to perhaps 30 percent by leasing. The rationale behind renting is that they are not bound to that particular configuration. Nevertheless, very few in my experience take advantage of this flexibility in leasing; they keep the original configuration, or add to it, for three, four, five, or even more years. What a waste of assets!

Here is an example of how leasing of a used computer saved one company a lot of money. Dominion Cellulose, Ltd., of Toronto was fast outgrowing its 360/20, the smallest machine in IBM's 360 line. Through Dearborn Computer Leasing, Ltd., Dominion leased a 360/30, a much more powerful machine, with twice the internal memory greatly expanded disk memory and other generally faster peripherals. The net result is a 70 percent increase in "throughput," yet monthly charges under the new three-year lease are the same as the rental on the replaced system.

FACILITIES MANAGEMENT

Ross Perot, the "Texas billionaire,"[1] made facilities management famous. His company, Electronic Data Systems, Inc., would take over the crippled computer operations of large companies and make them hum. According to insiders in EDP, the secret of his success was selling or utilizing for his own account the excess time on computers his organization was hired to manage. At first facilities management was available only to large companies with very big computers, but by 1972 I had discovered an example of a small company that has worked out a facilities management arrangement with a long-time computer expert based on a used IBM 1401 computer. I visited the facility and was impressed by what management told me. At a time when there were severe demands on them because of a relocation, they had been able to devote themselves fully to those problems and leave the big problems of setting up an EDP operation to a man who understood EDP far better than they did. In view of the demands on the time of financial officers, as outlined in this chapter, this aspect of facilities management should have great appeal.

---

[1] For years my then wife was a great admirer of Ross Perot. On one occasion, irritated by her raptures over his great success, I explained to her that Perot was merely a billionaire on paper. If he were to have attempted at that time (in the late 1960s) to liquidate his paper holdings in Electronic Data Systems, Inc., he would only be worth "a lousy hundred million."

REMOTE EDP

An example of a distributing company that turned its EDP over to a service bureau some hundreds of miles away is presented in Chapter 13. As the example makes clear, the cost benefits were and remain impressive. Now you might have some qualms about turning your entire EDP operations over to an organization that makes a point of also handling your direct competitors. (That's why the service is comparatively inexpensive. Your competitors' problems—and the solutions—are close to yours.) However, these service organizations take elaborate precautions to maintain the secrecy and confidentiality of your data—or they would not remain in business for so many years.

DECENTRALIZED EDP

At one time years ago, the great pundits in computers foresaw a day when a comparatively small number of super-size computers would be handling much of the nation's EDP over remote lines. These "computer utilities" have not come into being. In fact, the trend has been just the opposite, with greater and greater decentralization of EDP. That's why IBM's System/3 has been such a great success. Instead of linking all of a company's branch operations up to one or two giant computers, the big companies have instead been offering divisional managers their own computers in the form of System/3s and competitive systems of comparable size.

Decentralization has been spurred by the high cost, unanticipated complexity, and comparative unreliability of remote links as well as the steady increase in power and capability of small computers. The ultimate in compact computer power is the desktop calculator, which has bridged the gap between calculator and minicomputer.

In 1969, E. E. Vanbronkhorst, treasurer of Hewlett-Packard Company, told me that his company has been pleasantly surprised to discover that about 90 percent of the problems that its scientists formerly solved on big computers via time-sharing services could be solved on the Hewlett-Packard Model 900, the first of the "scientific" calculators. (The calculator would be mounted on a typewriter table with a flag attached for visibility. Whenever an engineer or scientist in a lab needed the machine, he could quickly locate it and, if unused, wheel it to his workplace.)

The 900 is primitive compared to the machines that have replaced it. Instead of buying a big computer to meet the needs of its technical personnel, companies should instead consider buying one or two of the desktop units (which, with printing accessories, can cost upwards of $10,000). The rare problem too complex or too cumbersome to solve on a desktop unit could be taken to some service bureau with a computer big enough to solve the problem efficiently.

In indicating these five alternatives in data processing, no one method is recommended. The purpose is merely to suggest viable alternatives to heavy capital expenditures in computer hardware. As long as you can suppress the ego factor in EDP—in both top management and DP management—and recognize that "possessing" (most companies rent or lease) one's own brand-new[2] computer is not essential, there are real opportunities to conserve capital for more productive investment.

FINANCIAL OFFICER AS DIPLOMAT

Inevitably, in choosing one capital improvement over another worthy proposal of lesser urgency, feelings will be hurt and egos ruffled. In conveying the decisions of the company's financial committee to those whose proposals have been either turned down or set aside for consideration when more capital is available, the financial officer has to take on the mantle of the diplomat—and teacher. The latter is the more significant role. By maintaining the morale of the executives whose pet projects have been rejected, the financial officer performs a real service. But in teaching these executives how a decision is reached on a capital project and in stimulating in them the capacity to conceive of less-costly alternatives, the financial officer does much more for the company.

Most executives will not rise to the occasion; they will not return with simpler solutions to the problem (perhaps there are none). Some, however, will not see rejection as a defeat but as a challenge. They will go back to their drawing boards and return with simpler or more elegant solutions, those that not only require less capital, but also pay off much faster or entail less risk. Nurture those execu-

---

[2] Few businessmen are aware that the computer system they rent may not be brand-new. The mechanical peripherals, those subject to the most wear, are probably new, but the central computing unit, the CPU, may not be new, but simply refurbished after it was removed from the premises of a prior user. The manufacturer merely certifies that it performs as good as new. And it will.

tives who can bounce back with better alternatives, especially those who can bounce back after a second rejection. They're gold.

CREDIT POLICIES IN AN AGE OF SHORTAGES

The advent of the energy crisis gave many companies an opportunity to make one long-cherished move: tighten credit policies. "Have forced slow-pay accounts to reform their paying habits." "Money costs too much today to finance our customers; they pay or go somewhere else." "Sell to customers who pay their bills within a reasonable time." These are quotes from executives of various smaller companies describing what they did as interest rates climbed and production or inventories dropped due to shortages.

The trouble is, you can apply too much pressure to slow payers. Then when business turns down and you are only too happy to again accept orders from those slow payers, they may still be too angry to buy from you. The happy medium is a restrictive policy on credit coupled with maintenance of close relations with long-term customers similarly caught in a money crunch. Use local salesmen to keep close tabs on customers and their credit standing, as recommended in Chapter 7. When your local representative determines that a good customer is making a real effort to maintain payments, work with that customer as long and to as great an extent as your own circumstances permit.

"PASSING" YOUR DIVIDEND

Assuming that your company has high enough earnings to pay a dividend to shareholders, isn't this a good time to consider "passing" up payment of dividends? Conservation of assets has a higher priority than payment of dividends, particularly in view of all the opportunities to invest money in ways that reduce a company's dependence on scarce materials or energy.

Of course, there's also an ego factor in dividend payments. Is yours one of those rare companies that proudly advertises the fact that it has not missed a dividend in 20 or 30 or even 40 years? If so, maybe this is the time to swallow a bit of pride and forward to shareholders instead of a dividend check an honest statement detailing just why the cash that would normally have been assigned to dividends must be conserved to strengthen and build the company against better times.

There is one compromise to consider in dividend payments. If the officers of the company are also major stockholders, it is quite legal for the dividend to be paid only to "outside" shareholders, with "insiders" denied. This step has been taken in the past—and it was highly appreciated by the outside, small stockholders (some of whom may be your lower-salaried employees).

CUTTING THE COST OF INSURING VEHICLES

In Chapter 6, there is a strong recommendation to review insurance coverage of swollen inventories. Naturally, you are likely to end up paying higher premiums on both incoming and outgoing inventory. To compensate it may be possible to cut premiums elsewhere. An excellent opportunity may exist in your coverage of company cars and trucks. Larger companies that operate many hundreds or thousands of vehicles have long since chosen to be self-insured for such hazards as collision, fire, and theft. Because they can spread the risk over many vehicles, they have found that whatever costs they have to bear for collisions, theft, or other damage to company vehicles is historically lower than the premiums. This should be obvious from the fact that the casualty insurance carriers usually pay out no more than 60 to 65 percent of what they take in as premiums.

Companies that operate as few as 30 or 40 vehicles might well do the same, particularly if these vehicles are located in high-rate areas such as New York City. And close examination of accident records over the past five years might even show that companies operating as few as ten vehicles should be self-insured for collision if their mature, responsible employees have compiled a very low accident rate.

What if an examination of accident records for company vehicles shows that certain employees are accident prone? In other words, if the driving records of certain employees are excluded, the rest of the company is blessed with a very low accident rate (or you may find that the accident-prone employees are no longer with the company or have been transferred to jobs where they don't drive company vehicles). If the accident-prone employees are still driving and by the nature of their job must drive, consider coverage in which only the vehicles they drive are covered for collision.

This presumes that they have each been assigned to company cars which only they drive. On the other hand, if the accident-prone chauffeurs drive trucks or other vehicles not individually assigned them, you may find that it makes economic sense to assign them to other duties and then drop collision coverage on all company trucks.

To evaluate potential savings on insurance coverage of vehicles, ask your agent or broker to make a study of the following alternatives:

Savings over the past five years assuming that all coverage for collision, fire, and theft is dropped. (If all company vehicles are garaged at the same location, consider as an option the retention of only fire insurance.) In other words, calculate total premiums minus total collision repair bills.

Savings over the past five years as above, but with coverage only for accident-prone individuals driving company cars. (The "dangerous driver" may very well be the president or other top executive.)

Savings over the past five years with the "deductible" raised from $100 to $250; in other words, greater but not complete self-coverage.

No doubt you realize that there is no question here about dropping coverage for liability—hitting another vehicle or a pedestrian. Such coverage is mandated by state law.

If the company follows your recommendation to become self-insured on all or the greater part of vehicle operation, it makes sense to establish a fictitious Self-Insurance Account. To this "account" each year would be assigned the savings gained via self-insurance. (The Internal Revenue Service does not permit such contingency accounts in reality.) Then, in case of an accident, even one in which the vehicle involved was "totaled," you can prove to any who question self-insurance that the company is still way ahead. Of course, in the unlikely event that collision losses greatly exceed the cumulative total in the Self-Insurance Account, you know it's time to return to coverage via an insurance carrier.

INSTRUCTION IN DEFENSIVE DRIVING

If your company switches to self-insurance on comprehensive coverage or takes higher deductibles, there's an obvious gain in avoiding accidents—aside from the major question of preventing loss of life or limb. Fewer accidents not only prevents depletion of your Self-Insurance Account, but keeps vehicles and people too in operation full time.

Are there ways to cut down on accidents? One is by providing instruction in defensive driving. At least three organizations offer such instruction in different formats. Best known is the nonprofit National Safety Council, which has been offering a proven course in the United States and Canada for ten years. More than 6 million have taken the eight-hour course, which is offered through some 1,500 organizations. The charge per student varies from nothing to a maximum of $10 (although the Greater New York Safety Council has been charging $15). For greatest effectiveness and to avoid pulling your employees off the job for an entire day, the course is usually given in four two-hour segments.

The course is so effective that a number of insurance companies now offer discounts on premiums to those companies whose driving employees complete the course. As of early 1975, these insurers included: Concord General Mutual; Colonial Penn; Hartford Insurance Group; Trinity Universal; United Security; U.S. Fidelity & Guarantee; Hawkeye Security; American Fidelity; Excalibur; Southern; Dairyland; Green Mountain; Reserve; Security National; and State Mutual. (All insurers in Texas must provide a 10 percent discount to Texans who complete the course.) Even if your carrier is not among these, you should be able to negotiate lower premiums based on lower losses.

To arrange for the course to be given on your premises to a group of employees by a qualified instructor, contact one of the 80 local branches of the National Safety Council or the latter itself.

A multimedia course including videotapes is offered by Instructional Resources Corp. Developed originally for the Bell System, the four-hour course (also given in two segments) is now given to the employees of 150 corporations. Some 250,000 people have taken it since 1972. The course costs $1,700, plus $5.75 per student for an instructional kit. A group leader is required, and it takes about three hours to learn this role.

In addition to the course, Instructional Resources also offers driver-training workshops limited to 12 students. These workshops, which cost $40 per student, are offered in Atlanta, Dallas, Houston, New York, and San Francisco. Or the supplier will send an instructor to conduct a workshop on your premises, again limited to 12 students, for $300 plus travel expenses.

What if your employees driving company vehicles are scattered so that it is not possible to bring them together for the courses and workshops that require instructors or group leaders? It might be possible to arrange for them to join some other organization's course. There's another alternative. One training organization, Porter Henry & Co., developed a home-study course in defensive driving for a client, C-I-T, that operates a large fleet of cars. Two years after the course was instituted, accidents dropped a whopping 60 percent.

Now available generally, the course, which is called "You're in the Driver's Seat," consists of six pocket-size programmed instruction booklets ranging from 110 to 126 pages in length. Each takes about an hour to complete, plus some road practice. Apparently very little administration is required. Drivers taking the course simply hand in or mail in the tests and receive the next booklet.

Cost is $10 per course, or $100 for an administrative kit consisting of ten courses plus a 16-page administrative guide. If you order one course (to evaluate it) the cost is $20. Porter Henry has also arranged a "sweepstakes" with valuable prizes for those completing the course to encourage participation.

Companies subscribing for the course also encourage employees to pass the booklets on to their spouses and children, a smart move if company cars are also driven by family members.

Porter Henry is also developing similar courses in preventative maintenance ($4), handling hazardous cargoes ($4) and driving over-the-road vehicles ($10).

BEWARE OF SWOLLEN INVENTORIES

During the energy crisis many companies panicked and stocked up on raw materials or finished goods out of all proportion to normal requirements. In all too many instances, they suffered. At the very least, they had to pay very high carrying charges on that inventory in terms of interest, storage space, and added insurance coverage. (Carrying charges on inventory are climbing, and many companies now use the annual figure of 25 percent and higher.) At worst, they suffered sharp losses as the value of that inventory plummeted in 1974 with the end of the energy crisis and the advent of a world-wide recession. Other companies suffered in varying degrees through deterioration or obsolesence of material during months in storage.

The financial officer is not responsible for the purchase of materials of poor quality or questionable utilization, but he can help make sure that inventories do not become so large that the company runs out of working capital maintaining them. First, the purchasing and production departments must be aware of limitations on incoming and outgoing inventory. The simplest criterion to set up is the familiar inventory-to-sales ratio. Second, the financial department has to receive regular, prompt, and accurate reports on the amount of inventory, including the sometimes elusive work-in-progress, to make sure that the limitations are not exceeded or, if so, that the financial department has approved the exceptions. The manufacturer that is the subject of the second case history at the end of Chapter 4 suffered because of a breakdown in communications between the purchasing and production departments and the financial department. By the time the controller found out that the inventories were so much higher than he believed, the damage had been done.

FIFO TO LIFO

By now you are aware that many manufacturers have switched their method of evaluating inventory values from first in, first out (fifo) to last in, first out (lifo). The effect, of course, is to eliminate some of the swollen inventory profits that resulted from sharp inflation in raw materials.

Presenting a much more conservative balance sheet makes sense in an area of such instability. To show swollen profits in one reporting period followed by shrunken profits in succeeding periods reduces confidence in your company. And this is certainly a time in which you need the confidence of bankers and other sources of working capital, suppliers, customers, and finally shareholders.

BEWARE CORPORATE RAIDERS

But there is also a danger in an overly conservative image: you become more attractive to corporate raiders. These financial pirates are always on the outlook for sound companies who are in reality much stronger than their published statements would indicate. Sometimes they are tipped off to an asset-rich company by an insider or an accountant.

So you now have a new concern. Instead of spending a lot of time seeking acquisitions, you may instead be forced to expend much effort to beat off an unwelcome invitation to join another organization whose interest is not in preserving your company but perhaps in dismantling it. To make your company less vulnerable to corporate raiders, do what others are doing: change your by-laws to provide for election of no more than one-third of your board of directors in any one year. In other words, arrange the terms in office of your board like the Senate of the United States instead of like the House of Representatives.

SPECTACULAR ACQUISITIONS

Earlier in this chapter eschewal of aggressive acquisition policies is suggested as one way that financial executives will be able to meet the great demands on their time because of current conditions.

This does not mean that all acquisitions are to be avoided. Rather, companies should wait for ripe opportunities to drop into their laps. And there will be such opportunities. Excellent companies, those that have established fine records over the years, will be forced to sell out under today's tough conditions. Acquisition prices will be bargains, especially compared to the ridiculous prices paid for some companies in the late 1960s. To pay for such desirable acquisitions, companies will need cash—another great reason for conserving assets today.

THE FINANCIAL OFFICER AND THE WASTE AUDIT

Because of its great potential in generating profits (a penny saved is a penny earned) the Waste Audit should most likely be supervised by the president of the company. However, if the president decides that he cannot head the committee preparing and supervising the Waste Audit, then a likely candidate for chairman of this committee is the financial officer. The Waste Audit is a meticulous compilation of figures that helps to depict the company's status and how it is moving in a significant number of ways; who better to compile such a report than the man who compiles that even more significant report with the same objectives—the financial statement.

SELECTED REFERENCE

"All About Used Computers." Boston, Mass.: American Used Computer Corp., 1971.

chapter 4

Production in spite
of disruption

THE BURDEN OF FUNCTIONING in an age of adversity falls heavily on
the production department of manufacturers. Whether the problem
is scarcities in raw materials (either current or ones that could revive suddenly), disruptions in supply due to strikes or shortages of
box cars, declines in quality of purchased parts, or massive cancella-
tions of orders, the production manager never has it easy.

Under such conditions, it is easy to understand why discipline
declines: you can't get effective work out of employees afraid of being
laid off because of disruptions or declining business. Yet if there
ever was a time in which maintenance of discipline pays off, it is now.

Flexibility also pays off. New ways of working or processing must
be considered to hold down costs and cope with disruptions.

But the most effective way in which manufacturers can overcome
the serious problems of the day is a new way of controlling incoming
inventory. More about Materials Requirements Planning (MRP)
later.

QUICK RESPONSES ESSENTIAL

The engineering departments of manufacturing companies in
particular must learn to adapt to disruptions. When the purchasing

agent comes to the engineers and asks them if he can accept a substitute or less costly material that the supplier claims is "just as good" as the specified material, he needs a response in hours not days. Otherwise the substitute will be sold elsewhere. The usual leisurely pace of engineering is not to be tolerated when such problems arise.

Now there are legitimate circumstances under which no engineering department can approve a change in materials on short notice. That's when the material specified has been chosen because it has passed various environmental or life tests. Rushing or compressing such necessary tests is rarely possible.

Here's how smart companies are handling this tough problem. They are asking their engineers to specify substitutes at the time of design—in other words, *anticipating* possible shortages. Now the blueprints for the product can't be witheld from production while alternative materials are tested thoroughly. Concurrent testing of the alternative materials must be done while the product goes into production using the preferred or lower cost material or while the engineers search the technical literature for reliable data on the performance of the alternatives. Then, if the need for a substitution arises, the engineering department can make a far more intelligent and rational recommendation—and quickly.

Obviously, the engineers can't make thorough tests or literature searches on every single material used to manufacture the company's products. This would be comparable to the labors of Hercules, and the cost would be prohibitive. The engineers must concentrate on the most likely substitutions. This means that the close communication between departments indicated earlier must also exist between purchasing agents and engineers. As the purchasing agents become aware of potential shortages in key materials, this information has to be conveyed to the engineers. One week the shortage will be developing in coil steel; the next in copper; the following in polyurethane; and so forth. Conversely, as shortages evaporate, the engineers must be told so they can shift priorities.

RELAXATION OF SPECIFICATIONS

Outright substitution of materials is the most serious problem. In many circumstances the problem will be lowered quality from the supplier. In other words, the supplier is delivering what he terms as the specified material, component, or subassembly, but in actuality it is somewhat "off spec." To what extent can such lower quality or fuzzier tolerances be accepted? How much will it degrade the performance of products in which it is incorporated? Will the less desirable component, material, or subassembly be apparent to the company's customers?

Just as in substitution situations, the engineering department must respond quickly to requests for waivers on quality from the purchasing or production department (sometimes the presence of off-spec parts does not become apparent until the production department starts to include them in manufacture).

Now all of this sounds as though the work load of the engineering department will be vastly increased, even doubled. How can this added burden be assumed unless the company hires more engineers? The answer is that the shortage tends to compensate for the added engineering burden. In a time of shortages, when the customer suddenly finds himself in a seller's market, he becomes more tolerant of changes or substitutions or even lowered quality. When production is limited by materials or energy shortages, there is not as great a need for new products—the customer will easily accept last year's design. So the engineering department can shift to problems of substitution and respecification and drop or postpone work on brand-new products.

WHEN TO EXPAND MODULARITY

When scarcities occur, it is obvious that providing raw materials, subassemblies, and components for a family of products with a high degree of modularity is simpler than for a group of similar products with little if any modularity. The trouble is, when shortages are prevalent it is too late to promote modularity: you're forced to stick with present suppliers.

Now that many of the material shortages plaguing manufacturers in 1974 and earlier have evaporated, companies should make a strong effort to expand modularity in their product lines to protect themselves in case the shortages reoccur. Here are some examples:

If there is a great variety of hardware used in assembling products, strong efforts should be made to consolidate on as few different types as possible, even if this means that in some applications the hardware is too "strong" for the particular job. If a given nut and bolt were selected on the basis of required holding power, but it is only one size smaller than another nut and bolt used in far greater number, then consider dropping the smaller size.

If various gauges of sheet metal are used in the construction of some appliance or piece of equipment, is it possible to use only one gauge or a fewer number of gauges?

In assembling electrical motors, generators, and solenoids, are many different thicknesses of magnetic material specified? Is it possible that only one or two thicknesses would suffice? (Some years ago an impatient assembler of starters for aircraft ran out of the specified thickness of magnetic material. He used a different and more common thickness instead and discovered that there was no change in performance. The company awarded him a small bonus.)

ACCURACY OF ENGINEERING RECORDS

There is one more injunction for the engineering department in a time of disruptions: high accuracy in engineering records. Even under the most stable of conditions, accurate bills of material and blueprints should be the standard. However, if the more sophisticated inventory control discussed later in this chapter is to be implemented, such accuracy is absolutely mandatory.

FLEXIBILITY IN SHIFTS

More and more companies that operate more than one shift are discovering that much is gained by arranging for a short overlapping of shifts. The overlap need not be more than 15 minutes, and it could even be as short as 5 minutes. The prime gain is in productivity. Machines that are usually shut down before the end of a shift are kept in operation. Assembly lines that might have been shut down between shifts are kept running. Quality as well as productivity go up. Ofttimes, machines that are shut down don't run as well until they "warm up." Continuously run machines tend to be more accurate.

It's easy to arrange for overlapping of shifts when a plant only runs two shifts per day. But what about a plant that operates three shifts per day? Overlapping would require paying some overtime each day, approximately one hour per week. The answer is to eliminate that third shift as much as possible. The third or "death" shift is notoriously low in productivity, which is one reason that few companies work three shifts per day. To meet the need for increased production, companies should consider other ways to raise output.

MORE EFFICIENT MACHINERY

One obvious way to increase output is to employ more efficient machines. New technology in processing and production machinery in all industries is becoming available all the time. Yet manufacturers are sometimes incomprehensibly slow in adopting them. Steel manufacturers outside the United States have gotten the jump on American steelmakers by introducing newer and much more efficient processes for making all grades of steel. As a result, Belgian or Japanese steelmakers can ship their products across the Atlantic or Pacific oceans and sell them in the United States at prices below those of American steelmakers. And lower wages have little to do with the markedly lower prices.

The best example of shockingly underutilized production technology is numerical control (N/C). I began writing about numerical control 20 years ago when it was first introduced. In the beginning N/C machines were incredibly expensive, and only companies in the defense industries, whose machines were either paid for by or loaned to them by the government, were able to utilize them. By the early 1960s the technology had been in effect simplified so that it could be applied to much smaller and less costly machines that small job shops could well afford. I was quite into N/C at that time because I was acting as an advisor to a leading manufacturer of numerical controls.

Today, more than a dozen years after the introduction of low-cost N/C, it is shocking to find out how few N/C machines are in service in the United States. Out of some 2 million metalcutting machines in the United States, only about 30,000 are tape controlled. In sales of new metalcutting machines, only 20 percent of the dollars are being spent on N/C machines by American manufacturers, who have the distinction of owning the most obsolete plants among all industrialized nations (of course, U.S. tax laws have a lot to do with that, but government measures will not be discussed in this book).

In terms of productive capacity, the percentage of numerically controlled capacity going into service is higher than 20 percent. A numerically controlled machine can out-produce a similar machine that is manually controlled by a factor of three to five. That's why N/C machines are so significant today: they can cut costs sharply. Beyond that prime advantage, they offer other important advantages: faster set-up time and less waste.

Faster, therefore lower-cost, set-up is especially important at a time of high interest rates. As set-up costs decline, manufacturers can afford to make shorter and shorter runs, which means lower carrying charges or that the company is in a better position to afford to schedule a short run when shortages of key materials do not permit a more economical long run.

There's still another reason for advancing into N/C: it is the prelude to the next higher level of productivity and flexibility in metalcutting, which is already upon us. Computer-managed parts manufacture combines N/C machines with automatic tool changing and computer-directed mechanical transfer of pallet-mounted parts in a system that enables a few unskilled men to do the work of ten times as many skilled machinists.

In this system, which is characterized by extremely short set-up times, an economic batch can be just one complex part. A dream? No, this is being done in Japan, East Germany, and since 1972, at the Heavy Machining Center of the Ingersoll-Rand Company in Roanoke, Va.

WHEN INVENTORY GETS OUT OF HAND

During the 1972–74 period of increasing shortages, manufacturers who had somehow survived for years with what one general manager called semiformal inventory control systems found themselves in deep trouble. With traditional suppliers no longer able to give them what they wanted within any reasonable time (which was in effect the "safety factor" on which they had depended), they were in deep trouble. Most were forced to buy large quantities of certain needed materials, quantities far beyond normal requirements; at the same time, they were very short or completely out of certain other key raw materials or parts. In other words, their inventory of incoming materials was seriously out of balance, to a damaging extent that often was not realized. As a result, back orders climbed sharply, which meant much customer dissatisfaction.

CASE HISTORY: TRAUMA OF FORMALIZATION

The management of a manufacturer of pipe-hanging hardware for buildings and plants, Fee & Mason, a division of ATO Corporation, was one small manufacturer (about 100 employees) that was penalized by an inadequate inventory control system. Management decided to institute a formal system in late 1973 and contracted with VanDeMark Associates, a consulting firm specializing in companies its size, for aid.

The prior system had been informal to the extent that the purchasing agent ordered materials strictly on the basis of historical demand. The new formal system is based on the familiar concept of the economic order quantity (EOQ). EOQ, developed about six decades ago, is especially applicable to companies, distributors as well as manufacturers, with a relatively stable product line and flow of goods which facilitates forecasting.

For EOQ to work, the following must be known: inventory carrying charges, which are made up of interest, insurance, and the cost of storage; set-up costs, which are costs in labor and any other expendables to prepare the required machine or processing equipment for a run; order preparation costs, which usually don't exceed $10; and demand for the item. The point at which any required material is reordered is based on that quantity set as an order point.

In the system as set up at Fee & Mason, the EOQ and order point are recalculated frequently. This is not as difficult as it might appear. VanDeMark has created some circular slide rules called calculators for determining EOQ and order points in less than a minute. With instruction manuals these plastic devices cost $25 apiece. Recalculation may be required by a number of factors such as a redetermination of how long it takes for the supplier to deliver (based on the average of the last three buys). However, during late 1974 every single EOQ and order point was up for recalculation because the annualized carrying charge (k) had been increased from 25 to 35 percent. (As a result, all EOQs and order points naturally dropped; for instance, one type of bar stock that formerly had been assigned an order quantity of 690 units was now up for reorder in quantities of 600 units.)

Based on the relative simplicity of the inventory control system at Fee & Mason it should have been fully operational by late 1974. Unfortunately, this did not happen. One deterrent was the loss of the executive assigned to man the system (he was aided by an assistant and only one clerk). In addition, there was some hostility and much skepticism towards the system among those whose usual way of doing things was challenged.

The major obstacle to implementation, however, was the lack of an accurate inventory count. While awaiting the annual physical inventory, an interim hybrid control system was set up.

After the annual inventory, management was shocked to discover that stocks on hand exceeded the EOQs for those materials by factors of two, three, and even four times. Complete reliance on the new system began on October 1, 1974. By late November, when I visited the Fee & Mason plant in Manasquan, N.J., early favorable effects were evident. Inventories of both incoming and finished goods were dropping, yet backorders were also declining (although still far above the desired level). Because the plant was operating on a two-week cycle, there was no longer much need to "expedite" rush orders from favored customers; since everyone was getting faster service, the production schedule was adhered to, and inventories continued to drop in succeeding months.

Another reason for faster delivery was the decision to shift from larger stocks of finished goods to larger stocks of component parts. The assembly labor factor in this company's 3,500 different products is high, in some instances it represents close to nine tenths of the manufacturing cost. In addition, there are many shared components among the end products. Thus, if there is a sudden demand for a given product, it can be assembled quickly from components in stock (often stimulating new production orders for those components that have fallen below their order points).

The material control system at Fee & Mason was still in the "shakedown" stages in late 1974. At that time it apparently required one or perhaps two more quarters before it would be fully operational. By that time, top management might start to think about advancing to a computerized system.

THE NEXT LEVEL OF SOPHISTICATION

An inventory control system based on EOQ can do wonders for a company, as shown above. For companies with semiformal or no real inventory controls at all ("when the foreman checks the warehouse and finds we are out of what he needs, we order more"), an EOQ system is a tremendous step forward—and may be all the sophistication that the company can absorb initially. But is it the last word?

"No," is the answer. In the mid-1960s the leading experts on inventory control began to evolve a system that did much more than provide the approximations, albeit good approximations, of what was needed to maintain production and meet customer demands. The objective of this new system was to insure that the exact quantity or amount (it also applies to batch processing of nondiscrete materials, such as fluids, powders, and pellets) of material required is on hand or is delivered not too long before it is required, which holds down those excessive carrying charges. And if the customer changed his mind and either canceled, modified, or requested postponement of delivery of an order, the system would adjust quickly to make sure that production had the wherewithal to deliver according to the new schedule.

Many of you are, of course, aware that such a system has not only been developed, but also applied in scores of manufacturing companies since the late 1960s. The results are often spectacular, as shown by these four examples.

Pretax earnings have jumped a whopping $1 million at Moog, Inc., since the installation of a sophisticated production and inventory control system for a plant in East Aurora, N.Y., that accounts for about 60 percent of the annual $50 million in sales of this manufacturer of servocontrols and numerical controls. The system is based on IBM 370/135 computer.

Safety stocks are down 75 percent, open orders are down 65 percent, and the "shop floor is no longer disorderly" at a New England manufacturer of mechanics' hand tools since the installation of a sophisticated inventory control system.

At U.S. Gauge, a division of Ametek, Inc., in Sellersville, Pa., the secondary benefits of a sophisticated inventory control system first activated in 1971 on an IBM 360 (since transferred to a 370/135) include knowledge of future investment requirements, minimization of paperwork through exception reporting, and reduction in the amount of manual clerical labor. This is in addition to the primary benefits for which the system was installed.

Employment has dropped from 300 down to 150 while production jumped 50 percent at a West Coast manufacturer of analyzers for gasoline engines. At the same time, quality, indicated by a sharp drop in returns from customers, is up too. The president frankly admits that his company would not have survived without sophisticated inventory control.

How can all these remarkable benefits be ascribed to a sophisticated inventory system known as Materials Requirements Planning (MRP)? By analyzing just what the system does, it is easy to understand how MRP achieves such a salutary "ripple effect" throughout a batch manufacturing or processing operation.

Total inventory goes down, which is the prime reason most companies institute MRP. This means that carrying charges, which as we have seen are as high as 35 percent per year at some companies, go down. Requirements for storage space may drop so much that companies can eliminate costly and clumsy storage facilities outside the company. (Ways to hold down the costs of temporary or permanent storage are detailed in Chap. 13.) Nearly all obsolete inventory should be eliminated because the company only buys what's needed soon so that incoming material does not sit around until it inevitably becomes obsolete.

The effect of MRP on production is even more striking. High-priced machinists never have to stand around waiting for work. If the system works, the parts or whatever is required are on hand. The system should also improve morale; once workers and foremen gain confidence in the system, they know that foul-ups leading to layoffs are a thing of the past. Production, as noted in some of the examples cited above, may expand without adding to the work force.

"Rush" work should be eliminated because the system is constantly updating priorities as sales requirements change. Thus, unduly costly set-ups for processing of a small number of desperately needed parts are avoided. And it is just those last-minute rush orders that result in the most errors (again, the best way to avoid waste is to make the product right in the first place). Expeditors on the production floor and in the purchasing department are no longer essential, and the level of expediting should drop off sharply. Only items of highest priority would ever require expediting, and complex products that the company was fearful of creating and selling can now be handled profitably.

HOW DO YOU GET STARTED?

With so much going for it, you would assume that MRP is being instituted throughout those industries based on batch processing (which make up the vast majority of manufacturers, but exclude the giant mass producers and processers with continuous production lines). Not so. Acceptance of MRP has been slow for a variety of reasons:

Fulfillment of prior conditions, which are absolute accurate control of incoming and work-in-progress inventory—knowing what's in inventory and where it is located; accurate record keeping; and completely up-to-date and accurate bills of material.

A computer is just about mandatory to implement MRP, and many smaller companies are not or do not believe themselves capable of handling what they see as a very complex computer system.

Some executives in both low-level and high-level management see the system as a threat to their positions.

The old system has been working "well enough."

ABSOLUTELY ACCURATE RECORD KEEPING

If you've been running your business right, you don't have to be told that discipline must prevail in inventory control, in record keeping, and in the recording of engineering changes. Sloppy control of what goes into and out of inventory is an invitation to pilferage and a depressant on profitability. Even if the motivation of those who withdraw items from inventory without following proper procedures is completely laudatory, such as the expediters who need items to maintain production, such lack of discipline is not to be tolerated. Similarly, salesmen must not be allowed to withdraw samples for favored customers without filling out all required forms and obtaining permission for the withdrawal—which should deter this common practice. Conversely, when unused or excess materials are returned to stock, that act calls for the execution of proper credit forms.

Even if your company never institutes a sophisticated inventory control system, record discipline must be instituted. Now some executives may believe that such accuracy is impossible to achieve with the company's low-salaried employees. The rebuttal of inventory experts to this weak excuse is that we are all familiar with an organization that for centuries has controlled its inventory of merchandise with near-absolute accuracy and no tolerance of errors—in spite of its reputation for paying poor salaries. What is this nonpareil business? Of course, the experts mean your local bank.

Achieving accuracy in inventory records generally calls for two steps: the development of good forms and proper procedures for insuring transcription of part numbers. Fortunately, there are plenty of models for good forms. Choose as a model a form that is detailed enough to match your needs, yet simple and straightforward enough not to frustrate semiskilled workers, especially those not too adept in English. (If you do employ many workers of Hispanic origin, consider printing the forms with Spanish headings under those in English.)

Errors in part numbers can cause real foul-ups. Transcribing just one digit incorrectly is enough to introduce a massive mistake in what the inventory control specialists, purchasing department, and the accounting department believe to be total on hand. How to prevent such errors? One familiar way is to attach a document to items with the part numbers already noted. When the item is drawn out of inventory, that document is detached. In manufacturing the document is usually a punched card; in retailing it is the well-known Dennison tag.

What do you do if it is difficult to attach such error-eliminating documents? (With a little ingenuity, you can attach a punched card to just about anything.) For instance, what if the item required is small, of low cost, stored in large numbers in a bin or box, and only one or two are required? Now someone has to write down the part number. To avoid errors in such situations some companies go to the trouble of insisting that two people get into the act—one to write down the number and the other to read it off the label on the container.

If you have a computer, there's an even better way to eliminate errors in transcribing part numbers: revise all part numbers so that they include a last "check digit," a number that is the arithmetic sum of all the preceding numbers by one of the well-known formulas of addition and subtraction. When such a part number is entered into the computer, it immediately applies the formula to the number. Any number that does not correspond with its check digit is thrown out, which should send someone back to the inventory control group to find out where the error was made.

Accuracy is also essential in bills of materials, as mentioned earlier. At the time of product introduction, the bill of material for that product is, of course, accurate. As the product is upgraded or new ways are found to cut its cost of manufacture, many changes are made in the product. Unfortunately, the changes are not always reported properly to all those affected by them. For example, the number for a part no longer required is not eliminated. The result is that purchasing may continue to order the part, the stock room maintains a supply of it, and—worst of all—through some error, the part is drawn out of stock and incorporated in an end product where it may very well degrade performance.

More than accuracy is needed. According to consultant Oliver Wight, the bill of material must also represent the way the product is made, not the way the engineer would like to think of it. As a result, bills of material sometimes have to be restructured to match the needs of MRP. Avoiding such unnecessary problems is simple: the discipline in record keeping demanded of warehousemen, foremen, and production workers is also essential in the engineering department and drafting room.

WHAT'S NEXT?

Assuming that employee discipline with respect to all aspects of record keeping has been instituted (or is being instituted parallel with the usually time-consuming institution of a sophisticated inventory control system), how do you proceed? Getting everyone into the act is the next order of business. MRP, or any sophisticated inventory control system, requires complete cooperation from those involved at the beginning of the process to the moment when products are completed.

1. The sales department has to quickly transmit sales orders, or any changes in previously received sales orders, to the production department.

2. The production department has to review the order immediately to find out if it can be assembled or fabricated with standard parts or materials on hand or those easily obtained, or if special parts or materials are required and must be ordered well in advance. If special parts are required, purchasing may be asked for lead times on delivery. Then it must be determined when work can begin on the order and when it will be finished. In other words, everything has to take its place in the Master Schedule.

3. The purchasing department has to order required parts and

materials beyond those on hand or on order to accommodate the new orders—and make sure that unusual parts and materials required will be delivered on time.

4. Most important of all, top management has to let everyone know that it is wholeheartedly behind the development of a sophisticated inventory control system. This means that management can never show impatience with what seems to be slow progress. Also, management has to understand that the executive and any assistants assigned to manage the system cannot be given other distracting duties to perform. On the other hand, if any executives obstruct the implementation of the system, they have to understand that any subtle sabotage will not be tolerated.

Everyone has to understand exactly how the system works. This is not the place to present a long exposition on MRP: its workings are adequately detailed in various publications and even on videotape. The best way to describe MRP is to call it a dynamic tickler file. In contrast with earlier systems that provided good approximations as to what was needed but did not adjust readily to changes in sales, MRP is designed to provide exactly what is required to complete a product and adjusts quickly to changes in sales—or the failure to deliver a required component.

To those who have not dealt with production problems in batches, this may not appear to be such a great accomplishment, but consider this situation. In a complex product with perhaps ten stages of assembly, MRP is the means by which a given component which is required at the initial, third, and eighth levels of assembly and is also used in many other products of that same plant and various levels of assembly is provided in the quantities needed *and on time*.

TIME-PHASED BILL OF MATERIALS

There's one essential in MRP that can't be avoided: all bills of material (by now they should be up-to-date) must be exploded along a time axis. Because intervals between assembly steps may not be known accurately, this requirement could take a lot of time and effort. Drudgery yes; brain-taxing, no!

TRAINING IN MRP

How do you train your employees and yourself in MRP? By far the best source of information is the American Production and Inventory Control Society, one of the nation's strongest advocates of MRP. Through its local chapters, this 15,000-man organization offers seminars in many localities throughout the nation. And you don't even have to be a member to sign up—usually there's a slightly higher charge for nonmembers. But it makes sense for your top inventory control people to join the nearest local chapter of APICS and even attend the national conventions.

There are even free courses for management. I observed an excellent introductory course offered by International Business Machines Company. The course is based on a videotape presentation supplemented by a textbook. According to IBM's Jim Clark, who helped prepare the course, a sizeable minority of those who've taken it were not even IBM customers. To arrange to take the course, which runs one full day, contact your nearest IBM sales office. They will forward your request to the nearest IBM Manufacturing Industry sales office. IBM will even present the course in your plant if you have a large enough group. Naturally, the course makes a good case for computerization, but that is a valid point.

The various consultants who help companies set up MRP will also help train your employees.

WHY A COMPUTER IS NECESSARY

In the examples of companies utilizing MRP cited earlier in this chapter, a computer was used in every instance. Is a computer essential to MRP? When the concept was under development in the 1960s, there was nothing in it that made computerization mandatory. In fact, compared to the statistical order-point systems, MRP depends on the simplist of mathematics—addition and subtraction—rather than sophisticated statistics.

If your product is not too complex, it might be possible to implement MRP manually—as long as too many changes are not required. And that's where the requirement for a computer is indicated as a practical matter. Only a computer, which essentially performs additions and subtractions at incredible speeds and in staggering numbers without tiring, can handle the job. The computer can make comparisons between inventory totals and the time-phased bill of materials without effort. If need be, the plan for components can be revised daily, although as a practical matter, weekly revisions are the norm. In contrast, a manual system would be hard-pressed to update each month or every other month.

WHICH WAY TO COMPUTERIZE?

Does the computer on which MRP runs have to be on your premises? It does in the great majority of instances, but it is not essential. The computer can either be at a nearby or even remote service bureau (although this approach did not work in Case History B at the end of this chapter). However, the computer you use must be equipped with disk memory. It's the disk that permits such rapid comparisons.

"ECONOMY" COMPUTERIZATION

Don't be scared away from MRP by the notion that computerization with disk drives is terribly expensive. At one time adding a disk drive to a computer entailed a high expenditure. Now small systems with disk drives are available for under $1,000 per month. A tremendous expansion in use of small computer systems should result from IBM's introduction of its System/32, which can be leased for three years under a "Term Availability Plan" for just under $1,000 in a configuration that includes 5 million "bytes" of disk storage and a 100 line-per-minute printer.

There are viable alternatives to the System/32. For example, NCR has introduced its Century 50/Mod 1 for only $1,050 per month on a five-year contract; on a one-year basis the monthly rate rises to $1,275. Smaller suppliers, such as MAI's Basic/Four and Qantel, are leasing disk-oriented systems for about $600 per month. This includes maintenance but not programming. Basic/Four has been used in a sophisticated inventory control system at Pactra Industries, Upland, Calif., since 1972.

As suggested in the previous chapter, used computers are a bargain. If your company needs more power than is available from these smaller systems, fully debugged and well-maintained 360s and Univac 9300s, all capable of supporting many disk drives, cost but a small fraction of their original price. According to H. M. Surchin & Co., Inc., a leading dealer in used equipment, there has been a very sharp decline since mid-1974 in the prices of used 360 systems. For instance, the central processing unit of a 360/30, a surprisingly powerful machine, can be purchased for only $18,000. This is less than 10 percent of its original cost.

There's another low cost alternative. Smaller manufacturers

should welcome the introduction by a large, well-established company of a low-cost, disk-oriented system. Hewlett-Packard, which is the 241st largest manufacturer in the United States according to the 1974 "Fortune 500" list, sells a system including programming that costs only $28,000. It leases on a five-year basis for only $787.50—maintenance is extra.

What's so unusual about this desktop system is that the central processing unit, CPU, is not a minicomputer but a 43-pound calculator. However, the calculator is the powerful, programmable HP Model 9830, which sells for $6,800. To this typewriter-size calculator can be added a two-platter disk memory for $13,645, a required interface device, and a thermal page printer for $3,145. Two versions of inventory control programs are offered: one that keeps track of up to 1,700 parts for $500 and a second that keeps track of up to 5,000 parts that only costs $100 more. Programs for other tasks, such as payroll, accounts payable and receivable, and general ledger, are also available for this system.

One disadvantage of this system is immediately apparent: it would take a lot of time to enter the required data base into the system via the keyboard on the calculator. (Once the data base is entered, using the keyboard for daily entry of data is not so burdensome.)

To compress this chore, HP offers a reader that senses pencil marks on cards for another $3,125 plus $525 for an interface. (It would be handy if a company using the system could rent the reader only for the initial period of establishing the big data base.) If the volume of data to be entered initially into the system is not great, then a low-cost card reader that costs only $580 can be used. Called the Model 9870A, it weighs only 18 ounces and can be held in one's hand. It can also be used instead of the keyboard for entering data on a daily basis.

After the data base is entered and kept up to date, a complete report on the availability and history of any part is forthcoming in only two seconds. The information could also be presented on a TV terminal, naturally at a much higher cost. HP offers a CRT terminal for this system at $2,835, and it requires an added interface card in the calculator at $430.

Incidentally, the calculator can still be used for scientific, business and engineering calculations when it is not working on inventory or payroll or other EDP tasks.

Among the companies that are using this system are Graham

Plating, Johnson Engineering, Scenic Airlines, Franco Chemicals, and Neurodyne-Dempsey.

In addition to the above, Burroughs Corp. has introduced six smaller computer systems, some directly competitive with IBM's System/32. The smallest system in the group, the B 702, rents for $860 per month on a one-year lease. On a three-year lease, the monthly rate drops 5 percent with a 7 percent drop on a five-year lease.

SOURCES FOR REQUIRED PROGRAMMING

An inventory control program is essential for computerized MRP no matter where the actual EDP is handled. There are various sources, such as the computer manufacturer, the service bureau that handles your inventory control, custom software houses, other manufacturers willing to sell or rent their programs, and yourself (see Case History A at the end of this chapter).

Most of the computer inventory programs by far are supplied by the computer makers. Usually, the program is rented on a monthly basis, but you can buy it outright too. To induce customers to buy their computers, some companies, those who have not "unbundled," offer the required programming as part of the deal, with no separate price tag on the initial programming.

If your inventory control is handled by a service bureau, that organization may supply the programming. It may have been developed on a custom basis by the service bureau or rented from the company that supplied the computer to the service bureau. Or the service bureau will contract with a software specialist to develop and maintain the necessary programming.

You can also contract with a software specialist to develop a program that suits your special needs, or you can rent or buy a "proprietary" inventory control program developed by the specialists.

According to consultant David O. Nelleman of the Chicago office of Arthur Anderson & Co., very few of the proprietary programs on the market are satisfactory. He sees two big deficiencies: poor documentation and lack of front-end validation. Poor documentation means inadequate plain-language backup for the specifics of the program, which means that your people will be handicapped when they need to modify the program—and you can be sure that modifications will be needed as your needs grow. Front-end validation means the capability of rejecting invalid data, such as part numbers lacking a digit (and the last digit is crucial, since it is commonly the "check" digit). As you can see by Case History B, inadequate proprietary programming is a very real pitfall.

Some companies, especially those which have been into MRP for years, developed their own inventory control programs. It is still possible to do this, but there is less and less need for it now that so many inventory control programs are available. As one expert put it, "Why reinvent the wheel?" Some of the companies who developed and refined their own programs might be willing to rent or sell the program to *noncompetitive* manufacturers with similar inventory control problems. Conversely, if your company develops its own inventory control program, or any specialized program for that matter, you could gain some additional income by renting or selling the program. You could also benefit by requiring your licensee or customer to make available to you any improvements they come up with in the program.

You can find out about such programs through several sources, such as the various computer "user" organizations and a directory published twice a year by International Computer Programs, Inc.

HOW LONG TO GET STARTED?

At this point you should be aware that implementation of a sophisticated inventory control program can take a long time. Don't be shaken if you discover that as much as 18 months is required. Consultant Nelleman knows of smaller companies that have been fully "on stream" in only three to six months, but these are the exceptions. They got started so quickly because they already had established discipline in record keeping.

Most manufacturers take much longer because they must not only reeducate employees, but also establish the discipline that is essential.

WHEN TO GET STARTED

Picking the right time to get started can speed up the entire process. A period of relative calm is a good time to begin. To its chagrin, one manufacturer picked exactly the wrong time to take such a major step as introduction of MRP. Not only was it bringing out complex new products, but simultaneously, it was preparing for a strike. Of course, the new system was a flop, and production and purchasing were quickly forced to fall back on costly and frantic expediting.

Before getting started, it makes sense to conduct a feasibility study. The study does more than smooth the transition; it also helps convince the usual skeptics and scoffers that the system will work.

To help the shift to the new system, a manufacturer of lighting fixtures put its staff through many dry runs on MRP before throwing the switch. Some consultants suggest installing MRP on a pilot basis at first. This could involve a product line with few parts or sub-assemblies interchangeable with lines. However, IBM's Clark disputes this piecemeal approach. He warns that you could get into trouble as soon as any components are being managed by two different systems.

WHERE TO GO FOR HELP

There are three ways to go in installing an MRP system:

1. Hire a consultant.
2. Depend on your computer vendor.
3. Do it yourself.

Unfortunately, there are not that many consultants available to help companies install MRP. As more and more companies turn to MRP, knowledgeable consultants will increase in number. For recommendations on savvy consultants, consult the nearest chapter of APICS. (Also see Directory under "inventory control consultants.")

The computer makers obviously have a strong stake in implementing MRP. Manufacturers without computers will require systems, and companies with computers will need to add more internal memory and disk drives. Your friendly computer salesman will also arrange for you to visit successful installations, which is a smart way to learn more about MRP.

Doing-it-yourself may be the slowest way to go but could be the surest because you proceed at a pace that enables your people to absorb their lessons.

THE NEXT STAGE

Once your MRP system is up and running, it's time to consider how to make it even more productive. To reduce computer runs, some experienced companies are progressing into adjusting the Master Schedule for net changes rather than regenerating completely. Another advance is to work tooling into the system. Thus, the required tooling for a job will arrive at a work station at the same time as the materials or semifinished parts. The computer can even be programmed to schedule operations on similar parts on the same machine in order, which cuts down on set-up time.

CASE HISTORY A: VIRTUES OF ANTICIPATION

When Norman Gusoff, controller of Edson Tool & Manufacturing Co., Inc., initiated the development of a computerized inventory control system for the Belleville, N.J., fabricator of metal enclosures, he had no idea that five years later the system would be essential in maintaining gross profits during periods of severe shortages. Since Gusoff had not heard of MRP in 1969, he called the system E.P.I.C. (Edson Programmed Inventory Control). Although differing in some respects from MRP, the system is very close to it in form and produces the same results. The example is so instructive because Edson, with only 200 employees, is one of the smallest manufacturers to use such a sophisticated approach.

The system operated at first on a rented NCR 100 system, which was the lowest-cost computer system with the essential disk drives, available in 1969. In retrospect, some savings might have been gained by arranging for a long-term lease of the system. However, Gusoff was understandably loath to commit Edson to a long-term lease while venturing into such unknown territory. In early 1975, the NCR 100 was replaced by a lower-cost NCR 101 for a monthly saving of $300. The printer associated with the NCR 101 can only print 250 lines per minute, compared with 450 for the NCR 100 system, but the printer associated with the latter was mostly "loafing" along.

Edson's large metal enclosures are custom fabricated to designs and specs prepared by its customers, who are manufacturers of large communications and computer systems. Thousands of different hardware and plastic-insulation items and materials are required.

Here is the kind of information available on short notice from the computer (which operates in the batch mode) that is so crucial in coping with shortages and inflation.

Document A. Price changes for all items plus a history of the last ten buys.

Document B. Current inventory, quantities on order from which supplier, and when due for delivery for all items.

Document C. By job, a breakdown of parts and materials required in terms of quantity and cost.

Document D. A listing of all items by code and detailed description.

Document E. An analysis by consumption of direct materials with cross references to jobs for which required.

Documents B and C are used by the production department in the creation of a master production schedule. The rule for scheduling a a job is that none are started until materials for all bulky parts are in house. Sometimes easily stored small parts are fabricated beforehand to keep up work levels. To avoid layoffs, which could result in the loss of experienced workers among Edson's largely semiskilled work force, a very even level of production has been maintained with a rare short workweek.

Here's an example of how work levels are maintained. Let us assume that job 459, which is the next one scheduled for production, requires 15,000 rivets. Examination of Document B shows that only 6,500 are on hand. The plant manager scans Document C to find a job due for early fabrication that requires fewer than 6,500 rivets. Let's assume that he finds one, job 617, that only requires 5,600 rivets. Next, he checks further on Document C to find out what else is required for 617. If all other hardware items and materials are on hand, he will presumably schedule it next.

Now let's go back to job 459. Besides the rivets, only one other hardware item is not available. Various courses of action are possible. First, Document D can be consulted to find another rivet and hardware item that could substitute for the specified one. If the required number of those items are in house, and the engineering department determines that they can do the job, the customer will be asked if the substitutions are permissible. Usually, the anxious customer is more than willing to approve intelligent substitutions.

If no reasonable substitutes are in house, purchasing expediters can be assigned to either track them down or locate a supplier who can deliver the items originally specified. Or a combination of specified and substitute items can be sought.

While specific items of an urgent nature are sought, the purchasing department regularly reviews Document B for late deliveries, obviously concentrating its efforts on items in lowest supply for which future demand is highest.

Document E is consulted when a customer reduces or postpones an order or when a job is deferred because other materials are late in arrival. By referring to Document E the production manager can quickly determine where to reassign the materials previously required (but not yet consumed) for a given job.

Because jobs are scheduled when the items called for on bill of materials for each is on hand, which may not be the order in which contracts are let, jobs are sometimes completed weeks or even months before the contract date. When this happens, the customer may be asked to accept early delivery—which delights some. Naturally, he is asked to pay earlier, which is important for a fabricator whose needs for working capital, in common with most manufacturers, are running much higher than in the past. If the customer refuses early delivery, the completed enclosures are stored in a nearby public warehouse or in rented van trailers parked in an empty lot across the street.

The main contribution of the E.P.I.C. system to profits has been its effect on productivity: although sales are up one hundred percent since it was instituted, the work force has not increased. Edson's delivery record has not suffered either.

What else? Now the function of Document A is made apparent. To make sure that gross profits do not suffer, Document A offers a history of price increases for each item required to complete a job. When customers are presented with such strong evidence, they usually agree to price increases. Although the price increases have not kept up with the higher cost of materials, Edson has been able to maintain the same level of gross profit, but not the same percentage of gross profit as sales volume has naturally gone up due to inflationary effects.

Incidentally, the E.P.I.C. program is not for sale or rent. However, Gusoff is willing to part with one useful bit of information gratis: if your foremen are not highly educated, which is the case at Edson, avoid giving them instructions in the form of computer printouts, which seem to scare many of them. Instead, stick to the old method of providing instructions on blackboards—transcribed from the printout.

E.P.I.C. is not the only task assigned to the computer, of course. In addition to the usual accounting functions performed on the computer, a new chore was developed for it late in 1974 and early in 1975. Because of very rapid increases in certain costs, such as for heating and solvents, Gusoff realized the traditional way of assigning overhead costs was no longer valid in costing out a project. For instance, if several parts in a certain job required painting, those parts actually cost more than other parts that are not painted (painting involves heat to drive off more costly solvents). In addition, the painting involved a process that called for a high investment of capital. Because it is comparatively easy to break up the usual overhead rates (based on labor costs) on a computer for assignment to jobs, a new program has been developed. Again, when confronted with the new procedure for figuring overhead, customers accept it and the associated price increases.

CASE HISTORY B: TROUBLES COME IN BUNCHES

Successful computerization of inventory control is not easy, as one fast-growing equipment manufacturer sadly reported. And as is often the case, the initial failure to achieve computerization, compounded by other problems, such as high rates of interest, was enough to throw the company, which had just become profitable, back into a loss position—since reversed.

The company, whose president requested that its name not be revealed, had relied since its founding in 1969 on a rather primitive manual system of inventory control. As is common in such situations, too much vital information was entrusted to the memories of those in charge of production inventory. Even though these employees were dedicated, energetic, and resourceful, the growth of the company in both sales and complexity of product line doomed the manual system.

At the time the decision was made to computerize control of production inventory, the company's EDP was handled in batch fashion on an IBM 360/30 at a service bureau 20 miles away. Management decided to stick with this arrangement. Since the bureau did not offer an inventory control service, a computer program was needed.

That's where the first mistake was made. For $16,500, a proprietary program, actually a modification of IBM's Bill of Materials Processor (known as BOMP) was purchased and delivered to the bureau. Today, management realizes that it should have rented the program on a monthly basis until its applicability was demonstrated. ("Software" houses that sell proprietary programs will usually credit some portion of the rental fee towards purchase.)

Soon it was apparent that the program was inadequate. Because the company manufactures advanced electronic systems, engineering changes are frequent. Whenever a new part or subassembly was specified, the data on that superseded item was wiped out of the computer's memory. This was disastrous since the changes were never meant for immediate implementation: first, stocks of superseded items had to be used up. (In time, other, lesser deficencies in the program were uncovered.)

The next deficiency in the system was uncovered at the service bureau. All documents relating to inventory control were delivered each day to the bureau in the usual sequentially numbered batches. Unfortunately, the bureau did not set up tight controls for keeping track of the batches. Some batches were inadvertently set aside and either entered too late or not at all.

Lack of discipline at the service bureau was more than matched at the company. The accounting department did not receive copies of pertinent documents: they simply accumulated on someone's desk. The result was that accounting received them a month or so late. By that time, the listed items had been consumed in production.

Within a few months the accounting department's figures on the total value of incoming inventory varied from the production department's totals by several hundred thousand dollars.

Top management soon realized it had made a big mistake in not assigning people with no other duties to control of inventory. Understaffed, as is true of fast-growing companies, all sorts of subsidiary and collateral duties were dumped on the four-man staff. Now an inventory control staff, one executive and three clerks, is responsible only for processing one category of documents.

Not too surprisingly, the executive in charge of inventory control, who had come from TV-receiver manufacturing, a mass-production business that has much simpler inventory problems than the batch-manufacturing business of this company, was replaced by a man familiar with sophisticated inventory control systems.

The system now works, but not perfectly, and the company has lifted itself back into the black. In the meanwhile, it has committed itself to an in-house computer system based on a popular mini-computer. The wholely owned system, under development by a specialist in collaboration with company employees, will be devoted to the simpler accounting tasks at first. In time, inventory control will be taken over the new system, which supposedly will cost much less than a standard system obtained from one of the computer makers. Unfortunately, this new system has taken much longer to develop than planned. By late February, 1975, it still was months away from implementation.

chapter 5

Upgrading purchasing and buying

DURING THE 1973–74 PERIOD of intense shortages, companies fortunate enough to employ an effective purchasing agent discovered that he can make a major contribution to company profitability. As one expert put it, "If you've got a good purchasing agent, go out of your way to hang on to him; if you don't have one, go out of your way to hire one."

Hanging on to or recruiting a good purchasing agent makes sense for two reasons. First, in and of himself he is a desirable employee; second, by doing a good job he has established a sound rapport with suppliers, which is in itself an asset. The purchasing agent who has treated suppliers and their representatives like gentlemen during the usual buyer's markets is the one who gets special or better treatment during seller's markets. Those suppliers know that some day, sooner than expected as we have seen in so many once scarce materials, buyer's markets will return.

Special treatment does not mean necessarily that your company will get more than its share or that your allocation will be raised. What it does mean is that when additional supplies are available, perhaps not of the exact material purchased but close to it, your company will received preferred treatment. Or the "decent" purchasing agent will be made privy to inside information on other sources of needed materials. And when supplies become more available, your company should receive faster delivery.

AVOID DOUBLE, OR "PHANTOM," ORDERS

How does a purchasing agent establish desirable rapport with suppliers? One sure way is to avoid placing double, or "phantom," orders. At the height of shortages in early 1974 there was much placing of phantom orders. As a result, some suppliers of raw materials or components reported record-high backlogs. Subsequently we found out that most of those backlogs were phony. Within a matter of weeks, suppliers with overblown backlogs skidded from three-shifts-per-day production to layoffs.

Astute purchasing agents avoided phantom orders even when supplies were tightest. They knew what troubles could be caused when suppliers with phantom orders delivered simultaneously. (In actuality, simultaneous delivery is rarely if ever encountered: the purchasing agent realizes that he has over-ordered and cancels duplicate orders, to the chagrin or relief of those who lose the order.) Sometimes, purchasing agents forget to cancel phantom orders after a competing supplier delivers, which is what happened to one manufacturer. The materials, which arrived nine months after the order was placed, were returned, but the customer had to pay the shipping charges. If both original and backup orders arrive and are accepted, the company is stuck with excess stocks that are damaging in two ways: working capital and scarce storage space are tied up.

On the other hand, if the backup orders are canceled over and over again when the prime order is received, suppliers grow leery. Next time you place an order, they don't take it seriously, and that order may be crucial.

PANIC BUYING DID NOT WORK

At the height of the shortages in early 1974, many companies resorted to panic buying: ordering vital raw materials in quantities far beyond normal needs and from any source who would take the order. Sometimes companies ordered materials they didn't require in hopes of bartering them for needed items.

Looking back on that fortunately short period of near hysterical buying, we see that it was bad business. Overall it hurt the economy and business as well. Prices were driven up to wild levels, shortages were exacerbated, and too many companies dropped their standards and accepted and paid for low-grade goods. Even at the peak of scare buying, level-headed businessmen predicted that little or nothing would be gained. They refused to engage in panic buying. As one put it, "I can't predict my needs that far in advance to justify purchasing unprecedented amounts of any one item."

The staff inventory control expert for one big conglomerate told how he spent his days shuttling about the country to make sure that the organization's prescribed inventory-to-sales ratios were not exceeded by any one of the company's many subsidiaries and divisions. When the shortages began to evaporate, it became apparent that those who stuck to their guns were right, and the hoarders were hurt badly by sharply dropping prices for their high-cost inventories.

DETERIORATION OF INVENTORY

There's still another good reason to avoid buying too much: possible deterioration of stored materials. For this reason, some experts urge that inventory be "aged" just like accounts receivable. In other words, make allowance for losses over time due to natural deterioration, which is characteristic of many organic materials; obsolescence, which affects technically advanced parts; and damage due to handling, which can affect anything that's stored.

RESERVING CAPACITY

One of the ploys used by some truly professional purchasing agents is to reserve capacity with a long-time supplier. In effect, a substantial block of the supplier's capacity is tied up for a year or more in advance. Both should benefit from such an arrangement: the customer is assured of steady delivery of vital materials, components, or subassemblies; the supplier can gain through simpler scheduling, which permits him to make longer and more profitable runs. (Longer runs don't necessarily mean immediate delivery; at his discretion, the supplier can store the product of longer runs, delivering to the customer's schedule. Even though some capital is tied up in such storage, the overall result is lower costs.)

Now this is a smart move for all concerned as long as there is a genuine need for the item in question. However, in today's volatile markets, does it make sense to contract for long-term delivery of some needed material? What if your customers change their requirements? Suddenly, you're stuck with a disastrous arrangement.

The significance of predicting your customer's demand now becomes apparent. If you can predict demand for your product, you are in a much better position to reserve capacity with suppliers in times of extreme shortages.

Reserving capacity can also work when you don't really know customer demand. Inventory control expert George Plossl reports how one manufacturer successfully tied up much of a key supplier's capacity by a ploy that is more ruse than deception. The item was gray-iron castings, then very much in short supply mainly because so many founders have gone out of business due to inability to meet pollution requirements.

The customer made a deal with the founder to deliver 400 castings of "Block G" each month. Each month, however, before actual casting began, the customer's purchasing agent would inform the founder that a substitution was required. One month some 600 castings of "Block L" were ordered—no problem because the total amount of metal required was the same as 400 castings of Block G. The following month another substitution was ordered: 200 of "Block R" instead of the reserved item. Month by month such substitutions were ordered. Finally, the perplexed foundery boss asked if any of Block G were ever needed. At this point the purchasing agent revealed that Block G was quite obsolete: it merely represented a convenient weight standard for blocks actually needed.

Instead of playing games such as this with suppliers, it is much simpler and more mature to work out an honest and intelligent scheme for reserving capacity. This takes more than the mere act of reserving a given volume or weight of capacity. Close attention has to be paid to purchase orders for items included in that capacity because such purchase orders are usually not generated at a steady pace by an inventory control system, assuming you have one.

To simplify the approach, it makes sense to group similar products into families for which requirements can be predicted with greater certainty than for an individual item, especially if there is some level of modularity among family members.

Orders for given items making up each family group must be released to the supplier (founder, forger, etc.) at a rate that keeps the reserved capacity loaded. However, these orders need not be released until a week or two before the supplier is going to run them—thus affording maximum flexibility to you and avoiding as much as possible all rescheduling of production.

This controlling of release of orders means coping with two situations: weeks in which more orders are generated than the supplier can handle; weeks in which not enough orders are generated to match the capacity reserved. In the first situation, some orders must be held back until the next release date, which takes some discussion with production control; in the second situation, you have to confer with production control and figure out what to order ahead to match the reserved capacity. In both situations the normal working of a sophisticated inventory control system, as outlined in Chapter 4, is somewhat manipulated but hopefully not for long, as we have seen with the shortages that burgeoned then disappeared in 1974.

INCREASING "CLOUT" WITH SUPPLIERS

No small company needs to be told that big companies have more clout with suppliers. Gaining such influence is possible if the small supplier can induce some large customer to buy vital raw materials, components, or other items directly, often for several other small suppliers. This happened during early 1974 and is a possible purchasing technique to keep in mind for future shortages. Sometimes it was the supplier who initiated such arrangements, which were entered into as much because the smaller party was short of working capital as to gain buying influence; less frequently, the small supplier suggested such unusual buying to a customer who needed his product desperately. Obviously, no small company should suggest this approach unless it has exhausted all other means of obtaining critical materials.

Another obvious way to gain influence with suppliers is to place larger orders. This is a patently risky procedure since the excessive quantities purchased might decline in value or customers may no longer require the products fabricated out of those materials. To aid small suppliers in purchasing larger quantities, some big companies placed sizeable orders in turn. To avoid being wiped out in case the big customer changes his requirements, smaller companies who enter into such agreements must ask for a real show of earnest in the form of down payments.

"HEDGING" IN GOLD

Buying for suppliers has taken an unusual twist in the electronics industry. Gold is an important raw material in electronics because it has two unmatched characteristics: the lowest resistance of any metal and very high resistance to corrosion. It is also easy to work with. About 12 to 13 percent of the world consumption of gold goes into electronics. For some items, such as high-quality connectors, the gold used in their manufacture represents two fifths of the cost.

To protect themselves against inflation in gold prices, some large industrial firms are buying or planning to buy gold futures on the various U.S. exchanges that are trading in gold since the December 31, 1974, expiration of the ban on ownership of gold bullion by American citizens. Instead of actually taking delivery of the gold represented by the futures, the futures are usually sold for a profit, and the proceeds are used to buy gold at the "spot," or market, price. Gold purchased in this manner is then assigned to suppliers who do not have the capital to trade in gold futures.

In a variation of the above procedure, the big customer shares the cost of maintaining gold futures with small suppliers of items utilizing gold.

COPING WITH LOWER OR ERRATIC QUALITY

During periods of scarcities, the quality of items purchased often drops. Companies have coped with this problem in three ways:

1. Accepted the goods in hopes of salvaging some of it and selling the rest elsewhere.
2. Abandoned sampling techniques for checking quality in favor of one hundred percent testing.
3. Tried to help suppliers overcome quality problems.

The first solution is born of desperation and is hardly likely to work. Companies who lowered their quality standards or even abandoned incoming inspection found that they were stuck with goods they couldn't use and no one else would buy. This is no way to go.

Companies that experienced erratic quality from suppliers during the period of shortages were often forced to drop sample testing in favor of testing every single part or subassembly. In return for this added investment in time and machines, they often found that they could "pass" a substantial majority of the items and thus keep their production lines going. The rejected twenty or twenty-five percent of the items were returned to the vendor for credit.

To avoid so much testing, it makes sense to attempt sample testing again at regular intervals. When and if the vendor appears to have reestablished his normal quality levels, complete testing can be abandoned.

The 3M Company was one of those that met the quality problem by extending the aid of its large engineering force to small suppliers who could not maintain former standards. Sometimes the problem could be corrected. In other instances in which it was found that the supplier's suppliers were providing feed stocks of lower quality, the situation could not be rectified quickly.

RESISTING EXCESSIVE DEMANDS FROM BIG CUSTOMERS

At the height of the shortages in early 1974, some big companies tried to impose their clout on small suppliers in a particularly demanding manner. Specifically, they attempted to insert clauses in purchase orders to the effect that the supplier would agree to purchase all materials required for the job within a short period of time, say 30 days, before commencing the job. Since these purchase orders involved contracts for delivery of custom-made items over many months, such purchase orders, if complied with, in effect required the small supplier to tie up a lot of capital and storage space for months.

Suppliers receiving such orders were wise to reject them. Any purchasing agent forced to cope with such purchase orders was placed in an impossible position. Even if a supplier had the capital and storage facilities to handle the order, he was foolish to accept such terms. Acceptance might have meant that such terms would apply beyond the period of scarcities.

RESISTING TIE-IN SALES AND UNCOVERING FRAUDS

Purchasing agents are subjected to other pressures during an age of shortages. Suppliers of scarce goods sometimes promote tie-in sales of goods or merchandise for which they are experiencing low demand or which are particularly profitable to the supplier. All such pressures should be resisted. Remind such unscrupulous suppliers that seller's markets are not forever.

Purchasing agents may also be plagued by hard-selling peddlers of all sorts of gadgets, pills, and potions that supposedly extend gasoline or heating oil. The chances of any of these "miracles" working is quite remote.

GOOD FORMS CAN SIMPLIFY PURCHASING PROCEDURES

As is true of other aspects of a business, the purchasing department's efforts can be upgraded by new forms. In the example cited here, buyers were able to concentrate on the more significant aspects of their job because a new form eliminated much checking on the status of outstanding orders. Even though the firm involved, Burt Capel Company, San Rafael, Calif., is a retailer, the concepts apply to any business.

The need for a new form was realized when management found that there was much confusion on the status of goods on orders and the correct pricing of items when received. In addition, the company could not keep accurate stock accounts, in part due to poor control of back orders from suppliers.

Replacing three forms, the new, efficient form was designed by the head of the company in collaboration with a specialist in purchasing forms from the supplier, Moore Corp. One unusual feature of the new multipart form is that it is perforated both across the top for ease of removal and vertically about an inch from the right-hand margin to create an internal notification strip. Here's how the new form is used:

1. As the buyer completes the top part listing his purchases, carbons transfer all the information to the other parts so that only one writing is needed. Items the buyer does not want back ordered in the event the vendor is out of stock are indicated on the form.
2. The complete set of forms is sent to the purchasing manager for checking against departmental budgets. If approved, parts one and two are then forwarded to the supplier, but the internal notification strip is retained. Part three is retained by purchasing, and part four is sent to the receiving department. Part five goes back to the buyer to be used for expediting late shipments

and for initiating new orders (perhaps from other suppliers?) to obtain those goods not in the vendor's stock.

3. The vendor keeps part one, which becomes the purchase order. Part two is returned as notification of shipment with indications of goods to come later as back orders.

4. The copy sent to the receiving department has the quantity ordering column blanked out by crosshatching. This forces the checkers to count each item received from the supplier. The internal notification strip is now forwarded to the advertising department so that it can begin promotion of the goods involved.

According to Burt Capel, the head of this retailer of automotive accessories, the new procedure: saves the buyer's time so that he can do his prime job better; has reduced errors by forty percent; has made promotions coincide with availability of merchandise; and kept the company competitive with updated price information.

The many suppliers of forms can provide dozens of examples of efficient forms and associated procedures in effect at other companies, including those in similar lines of business. If your purchasing agents are wasting time because of obsolete forms, now's the time to design new ones. In times of scarcities, purchasing agents spending many thousands of dollars should not be impeded by the lack of a good form that costs ten cents.

CLOSE COLLABORATION WITH OTHER DEPARTMENTS

In other parts of this book, the need for close collaboration between purchasing and other functions, such as production, is underlined. In particular, purchasing agents are urged to read chapter 4, with its discussion of sophisticated inventory control systems that really simplify the work of the purchasing department.

As shown in chapter 11, there is also a big payoff in close collaboration between purchasing and shipping. To create backhauls for company vehicles, the shipping department has to know about incoming shipments that can be picked up by company trucks in that locality. In most instances, the company truck will be in the vicinity of the supplier plant or warehouse a day or two after the load is scheduled for shipment. Sometimes the company vehicle will be in the vicinity a day or two early. In either instance, the purchasing agent has to inform the supplier that the load will be picked up by a company vehicle on such and such a day. If the vehicle is to arrive early, the supplier may be able to expedite preparation of the order so that a backhaul is available.

In a period of shortages, the opposite situation may prevail. The company needs some goods so badly that it is necessary to dispatch a company truck for them instead of waiting for the supplier to deliver in one of his vehicles or via common carrier. When this happens, the purchasing agent should confer with the shipping and sales department to find out if a customer located in the same vicinity will accept early delivery of a shipment.

chapter 6

Security's role in asset conservation

IN AN AGE OF ADVERSITY companies can no longer tolerate any of the losses that were too often ignored or played down in more normal or affluent times. That's why your director of security, or whomever is entrusted with company security, has gained in importance. In particular, if scarcities reoccur, new responsibilities are thrust on the security director, such as:

To cover the full impact of loss of vital materials, new forms of insurance must be procured.

Protection must be extended to once-prosaic materials, including periods when they are in transit (threat of hijacking).

In the event of a serious fuel shortage, company vehicles must be parked where their tanks cannot be drained without detection, or locks must be mounted on the tanks. Similarly, vehicles belonging to employees must receive extra protection during the day, but especially after dark.

If the plant must be manned after dark because of rationing of electric power during the day, extra guards must be hired. Conversely, if cleaning hours are shifted to coincide with working hours, special efforts must be made to check out the cleaning

personnel, especially if they are supplied by a contract maintenance service because they may have access to files that are not
locked during the day.

Scrap materials, for whose removal the company may once have
had to pay, must be stored where they can be protected easily
instead of leaving them scattered about company premises.

Purchasing may have to be assisted in detecting and rejecting
the many fraudulent products for which extravagant claims of
gas-saving or fuel-saving are made. The same is true for unethical brokers selling shoddy goods in a climate of shortages.
In addition, employees may have to be protected from slick
salesmen who come onto company premises. Fellow employees
may also be selling fraudulent gas-saving gadgets. (One way to
keep such bloodsuckers away from employees is to ban all
visitors not engaged in company business from the premises.
In years past I have ordered aggressive insurance salesmen to
leave company offices. Under today's tough conditions there is
no reason why management should tolerate such distractions to
productive work as insurance salesmen, drug peddlers, bookies,
policy runners, debt collectors, and representatives of local
charities. Charities could be accommodated in a single appeal
at year's end. The rule should be no personal business conducted on company premises.)

ADEQUATE INSURANCE COVERAGE

Should the intense shortages of 1973–74 reoccur, companies must
review and upgrade their insurance coverages in many ways.

Because of the great inflation in value of inventories of certain
scarce materials, the upper limit on insurance policies must be
raised.

Because scarce materials cannot be replaced quickly or at all
(under allocations), their loss could hurt the company far beyond their cost. The company will also lose the opportunity to
make a profit on their conversion into finished goods or on their
sale. Therefore, coverage must be extended to loss of profits and
also to cover "interruption of business" while they are replaced,
which could take months.

Many companies may stockpile materials or finished goods beyond the approved capacity of storage places or in rented storage that is not equipped with proper sprinklers. This puts them into a higher risk category and requires a higher premium. For example, during the paper shortage, one printer stockpiled paper flush against the sprinklers in his warehouse. Fire regulations require that goods be stacked no closer than 18 inches to sprinklers. His insurance carrier gave him two options: remove an 18-inch layer of paper or accept a higher premium. The printer chose the latter.

DETERRING HIJACKING AND THEFT

Companies that never before faced the threats of hijacking and theft of loaded vehicles must now cope with this new problem in the event of scarcities. In years past trucks with an amazing variety of products have been taken by thieves. The products include tools, peanuts, razor blades, cheese, aluminum, and just about anything of value. Scarcities expand the list of marketable products of interest to the hijackers and truck thieves. (Far more trucks are quietly stolen than are ever hijacked in the usual bold manner.)

There is plenty of sound advice available in the literature on deterring attacks on vehicles. Here are some simple suggestions that are easily applied.

Give special priority to high-value cargoes. In other words, unload incoming ones first or complete the loading of outgoing ones the same day so that they don't sit partially loaded overnight.

Check the background of all employees working on the shipping docks with great care and reject those with questionable associations. If you are suspicious about any drivers or helpers on trucks operated by common carriers, ask the carrier to exclude them from your premises or change carriers. There is very strong evidence that high-value cargoes are "fingered" by insiders for the thieves and hijackers. (Unfortunately, new laws make it difficult to ask job applicants directly if they have criminal records.)

If loaded trucks or trailers must remain in the shipping area overnight or over a weekend, park them with their tails flat against a wall and then block their paths with another trailer to which a king-pin lock has been mounted.

At the loading docks, separate incoming from outgoing vehicles.

Remove all pay phones from the shipping area. Provide a phone gratis for chauffeurs to call their home offices, but place it where your dispatcher can overhear the conversations.

To prevent theft of vehicles or their contents, instruct your chauffeurs never to leave vehicles unattended with the ignition key in place or with doors to the cargo compartments unlocked. (Many drivers are in the habit of leaving trucks unattended with the motors running.) To help insure that drivers follow this rule, vehicles should be properly tuned so that they start up easily once the ignition is shut off: many drivers leave diesels running, especially in winter, claiming that they can't restart them easily. This is a fallacy since a big diesel, even in the dead of winter, takes hours to cool. If your drivers can't be disciplined, install a Babaco, Everguard, or equivalent "senior" alarm with the locks on the ignition and cargo doors keyed alike. This forces drivers to remove the key from the ignition to open the doors to the cargo compartment.

Of course, chauffeurs must be under strict orders to lock cargo doors any time they are away from their vehicles, such as while making deliveries or stopping for fuel or prescribed rest periods. If valuable merchandise is still missing from company trucks in spite of this simple measure, then it is obvious that the driver himself or his helper is the thief.

One way that companies protect valuable cargoes is to place seals on the doors. However, this only works if the vehicle makes a single delivery, and some clever thieves have found ways to circumvent the seals. An alternative is the new "electronic seal." This device, which costs about $1,500 installed, creates a tamper-proof record of times of each opening and closing of cargo doors. What's more, if the door is not locked and the keys removed within 30 seconds of a door closing, an alarm sounds. Thus, if a truck is supposed to make eight deliveries and the device records nine door openings, direct evidence of an unauthorized stop is available. Of course, once chauffeurs are informed the devices have been installed on vehicles, they will not make any unauthorized stops. They could still arrange to divert valuable merchandise while stopping at a customer facility, but this is not easy to accomplish. The "SS-1" electronic seal is a product of Intelligence Services, Inc.

DETERRING OTHER CRIMINAL INSIDERS

Besides the dishonest chauffeur, there are other insiders who represent a greater threat than the outsider, as all experienced security directors are aware. Here are some simple ways to cut down on such losses:

Remove all clothing lockers to spaces near those exits used by employees. This makes it very difficult for employees to carry out valuables concealed under overcoats and hats and in umbrellas and overshoes.

If cash is missing regularly from registers, install a rubber mat with built-in electrical switches behind each register and plug the register into it. Thus, only those who stand behind the register can operate it, and no customer reaching across the counter can open the register and grab any cash. If this does not end the thefts, install an event-actuated camera aimed at the register. It will take a picture every time the register is opened. Thus, you know whom to confront if cash is missing.

Insist that all employees involved in handling of cash or issuing or authorizing of checks take annual vacations. Too often in the past it has been the over-diligent employee who never takes vacations that has been revealed after years of embezzlement. Such criminals refuse vacations to prevent anyone else from performing their duties and upsetting their carefully set-up schemes.

At regular intervals, shuffle the jobs of those in sensitive positions where they can divert cash or valuable assets.

SAFEGUARDING GASOLINE, DIESEL FUEL, AND RELATED FLUIDS

During the winter of 1973–74, at the height of the energy crisis, many organizations were victimized by employees and outsiders. Scarce gasoline was stolen from pumps and siphoned from trucks while diesel fuel was removed from tractors. To prevent such losses in the future, companies should do the following:

Keep all fuel pumps and tanks under surveillance with high-security padlocks attached to the pumps (electric switches for the fuel pumps must also be put under lock and key). To make sure that guards include the fuel tanks in their rounds, a key station for watchmen's clocks should be added to the tank or pump area.

While eating lunch or if away overnight, chauffeurs should be instructed to park their vehicles in well-traveled, well-lighted areas where it is less likely that any fuel can be siphoned off.

Install coiled-metal guards in the openings of fuel tanks on all vehicles. These barriers to siphoning are cheaper (don't pay more than one dollar each) and much less bother than lockable caps. However, they are a nuisance at service stations because the fuel nozzles can't be left unattended in the opening to the tank in the usual manner.

Some employees siphoned off fuel from vehicles they were operating. This form of theft is easy to detect: the fuel consumption for the vehicles suddenly jumps by 100 or 200 percent. Detection simply requires good record keeping of the fuel consumed by vehicles. This should be standard practice at all times to help maintain vehicles properly.

One governmental organization that was plagued by thefts of scarce gasoline used a very clever means to detect the thieves. An aromatic was added to the fuel. The owners of all private vehicles that emitted the distinctive odor were immediately suspect.

During the last energy crisis only fuels were the target of thieves. However, during any future fuel shortages, other vital petroleum-based fluids may be stolen. For example, a shortage of antifreeze occurred during the winter of 1974–75. Other fluids, such as lubricating oil and hydraulic fluid, may be in short supply. They must be safeguarded by proper locks and careful record keeping.

Suppliers must also be checked for accurate deliveries. The most likely problem is simply a "short" delivery of gasoline or diesel fuel or heating oil. However, during the 1973–74 energy crisis some fuel companies were selling "regular" gas as premium. Those caught paid heavy fines. Detecting such substitutions of gasoline is not difficult: most of the petroleum companies dye their premium grades a distinctive color.

If your company purchases coal, you have to be alert to deceptive practices too. A number of power companies have accused their suppliers of two kinds of monkey business: mixing in excessive amounts of rock or dirt into coal or substituting lower grades of coal for thóse ordered. Careful scrutinizing of all deliveries plus frequent spot checking is necessary. "Layering" is the method of hiding lower-grade coal. Coal cars or barges are mostly filled with low-grade or "crop" coal, then a thin layer of the higher, specified grade is poured over the cheaper stuff. To detect such deceptive "topping," it's necessary to take samples from deep inside each coal car or to check after the car is dumped into the storage pile. Power companies detecting layering have refused to accept delivery and then instituted suit against the supplier.

If the lower-grade coal is not detected at the time of delivery, it should be detected when it is burned. Careful record keeping would reveal that excessive amounts of coal are required to achieve the normal day's production of heat or power and, if the coal is "dirty," an excessive amount of ash is accumulated. By that time, of course, it may be too late to take action against a specific supplier unless he's the only source for your coal. But you don't have to do business with him any more.

THE THREAT OF EXTRA GASOLINE

During the energy crisis of 1973–74, many motorists carried extra gasoline in unsafe containers in their vehicles, and some paid for their negligence with their lives. In the event of a new fuel shortage, there's a strong likelihood that many car owners will again carry extra gas inside or on top of their cars. Gasoline can be transported safely in "approved" containers with proper venting. However, in the event of a fuel crisis, there's sure to be a shortage in the containers as well. So motorists will transport gas in any available container, including large gas jars.

To protect lives and company property and the vehicles of other employees, companies should place an absolute ban on the bringing onto and storage on company property of any gasoline not in the tanks of the vehicles. Because the company is not in a position to inspect and approve the containers in which gasoline is transported, no exceptions should be allowed. Employees may counter with the argument that they won't be able to get to work unless they carry extra gasoline. The only intelligent reply is to indicate that the company is promoting car pooling, which is essential in the event of a gasoline shortage (see Chapter 18). For those employees whose homes are so isolated that car pooling is not applicable, the company should provide extra gas.

THE ROLE OF THE SECURITY DIRECTOR IN THE WASTE AUDIT

The director of security should not have direct responsibility for taking any aspect of the Waste Audit. By its very nature it is a "line" rather than a "staff" responsibility. Unless, of course, security is a collateral duty of an executive in a smaller company, and his main function is maintenance or personnel or some other job where taking a Waste Audit is required. Compilation of the Waste Audits performed in each department into an overall report could be assigned to the director of security because his real responsibility is conservation of assets. If the director is also the director of energy conservation, then this added responsibility is particularly appropriate. In a time when conservation of assets is paramount, the role of security need not be emphasized. Criteria for investigations of losses should be tightened, not because so much more will be recovered, but for its effect on employee discipline. In other words, minor pilfering of office supplies, tools, hardware, and gasoline, which may have been overlooked in affluent times, must be choked off. Now's the time.

ADDITIONAL READINGS

Dow Jones-Irwin (1818 Ridge Road, Homewood, Ill. 60430) publishes four books that are excellent guides to insuring that your company's security program is sound and well administered:

B. E. Gorrill, *Effective Personnel Security Procedures,* 1971

Charles F. Hemphill, Jr., *Security for Business and Industry,* 1971.

Charles F. Hemphill, Jr., and John Hemphill, *Security Procedures for Computer Systems,* 1973.

Charles F. Hemphill, Jr., and Thomas Hemphill, *The Secure Company,* 1975.

chapter 7

Selling when markets are in disarray

THE DEPARTMENT that has to be the most reoriented, or perhaps reorganized, in an age of disruptions is marketing. It's not just that the selling style of an age of abundance is doomed in a time of leanness, but that the marketing department has to operate a lot smarter. "Smarts" must be applied in every aspect of marketing, but especially in forecasting sales. In addition, marketing faces other problems and challenges, such as:

Retraining personnel, the need for which applies whether the company is enjoying a seller's market or declining sales.

Upgrading the system of responding to customer inquiries.

Increasing the effectiveness of promotion.

Preparing contingency plans for severe gasoline rationing or curtailment of car travel because of the very high cost of fuel and cars, all tied into the ongoing problem of compensation for expenses.

Participating in the creation of new products and services that suit the times.

ACCURATE SALES FORECASTS—THE GREAT IMPERATIVE

In Chapter 4 the adoption of sophisticated inventory control techniques is urged. These techniques, best known as MRP (Materials Requirements Planning) depend for their success on accurate sales forecasts. In addition, accurate sales forecasts permit the company to invest its money much smarter. If the forecast accurately predicts an expansion in sales, then the company can invest in expanded production and/or distribution facilities with greater confidence. On the other hand, if the marketing department predicts a decline or leveling of demand, the company can prepare intelligently and with least disruption, such as by instituting a policy of cutting the work force by attrition.

Although sales forecasting is standard procedure for large companies, too many smaller companies never try it. Or, having tried it once unsuccessfully, they are afraid to attempt it again. Is such pessimism warranted? The experts willingly admit that forecasting is not an exact science (none of today's prophets, such as economists, are successful at prophesizing either). On the other hand, they claim that there's no better way to operate. Blithely predicting higher and higher sales (to keep up morale and please stock analyists) is certainly no intelligent approach.

Sales forecasting is basically a trial-and-error process, so the only way to learn how to do it *is to do it*. Your first forecasts are sure to be way off. In fact, forecasts should be presented in a format that indicates error. The "error factor" could be expressed in the statistically common manner of "plus or minus 7 percent," or in the form of a range of possibilities. The range could be indicated by high and low figures, perhaps with a mean. "Avoid highly sophisticated statistical techniques" is the advice of the experts. These techniques may only be fully understood by one individual in a smaller company. If he leaves or retires, your forecasting efforts may be crippled. Instead, forecasting should be a group effort, with the current projections subject to frequent review, at least once a quarter. In other words, the forecast is not an absolute that must be achieved, but an intelligent projection that changes as actual sales develop.

Begin by polling each member of the sales force, local sales representatives and export agents, if you do business overseas, for their projections for their respective territories. These individual projections are then reviewed by the regional or product managers. Criteria in this review are historic patterns for each territory, the level of over-optimism of the predictor himself (how realistic has he been with his predictions in the past), and the possible effect of new competition in the territory. The collective predictions must be adjusted by factors to which sales personnel in the field may not be privy, such as planned new promotional efforts and plans to add or eliminate products and services.

Share-of-market techniques apply if your company is a major factor in its industry or market. For instance, if your organization has long enjoyed a seven-percent share of the total market for its goods or services, and this market has been growing at an annual rate of five percent, then it is comparatively easy to come up with a reasonable sales forecast.

Don't forget that the accuracy of any prediction is more open to question in proportion to the remoteness of the event. Until you and your colleagues become more adept at forecasting, reviews should be frequent. In time, as forecasts become more accurate the interval between reviews can be increased. For the process to work, adolescent boosterism has to be set aside in favor of mature realism. The day when a sales manager loses favor or is even downgraded or exiled because he comes up with a conservative projection are past. And total frankness is essential too. If some new situation, such as a major customer going bankrupt, occurs to lower the prediction, then the sales manager must be frank enough to reveal this fact and lower his projections, and management must be mature enough to accept and cope with it.

If your company utilizes a computer, it can aid in preparing sales forecasts. Consult with your supplier on forecasting programs available directly from the computer maker or from other users of the same system.

RETRAINING THE SALES FORCE

Education is one of the prime functions of any manager, and this is especially true of the sales or marketing manager. A downturn or a seller's market are particularly good times to devote more efforts to educating and retraining your sales force. If you are in capital goods and enjoying the seller's markets so common in heavy industry, then your sales personnel indeed have the time available for retraining. On the other hand, if sales are level or down because of recession or a shortage of raw materials, instead of driving your sales force, with little or no added sales resulting, set aside time for retraining. Significantly, those who teach or lecture on "time and territory" management report that they have never been busier. But they mostly work for big companies.

If there was ever a time for salesmen to learn how to cover a territory with the least effort and expenditure of fuel and money, this is it. Obviously, one of the techniques to be stressed in retraining is how to use the telephone properly in sales. The phone companies were smart to stress the use of the phone during the 1973–74 energy crisis, and their sales were up sharply. If a salesman has been dealing with a given customer for a long time, a follow-up phone call can be nearly as effective as a visit. In fact, the phone call may be more acceptable than a personal visit. In a shortage economy, purchasing agents in particular are harried men. They don't have time for the obligatory luncheon, but they may be too polite to refuse an invitation from an engaging salesman with whom they have a long-term relationship.

Just what a salesman does for a customer may be due for revision. Instead of meeting the customer's traditional or expressed needs, salesmen must learn to probe for his real needs. Especially in a shortage economy, salesmen have to be able to offer alternatives. This takes effort because the salesman who can offer valid alternatives must be the one who analyzes and understands his customers' operations. There's another benefit to getting close to the customer: in times of scarcities, it helps determine if orders are for real or phantoms.

HOW AND WHERE TO ORGANIZE RETRAINING

Training or at least stimulating sales people to greater efforts is nothing new. It's a standard aspect of the traditional national sales meeting. Today the question is: "Do we still need a national sales meeting?" With the cost of ground and air travel, hotel accommodations, food and liquor inflating at a double-digit rate, can companies afford to bring all of their sales people together from all parts of the country? Some companies don't think so. Instead they are substituting regional sales meetings to which only the sales manager and those making presentations have to travel long distances.

What sort of accommodations are required? In keeping with the injunction to conserve assets, sales meetings can be held at more modest establishments with limited entertainment facilities. Obviously this implies all-day sessions with no time off for a round of golf.

Bargaining with banquet managers is not to be scorned. They're hungry for business and should be expected to lower their excessive rates for group meetings. And check their bills carefully. In years past I have been shocked by inflated bills for liquor submitted by supposedly highly reputable hotels. (In one instance I forced the manager of a big restaurant at a major airport to cut a phony liquor bill by 50 percent when I calculated that the twenty-five guests at the all-day meeting I chaired would have been intoxicated into unconsciousness if they had consumed as much liquor as originally charged on the bill.)

Instead of serving roast beef and steaks, substitute chicken and seasonal fish. Will your sales people grumble at your "cheapness?" Maybe, but at times when many sales people are looking for jobs, you're not risking much.

The telephone can be used to supplement or compensate for greater intervals between sales conferences. A consulting organization named Systems Consultants, Inc., has developed a system for setting up conference calls between headquarters and up to ten other company offices. Called the Integrated Telephone Conference System, it permits no-hands phone conversations between the widely separated groups. Although the system is not inexpensive and could cost as much as $10,000 for a large and elaborate installation, it is still less costly and much less time-consuming than a conference attended by employees traveling great distances. And once you've made the investment in the system, it can be used over and over again.

MAINTAINING MOBILITY DURING A GASOLINE SHORTAGE

"I once sold a million dollars out of the back seat of a VW, and I could do it again." This comment by a sales representative after the Arab oil embargo was imposed shows how some resourceful salesmen were prepared to cope with gasoline rationing. Aside from the obvious move to smaller cars, how can you maintain the mobility *and effectiveness* of sales personnel if gasoline is rationed?

Here's where time and territory management comes into play. It should be obvious that gasoline can be saved if salesmen schedule their visits to customers so that they cover the least miles. Accomplishing this may entail asking a customer to wait a day or two for a requested conference. Will this antagonize the customer? Some "difficult" customers are sure to resent a request for a switch to a later day or an earlier one so that the sales person can visit more than one customer in a given town. However, the great majority of customers are reasonable people. During the height of the last energy crisis many salesmen found their customers to be completely co-operative on the matter of adjusting visits.

Public transportation should be relied on too. Before the introduction of the automobile, traveling salesmen—they were called drummers then—depended on public transportation. (Remember the opening scene in "The Music Man?") In spite of the shrinkage of rail transportation, there's still good service between large cities, and all smaller cities and most towns are served by buses. Buses! Although they have the reputation of serving only the poor, I find them in general cleaner than trains and nearly always on time or even a bit early. (In spite of the national speed limit of 55 mph, few buses on superhighways appear to pay much attention to the limit, and their trip times are nearly as fast as before.)

Even though flying is more expensive than it was before the energy crisis, it can be cheaper—and certainly less time-consuming—to fly rather than drive. At current hotel/motel rates, it is certainly cheaper to fly (economy class of course) to some city several hundred miles away, take care of your business in one day, and fly back the same evening instead of driving back and forth with a one-night layover at a hotel or motel. (I've actually flown to Chicago from New York, spent a long and productive half-day there, and flown back the same evening. If the person or persons you're visiting can be induced to meet you at the airport, such quick turnarounds are even more feasible.) The one-night layover after a long drive may become mandatory with some companies as a result of the "fatigue factor" encountered by those driving smaller cars for many hours per day.

To return to the question of the smaller car, how can the salesman who must haul a lot of samples with him manage? Here are some alternatives to consider:

1. Small station wagons. However, anything stored in a station wagon is visible, which makes such items vulnerable if they ap-

pear valuable to passers-by. To protect valuable samples at night might require that they be brought indoors, unless the vehicle is parked overnight in a well-guarded garage. For further protection, salesmen's cars can be equipped with "senior" alarm systems (see Chap. 6).

2. Small and compact cars with "hatchbacks." Most would suffer from the same visibility-of-contents problem as the station wagon.

3. Carrying samples on an overhead rack, which calls for salesmen with strong backs. However, the racks, when loaded, not only increase gas consumption, but also make the car more prone to turning over and harder to handle.

4. Panel trucks equipped with noncommercial licenses so that they can travel on parkways on which trucks are not permitted. If the load compartment has no windows (in some states a panel truck must have at least one window other than those in the driver's compartment to qualify for travel on parkways), then any samples carried in it are more secure.

Here is another way to cut travel expenses and also save on gasoline. If the customer in a remote city is only a few miles from the airport, dispense with the usual practice of renting a car on arrival and go by cab. If you have to arrive the evening before the planned visit, rely on the motel's van that picks up arrivals at the airport.

Of course, if the customer is a great distance from the airport, a car must be rented. Here's one simple way to cut down on their cost: instruct your employees to reject the $2-per-day "complete coverage" when they rent cars. This high-cost coverage only buys $100 worth of insurance protection, eliminating the standard "deductible" in case of an accident. (Beyond that the car is covered for any damage as part of the standard rental contract.) Let's assume that on any given work day at least one of your employees rents a car and takes the added $2-per-day coverage (plus any applicable sales tax), then the company is in effect paying a $500 annual premium for $100 worth of coverage (250 working days per year times $2). That has to be the highest priced insurance in the world.

Be self-insured, which is the rule with most large companies, such as IBM. Even as an individual, it makes sense to be self-insured if you rent frequently. Over the past ten years I figure that I have saved about $400 by not taking the complete coverage—and I have never had an accident in a rental car. If I did, I would still be at least $300 ahead.

COPING WITH SEVERE GAS RATIONING

So far we have been assuming that gas is available but expensive. What if gasoline is rationed severely, and salesmen, even if given an extra allotment, can't maintain mobility? Then they would indeed have to fall back on public transportation. Here's one way they could still maintain contact with customers. Years ago many salesmen contacted customers by inviting all those in a given city to see a display of their samples in a suite at some centrally located hotel. There are still a lot of "drummers" who operate in this manner, particularly in the jewelry trade.

If you are forced to operate in this manner, try to make the most of it by introducing a note of nostalgia into the suite (nostalgia is very popular these days). The suite could be decorated in a turn-of-the-century motif, with the salesmen wearing suspenders and other haberdashery of the time. This may be corny, but it would take some of the sting out of requiring your customers to visit you.

Another obvious way to prepare for gasoline rationing is to start now to retrain those employees who drive great distances for the company in "conservative" driving techniques. There's lots of information available on driving with economy in mind. The Ford Motor Company makes a leaflet available through its dealers. An even more elaborate brochure available gratis is "Confessions of a Mileage Champion," by Ben Visser, an engineer who sweated 376.59 miles out of a single gallon of gasoline in a specially reconstructed Opel. You can obtain as many copies as you need by writing to Shell Oil Company, Dept. JM/1, P.O. Box 53083, Houston, Texas 77053.

Another useful free brochure entitled "Facts on Car Care," is available by writing to Firestone Tire & Rubber Co., Director of Consumer Affairs, 1200 Firestone Parkway, Akron, Ohio 44317.

Also see the discussion in Chapter 3 on defensive driving.

SPECIAL ALLOWANCES DURING AN ENERGY CRISIS

During the energy crisis of 1973–74, companies with many men on the road faced the problem of properly compensating them for the high price of gasoline. Even with most driving fewer miles, salesmen were still not reimbursed sufficiently under mileage allowances worked out before the price of gasoline took off. And because they were driving fewer miles, their actual costs of ownership per mile went up.

Companies were understandably reluctant to raise their mileage allowances permanently because they did not know how long the crisis would last. Here's how some companies handled the problem:

Increased the mileage allowance for each salesman based on the size of car he drove: standard, intermediate, compact, or sub-compact. Here's an example of how this worked. Let's assume that an employee in California drives his standard sedan 6,000 miles per quarter and he averages 10 mpg on the highway. This means that he is consuming 600 gallons per quarter driving for the company. If he paid an average of 60 cents per gallon, then his total cost for gas was $360. Previously, he had been reimbursed 12 cents per mile, based on an average gas price of 38 cents per gallon. His added costs per mile work out to 2.2 cents. Therefore, during the energy crisis his mileage allowance is raised to 14.2 cents per mile.

Raised their mileage allowances to the then 15-cents-per-mile limit set by the Internal Revenue Service and still paid special allowances based on the high price of gas in each region. (The I.R.S. requires special reporting when companies reimburse their employees at rates higher than those allowed by law. Obviously, no one wants to get into a category where extra paperwork is required to prepare their income-tax returns.)

TWO-TIER MILEAGE ALLOWANCES

Even without gas rationing, the higher cost of gasoline and other factors in travel is forcing companies to change the bases on which they reimburse employees. For example, more and more companies are switching to a two-tier system of reimbursing employees who use their own cars on company business. Paying those who don't use their cars much for company business a higher mileage rate recognizes the obvious fact that a car that is driven little each year costs much more per mile to operate. The difference in actual cost per mile between those who drive a lot and those who drive a little are greater than you might believe. The Hertz Corporation has made an analysis that shows that the cost per mile for an intermediate-size 1974 car driven 10,000 miles each year and kept for three years was

24 cents. If the same car is driven 15,000 miles, the per-mile costs drop to 18.3 cents and to just under 14 cents for 25,000 miles per year. These calculations were made in early 1974; they are no doubt higher today.

As a result of wide disparities in the cost of operating cars in different parts of the nation and between the city and suburbs, a growing trend is "customized" reimbursement. Rates are determined for each area, usually on a split basis: fixed costs per month, such as insurance, plus the variable costs based on mileage. The leading compiler of these rates is Runzheimer & Co., Inc.

NEW WAY TO PAY TRAVEL EXPENSES

With the cost of travel inflating steadily, any way of cutting these and attendant costs should be of interest. That's the appeal of the "Travelorder," a comparatively new concept in paying small sums—which is like the familiar letter of credit. They are issued on a once-a-week basis to those who travel. They provide employees with immediate funds so that they don't experience the usual delay in receiving checks from the home office. Each recipient is provided with a list of over 2,000 motels and hotels that cash the Travelorders. They are also cashed by commercial banks.

The advantages to the issuer of Travelorders are these: lower preparation costs—about $35 per year per man versus the higher annual costs of preparing travel reimbursement checks; the recipients are forced to file their expense reports promptly; and there is no need to mail expense checks to men on the road for long periods—they carry a batch of Travelorders with them, but can only cash one per week based on notations on a sort of letter of credit carried with them.

The Traveletter Corp. has also developed a new, lower-cost way to make small cash disbursements in the field, such as to merchants for promotional purposes. They are called "Rapidrafts" and, like the Travelorders, carry an upper limit on the amount for which they can be issued.

AVOIDING CROSSING THE I.R.S.

The importance of avoiding a reimbursement rate higher than that allowed by the I.R.S. is stressed above. You just don't want to impose added record keeping and tax calculations on loyal employees burdened by the other extra demands and concerns of an era of shortages. Here's a way to help avoid this situation: arrange to offer lower-cost auto insurance through a payroll-deduction plan. Obviously, this offer in all fairness has to be made to all employees, not just salesmen, and it should apply to cars other than those used by the employee but registered in his name or those of family members such as his spouse and children. The savings to the individual are substantial; the added cost to the company, especially if your payroll is computerized, is small. And employees are not forced to accept this valuable fringe benefit.

To find out how much can be saved per employee, ask each one to complete an information form to be submitted to your insurance agent. The form naturally must show how many miles the vehicle is driven each week. With car pooling, savings may be even greater than anticipated.) When the forms are returned to each employee with indications of rates based on a mass insurance plan, most will be only too glad to join.

There's another I.R.S. regulation of which you should be aware: if you provide a company car that the employee is permitted to use on personal business (this is pretty much standard), the employee must reimburse the company for such usage. Otherwise, the personal use is considered as extra income, subject to income taxes and social-security deductions. Common rates for such reimbursements are 6 cents or 7 cents per mile.

Incidentally, if personal use of the company car is permitted, the employee's spouse and minor children may also use the car. What if the children include teenage boys, the age group that traditionally has by far the most accidents? You can't specifically forbid use of the car by teenage boys, but many companies indicate that they would prefer that company cars are not driven by teenagers.

SPEEDING RESPONSES TO CUSTOMER INQUIRIES

If the mobility of your sales force is reduced, it is imperative that your system of responding to customer inquiries be updated: at a time when your salesmen may not be as visible, quick responses to inquiries maintains the "presence" of the company in a productive manner. Of course, fast response to customer inquiries makes good sense at any time. All of us have suffered the frustration at one time or another of requesting technical information or help from a company and then waiting an inordinate length of time for a response, or never getting one at all.

Although branch sales offices are often called on to supply information, it is headquarters that handles most such inquiries. This means that the system of responding to "sales leads" can be under the direct scrutiny of the marketing manager. Here are some suggestions to implement such an upgrading:

1. Establish a system of color-coding all incoming inquiries by the day of the week in which they arrived. Assuming that mail is only opened five days a week, only five different colors for "signal squares" are required, one of which is attached to each request as it is taken out of the envelope and stamped with the date of arrival. The signal squares would be imprinted with the numbers 1, 2, 3, and 4 on their edges, which means that the response system works on a four-week cycle. Let's assume that the color red has been assigned to Mondays, the day the most mail usually comes in. If the sales manager sets as policy the rule that all requests for technical brochures must be filled within two days, then a glance at the desks of those clerks assigned to the response system would reveal any delays in response time. (Each desk in the inquiry response section would be equipped with five colored "in" trays corresponding to the colors of the squares.) Obviously, this system depends on the maintenance of adequate supplies of technical literature, a problem when paper is in short supply. If the person in charge of ordering technical literature falls down on the job, the error is soon made apparent by the piling up of inquiries. If there is a run on a certain category of brochure or leaflet, the system should include a checklist reply form that is mailed to the respondent indicating that the company is temporarily out of the printed material requested but that "a copy will be forwarded as soon as available." Naturally, this also requires that the clerk use a carbon-copy type of label in responding to such inquiries to save the effort of typing up a new label when the printed material is indeed available.

In a variation on the above, the colors could correspond to the week, if one or two-day response is not needed and a response within a week is satisfactory.

2. Form letters to handle the great majority of responses should

be created. A comprehensive form letter can be more satisfying to the recipient than a hastily dictated individual response.

3. If you want to respond in a fancier, more individualized (horrible word) manner, yet avoid the great expense of specially composed and dictated letters, consider setting up a system based on word processors. If you are not familiar with these versatile office machines, they are essentially typewriters with memories. Everything that's typed on them is also recorded on magnetic tape or magnetic cards. To correct a message, only the part in error or to be modified is typed over. The correct part of the message is typed out automatically at the highest speed of the typewriter (about 200 words per minute). Some insurance companies have organized very sophisticated response systems around word processors, which are now available from more than 50 manufacturers. For instance, at the Colonial Penn Insurance Co. in Philadelphia, some 2,000 phrases and paragraphs, including many variations on salutations and closings, have been memorized on tape. Those clerks who respond to customer inquiries about their policies or about new or added coverage select the appropriate phrases to meet the customer's needs. Many of the standard paragraphs include blank spaces into which the customer's name or some other personal reference can be inserted via appropriate instructions to the computer that controls the system. In this elaborate system, the responses are actually typed out at high speed on a computer printer with a typewriter-like set of characters.

GETTING THE MOST FOR YOUR PROMOTIONAL DOLLAR

The great merchant John Wanamaker is known for his remark that "Fifty percent of the money I spend on advertising is wasted, but I don't know which 50 percent."

Is it possible to cut down on the wasted 50 percent? In these times one sure way is to emphasize hard sell in advertising and deemphasize or totally eliminate advertising that supposedly contributes to "image." Unfortunately, too much of what passes for hard sell promotion contains too much emphasis on image or ego. Years ago when I was the chief editor of a firm that published technical magazines and catalogs I went around the country giving a speech to our advertisers and their agencies entitled "Suppressing the Ego Factor in Advertising." The gist of my speech was that a strong ego was essential in executives trying to build up a company, but that it had to be suppressed in the creation of their advertising. As an editor I was aware of ads purportedly designed to move product that put too much emphasis on company facilities; history; being "first in . . ."; "largest manufacturer of . . ."; and other self-congratulatory phrases that really don't impress the astute buyer (at least of industrial products).

Instead of massaging their own egos so much, I urged my audience to concentrate on the customer's ego (which is true of most consumer advertising). For example, suggest that by specifying the product in question, the buyer will impress his superiors. I always got a great response to this speech, although I never followed up to determine if my audiences actually applied the recommendations.

The same applies to promotional brochures sent in response to customer inquiries (on "bingo cards" or otherwise). Suppress the collective ego of the company's executives in favor of emphasizing what the product does for the customer.

In view of the declining role of the individual investor and the dominance by so-called institutional money managers, there's little value in advertising whose apparent purpose is to promote the company's stock. Marketing managers with any spunk at all should approach the top management of their companies and urge that the dollars going into image advertising and financial promotion be diverted to product advertising.

Here are some other ways to stretch the company's advertising and promotional dollar:

Buy more fractional-page ads instead of full pages. In general, the cost of one full page is equal to the cost of about three quarter pages. Yet each quarter page will pull nearly as many inquiries as a full page, sometimes more.

Cut down on the amount of copy in ads. Most industrial advertising contains too much copy. On the other hand, some very successful consumer ads for phonograph records and books have consisted of nothing but long compilations of what's available.

Where the company is part of a larger organization, take advantage of the parent company's other and placements to gain volume discounts. Some publishing firms offer these volume discounts even if other divisions buy advertising in periodicals other than the one in which your company takes space.

THE SALESMAN AS ORIGINATOR OF NEW PRODUCTS

Salesmen don't have to be encouraged to come up with ideas for new products or modifications of existing products. In fact one has to be a diplomat to turn down all the ideas proferred by your company's salesmen without offending them. All too often, the idea is based on a salesman's contact with a single important customer who expresses an intense and continuing great need for the product in mind. Remember the story of the man who sold central airconditioning? He was convinced by a major home developer who indicated a need for a model with a capacity that fell between that of two existing models. By the time the company engineered the new model and put it into production, the home developer had gone into bankruptcy!

However, if company salesmen really do develop into consultants, they should become more reliable sources for viable products, modifications of products, and new services. The problem for management is to indicate the need yet at the same time make it clear that the overriding responsibility of all salesmen is still sales and customer service.

THE SALESMAN AS CREDIT MANAGER

Years ago I read a very informative little book titled *The Credit Side of Selling* by Edwin B. Mason. The book, unfortunately long out of print, shows how the salesmen can not only help collect credit data on customers and potential customers, but by working closely with the customer whose credit appears shaky, establish highly productive and profitable relationships that last.

If there was ever a time in which a company's salesmen should be mobilized to help provide sound credit information, this is it. They are out in the field where they can not only observe the customer and the level of activity in his facilities at first hand, but also pick up telltale little clues to a company's financial status from conversations with its competitors and other local businessmen.

To help salespeople, and sales representatives as well, gain insight into the financial condition of their customers, public information on finances should be made available. Salespeople can either request that their names be added to mailing lists for financial statements of their customers, which is the easiest way to do this, or such financial documents could be forwarded to salesmen as received. Of course, there's little point in receiving financial documents if one does not know how to interpret them. Understanding financial statements could be taught at regional sales meetings, or by easy-to-understand brochures that are widely available, such as the one published by the New York Stock Exchange, 11 Wall Street, New York, N.Y. 10005.

To help slow-paying customers with their problems may be beyond the capabilities and available time of salesmen. In many instances, small companies are in trouble because they don't know how to collect from *their* slow-paying customers. Does it make sense for salesman to be able to call on additional resources within your company to aid good customers in such trouble?

That's what some big companies, such as Benjamin Moore & Company, paint manufacturers, are doing. They are supplying information and aid to slow-paying customers to help them deal with delinquent accounts. Usually, the aid consists of mere advice, but good advice. In a few instances, big companies have actually taken the extreme step of underwriting legal expenses for distributors seeking to collect from those who accepted the first party's goods and failed to pay for them.

Obviously this is a special step that requires diplomacy in offering and implementing. Some customers, even those in deep trouble, will consider such offers nothing more than meddling. They are afraid that the entry of some heavyweight into the situation will antagonize the delinquent company all the more.

Naturally, if you go to all the trouble of paying for the expense of collecting, you want to make sure that any monies gained are returned to you. The mechanism to insure such payment is this: ask that any checks be made out jointly to you and your customer.

KEY ROLE IN PRICING

The marketing department obviously has a key role to play in setting prices for new products, and those long in production as well, assuming that your company does not deal in commodity items. Just as important is the need to gain acceptance for inevitable price increases in an inflationary era. In the latter role the new mature relationship between salesman and customers really pays off. The customer who senses that your company understands his problems will be more receptive when your salespeople ask cooperation with supplier problems, especially for steady increases in raw materials and just about everything that contributes to the cost of the product. One smart way is to provide salesmen with documented evidence of price increases in the raw materials that go into your products. This is still another reason why the mature relationship with customers is ultimately less demanding and more rewarding than the hail-fellow-well-met approach that too many salesmen still take.

SPREADING THE WORD ON PRICE CHANGES

The very mechanism of reporting price changes in an era of shortages is a challenge. When prices change rapidly, publishing of new price lists is a chore and costly too. By the time a customer receives the new price list, it may be obsolete. So it makes sense *not* to issue price lists.

An obvious alternative is to quote "price as of delivery." When the customer needs his order, he does not question such vague pricing. However, before pricing in this manner, explain the policy in person to important customers.

THE CHALLENGE OF "DEMARKETING"

Of all the challenges faced by marketing executives in an era of shortages, none is more difficult to handle than the need to adapt to overdemand. For decades we have been operating in buyer's markets. The comparatively sudden—and apparently temporary—shift to seller's markets raised new problems never faced before by most marketing executives.

One great danger is the growing indifference or arrogance of some salesmen or sales organizations towards customers, or one category of customers, such as smaller customers. Another danger is that top management will permit the sales organization to become attenuated.

In a remarkably prescient article published in the November–December 1971, issue of the *Harvard Business Review,* professors Philip Kotler and Sidney J. Levy of Northwestern University made the important point that marketing under seller's markets is just as difficult as marketing under the more normal buyer's markets—and it's all part of the marketing function. In other words, marketing is not just a "fair-weather function."

In the article, the professors cannily refer to marketing in seller's markets as "demarketing," which is the basis for their title, "Demarketing, Yes, Demarketing!" But their position is that there really is no such function.

They see two main ways to deal with overdemand: "demand containment," and product allocation.

There are some obvious ways to "contain" demand: reduce advertising and sales promotion; cut back on selling time or effort; increase prices, and not just in the obvious way, but also by eliminating freight allowances; and cut back on outlets, such as the elimination of undesirable dealers (i.e., those who have cut prices in the past).

Under product allocation the professors see customers treated under various alternative strategies: "first-come, first-served," "proportional demand" (every customer receiving the same lowered percentage of the previous year's purchases, which was the way diesel oil was allocated in 1972–73 even before the Arab oil embargo); a "favored customer" basis, which may be illegal and is certainly unethical; and a "highest bid" basis, which in effect discriminates against the cash-poor. The professors stress that the objective in product allocation is to "minimize the total disappointment of customers."

During the period of shortages, many companies reacted by dropping the least profitable products or those that required the scarcest raw materials. This is a dangerous policy, according to the professors, because a marginal product that is dropped may still be quite popular with customers who buy large volumes of products still in the line. The professors suggest ways to cope with this situation, including maintaining small stocks of the "retired" products to retain the goodwill of favored customers.

There is another viable alternative not offered in the article. This is to turn over production and customer lists of least profitable products to some smaller manufacturer who can make an acceptable profit on them because of his lower overhead; because he makes related products, which lowers the cost of production; or because his sales force can service the customers at lower costs (or a combination of all three factors). Another advantage of this approach is that the company losing the product line gains some income, although any income gained is usually not very large and is also in the form of royalty payments spread over a limited number of years, such as five.

For many years, some giant companies have been selling off product lines for which demand or profits have been declining. DuPont has done this with chemicals, and General Electric has done it with electronic/electrical mechanical products. General Electric has actually set up a formal organization (Business Growth Services) for the sale of declining product lines plus the results of research and development for which GE itself and other companies do not see enough potential, but which could meet the marketing requirements of a much smaller company. This operation publishes information on products and business available in the United States as well as products or processes available from Japan. "Selected Business Ventures" costs from $175 for one category of product to $725 per year for eight categories; "New from Japan" costs $275 for one category and up to $950 annually for five categories.

An example of a transfer of a product is cited in Chapter 8, the sale of a coal-stoker business by Babcock & Wilcox Company to the Laclede Stoker Company.

DANGER OF OVERREDUCING DEMAND

There is an obvious danger in applying policies of reducing demand and allocating production: you can go too far and damage future relations with customers. Setting up and applying such policies takes skill, and top management must realize this. In other words, top management should not see seller's markets as an opportunity to retire or get rid of high-priced marketing executives in favor of less-experienced, younger executives who have lower salary and bonus requirements. As we have seen, buyer's markets succeed seller's markets all too quickly.

IS THE WASTE AUDIT APPLICABLE TO MARKETING?

Can the concept of the Waste Audit be applied to marketing? Some companies have long applied the concept, in effect, by figuring out their marketing costs very carefully. They know the percentage of product cost that can be assigned to the marketing effort, just as they also know their manufacturing and distribution costs to a mil.

When the cost of marketing a given product or product line gets out of line, such as after a period of time when the naturally higher costs of introduction have been absorbed, an analysis is called for. Sometimes the increase can be ascribed to controllable factors and reversed. However, if increased marketing costs are not controllable but inevitable, perhaps because of increased competition, then the company should consider dropping or disposing of the line.

SELECTED REFERENCE

Fenvessy, Stanley J., *Handling Customer Communications.* Dow Jones-Irwin, Inc., Homewood, Ill. (in publication).

chapter 8

Creative responses
to adversity

OUR COLLECTIVE "SMARTS" are the most effective weapon in the fight against recession, shortages, inflation, and the lesser adversities. Working harder will help, and most Americans can work a lot harder before they are strained (and enjoy their work even more). But working "smarter" is what really counts.

Throughout this book are given examples of how people are working smarter to solve pressing problems:

Packaging designers who have sharply cut the amount of paper and/or plastics required to protect a given product.

Bridge and tunnel authorities that have reduced tolls for cars that carry more than one passenger during the commuting hours.[1] (In the same vein, some ski resorts have offered reduced rates to drivers who bring at least three guests with them to the resorts.)

Manufacturers of motorhomes who have converted to production of small buses.

---

[1] Reduced tolls or no tolls for car pools actually antedate the energy crisis. To cut heavy commuter traffic, tolls for car pools on the giant San Francisco–Oakland Bridge were in effect eliminated in December 1971, in a one-year experiment that was naturally extended during the energy crisis. The practice was emulated by many other bridge and tunnel authorities during the crisis.

Insurance carriers who offer lower rates to drivers who join car pools and thus don't have to drive to work every day.

The Westinghouse engineers who found that the common adhesive that attaches floor tiles can be used to make large cartons stick together inside of trailer vans so that they don't bounce and are thus not damaged by road shocks.

Intelligence and innovation can and must be stimulated by companies to help them solve today's tough problems elegantly rather than by brute force. And the ideas could come from any employee, or outsiders as well.

PROFITABLE OPPORTUNITIES STIMULATED BY ADVERSITY

Don't get the idea that our collective smarts must be entirely concentrated on reacting to shortages. There is another and even more positive response required. I mean the creation of entirely new or modified products and services that will generate *added profits* for companies in an economy ridden by shortages, inflation, and reduced sales of traditional products.

The first crisis that stimulated such new thinking was the energy crisis. Here are some examples of potentially profitable new products that could find a market in nations short of energy and, therefore, of products that are energy intensive in manufacture:

One federal agency hopes that a fluorescent lamp can be developed that can be screwed into the sockets that hold much less efficient incandescent lamps.

A low-cost, remote-control switch for overhead lamps that can be pasted on a wall to turn off signal lights now controlled only in large banks by a remote, wired-in switch is desirable. This device could be similar to the gadget used to change channels on the TV receiver. (If batteries are not required, so much the better.)

Windmills that generate electricity (which must be stored) should be developed. Once the Great Plains were landscaped with windmills that pumped water. With electrification of rural areas in the first third of this century, most of the windmills[2] were replaced by more dependable electric pumps. Today, a few new

---

[2] About 175,000 water-pumping windmills are left, but only half of them still work.

windmills that generate electricity are being installed, but are mostly imported from Australia. That they must be imported suggests a quicker way for an American manufacturer to test domestic markets for unusual products. Instead of going to the great expense of tooling up to make a product that might sell in an inflationary shortage-ridden economy, import the product whole from abroad. Even if your company has to take a loss on each unit sold—by pricing it at a level at which it could be sold profitably in the United States if mass produced here, the overall entry cost is still small compared to tooling up. And the entire test could get started in months instead of a year or so. (Don't be ashamed to put your company's name on foreign-made goods: U.S. manufacturers are among the leading importers, with the automakers pointing the way.) A brand new U.S. supplier of windmills is the Zephyr Wind Dynamo Co.—see Directory.

Cooking utensils with insulated sides and tops are being discussed. Metal pots and pans radiate a great deal of the heat they absorb. Less energy would be required in cooking if the utensils could be made with some insulator, most likely a cellular ceramic sandwiched between metal. Food in such utensils would obviously remain hot a lot longer after they were removed from the stove. Such utensils would obviously cost much more than pots and pans made entirely from metal. However, the prices for fancier copper utensils "essential" for gourmet cooking seem so high that insulated cookware might be able to compete.

An ignition device for gas stoves that replaces the wasteful pilot light on units is now in service. Caloric has added this feature to its new line of gas stoves. Reportedly of British origin, the ignition device is *not* the one offered and widely advertised by Robertshaw Controls Co. These ignition devices use electricity, but much less in terms of energy than the pilot light, since it does not "burn" steadily, only when required and for an instant. Although an electrical ignition unit could be "retrofitted" on existing stoves, it requires too many parts and too much labor to pay off.[3] An ignition system based on the piezoelectric phenomenon might work for new as well as old gas stoves. (Piezoelectric

---

[3] The Ad Hoc Committee on Appliance and Apparatus Efficiency of the New York State Interdepartment Fuel and Energy Committee considers the idea of fitting igniters on present stoves as "impractical." See p. xvi of the committee's report published on June 25, 1973.

materials are crystals that generate tiny electric currents when squeezed.) I saw such a unit demonstrated over 15 years ago in the laboratory of a lone inventor. The mechanical force came from the initial hand turning of the valve that fed gas to the burner. The inventor's work was supported by Arkla. Unfortunately, it never came to fruition. (About ten years later, Roper Corporation actually introduced spark ignition on its line of gas stoves. The energy-saving feature was reportedly withdrawn because it "gummed up" in use.)

Another possibility is to install a battery-powered igniter on existing stoves. Presumably, this would eliminate drilling holes through the back to permit the entry of a power cable. However, the battery would most likely have to be insulated against the heat. To appeal to the consumer, the unit would have to be highly efficient so that the batteries could last from four to six months.

Red China has provided an idea for small (several thousand tons per year) packaged fertilizer factories that could be sold in the underdeveloped nations that are so desperate for food yet can't afford fertilizer at the new high prices. China's "backyard" factories turn coal and water into ammonium bicarbonate. Packaged plants could be designed to convert coal, lignite, peat moss, wood, inedible organic waste, asphalt, or other low-grade petroleum into fertilizer. They would not have to be as efficient as large-scale fertilizer plants but would have to be easy to set up and operate.

COMPACT ENERGY STORAGE SYSTEMS

Compact energy storage systems should be attracting much attention, and they are. In Chapter 15 a system for storing heat in the form of molten anhydrous sodium hydroxide is described. This concept could be applied profitably to light trucks and other delivery vehicles that make frequent stops. In winter to keep the cab warm, the drivers nearly always leave the engines of such vehicles running. This is not only a waste of energy but leaves the machine vulnerable to theft. An NaOH "heat sink" attached to the engine could hold enough heat to keep the cab warm for at least ten minutes or more with the aid of a very small fan operating off the vehicle's battery.

Energy storage systems are needed because there are so many underutilized, cheap sources of energy that don't deliver 24 hours a day. The most obvious one is solar energy, but there is also wind energy and tidal energy. In addition, the conventional power utility does not operate at full capacity all day long, which means that some storage system could be used profitably for "peak shaving"[4] at every power utility in the nation.

The power utilities are, of course, well aware of the need for energy storage. Some have or are constructing pumped-water storage systems in which off-peak power is used to raise water from a river or lake up to a reservoir high in neighboring hills. When this energy is required, the flow of water is reversed through the pumps, which then act as turbines driving large generators of the same type used in hydroelectric plants. Pumped-water systems have a number of disadvantages, of which the first is high initial investment. They are not too efficient, recovering only about three quarters of the energy used to pump the water. Environmentalists are also opposed to the pumped-water systems because they require so much acreage in what are usually unspoiled highlands. In New York State, the environmentalists have been delaying the construction of the Storm King pumped-water storage system by years. (Consolidated Edison calls this project the Cornwall Pumped Storage Project.)

Perhaps the most significant disadvantage of pumped-water storage systems is that they can only be used where there are convenient highlands. So much of the Great Plains and many coastal regions don't have these.

The power utilities are also considering another more exotic means of storing energy: compressing huge amounts of air inside abandoned mines, which are presumably airtight. Without having made an extended analysis of this concept, I have a strong gut feeling that it would suffer from many of the same disadvantages as the pumped-water systems. First of all, a convenient abandoned mine is needed, which limits the concept greatly. Second, I believe that it would be no more efficient than pumped water, and perhaps even less efficient. Then I have the suspicion that it would be difficult to make many mines airtight, and any little tremor might disturb the

---

[4] To meet peak demands, nearly always in summer, the power companies must build additional generating and distributing capacity way over their average needs. For example, New York's Consolidated Edison experiences a summertime peak about 25 percent higher than its winter peak.

air tightness. (Although California is the most earthquake-prone area of the nation, seismologists indicate that many other parts of the nation could be struck by quakes.)

THE APPEAL OF GIANT FLYWHEELS

Fortunately, there is a new (really old) concept in energy storage that does not suffer from the major disadvantages of the two storage systems discussed above. Engineers and scientists are working to develop giant flywheels as a means of storing energy. Actually, all of us depend on the flywheel principle for energy storage. Our cars are equipped with flywheels to smooth out the inherently staccato nature of the internal combustion engine.

The flywheels on even the largest of trucks weigh pounds, whereas the weight of the giant stationary flywheels envisioned for energy storage would be measured in tons, in fact in hundreds of tons. Yet the materials used to construct the flywheels would be so strong that the entire system would most likely not exceed 50 feet or so in height (unlike flywheels on vehicles, these flywheels would nearly always be mounted on vertical axes). Assuming that the flywheels, together with associated motor-generator and a means for evacuating the enclosure in which the wheel spins, occupy a volume 50 × 50 × 50 feet, then they could be erected in the basements of many large buildings. They would serve two purposes. First, and primarily, their function would be peak shaving, holding down the highest level of demand by the building's occupants to earn a lower rate from the local power company. Second, in the event of a brownout or black-out, the flywheel could provide emergency power to maintain essential services, such as lighting and elevators.

How long would it take to pay off the added investment in a fly-wheel storage system? Let's make a conservative guess of ten years (most likely shorter). That would still be a good investment because during those ten years the system would add to the value of the building, and the investment could be recouped in the event of sale of the building. This is based on the quite reasonable assumption that the flywheel system is inherently long-lived and would last for decades, or for a period comparable to the life of the building.

In an excellent discussion of flywheels in the December, 1973, issue of *Scientific American,* Richard F. and Stephen F. Post postulate that a flywheel system capable of storing 10,000 kilowatt-hours would cost $325,000. It could deliver a peak of 3,000 kilowatts. The system would only occupy a space of $20 \times 20 \times 20$ feet. They suggest that such storage systems would be constructed by power utilities at local substations, most likely without requiring any expansion of the substations. The flywheels are certainly more desirable than present peaking equipment, which is usually the gas turbine. The latter burns a high-cost fuel which could become quite scarce. Flywheels not only require a much lower investment than pumped storage, but can be planned and erected in months compared to years for the former. Also, no environmentalists are likely to oppose the erection of compact systems in urban buildings where they are not even visible to passers-by. And, unlike pumped-storage systems, flywheel systems are erected where needed, not miles away with attendant transmission losses.

Is there any danger involved in flywheel storage, especially since the Posts, father and son, also urge that flywheel storage of energy be considered for propulsion of vehicles? The flywheels are supposed to spin at very high speeds, such as 3,500 rpm. At such high rotational speeds, there is a danger that the flywheel will break apart (the way some turbine engines on aircraft have destroyed themselves). In the latest designs for flywheels the materials under consideration are glass and plastic fibers of high strength. According to the Posts, when these fibers are overstressed they disintegrate into relatively harmless powders rather than breaking up into dangerous large chunks as would a metal flywheel.

What about using flywheels to propel cars? (The Swiss long ago built intracity buses that were propelled by flywheels that were recharged by electricity at each stop.) The Posts have figured out that a flywheel system storing 30 kilowatt-hours of energy would provide "reasonable performance" for a small car, or "a range of 200 miles at 60 mph." That's about the same distance a conventional car can travel on one tank of gas at that speed. In contrast to a storage system based on conventional lead-acid batteries, which would weigh about 2,000 pounds to deliver the same amount of energy, the sealed flywheel system would weigh only 500 to 600 pounds, including the entire drive system. And a flywheel system delivers energy quickly and can also be recharged in minutes, while slow-charging batteries never provide fast acceleration.

Flywheels have one other great advantage for vehicles: they can incorporate regenerative braking in which the energy used in braking or picked up while the vehicle is rolling downhill is pumped back into the flywheel. By means of regenerative braking, the range of a vehicle could be extended by 25 to 50 percent. What about long-term parking, such as leaving your vehicle at an airport for two weeks while you and your family are on vacation? Because the flywheel spins in a vacuum, it slows down very slowly. The Posts report that the rundown time for a rotor in a vacuum chamber is estimated at from 6 to 12 months.

Because the flywheel system is long-lived and relatively main-tenance free, the Posts suggest that the drive system from one vehicle could be transferred to a new chassis and body when the original one wears out, just as long-lived aluminum van bodies are remounted on new chassis when the current chassis is scrapped.

The Posts have licensed their flywheel patents to a newly formed company called U.S. Flywheels, Inc., with the stipulation that it develop an "urban vehicle." Wm. M. Brobeck and Associates has a contract with Electric Power Research Institute, the national research arm of the power companies, to develop flywheel systems. During the summer of 1974, Stephen F. Post built and tested a model fly-wheel unit at Brobeck Associates under federal sponsorship.

In this discussion of flywheel storage systems their greatest advan-tage has deliberately been left for the end; they have an efficiency ratio (energy out compared to energy input) of over 95 percent. What a contrast to the claimed "four for three" (i.e. 75 percent) efficiency of pumped storage and 75 percent for storage batteries when they are charged slowly (when charged fast, the conversion efficiency of storage batteries drops to between 75 and 50 percent).

NEW DEVELOPMENTS IN STORAGE CELLS

Even though flywheel storage is more efficient than storage cells, there is still a need for continued development in the latter. When comparatively small amounts of energy must be stored, such as from a windmill, the storage cell has it all over the flywheel. I believe that there are also opportunities for developing very large electro chem-ical storage systems based on materials other than lead and nickel. Just what form these systems will take I cannot say, but I am sure that chemists as well as physicists and engineers will have a big role to play in imaginative energy storage.

AVOID THE "HOSTILE" MARKETS

In seeking opportunities, companies and individuals should avoid what are termed *hostile* markets—those that are either extremely costly or difficult to break into or for which high barriers have been erected against outsiders.

Detroit is the prime example of a hostile market. In no field are greater barriers set up against outside innovation than in the auto industry. An official of the National Transportation Safety Board reported that his outer office is usually filled with frustrated inventors who had developed devices designed to improve the efficiency or safety of the automobile. Some had conceived truly worthwhile advances, but all failed to obtain even a hearing in Detroit. In fairness to the carmarkers, it should be pointed out that if they investigated every new idea offered to them, their engineers would never have time to design next year's cars.

CONVERSION OF GARBAGE INTO ENERGY

There's one form of new process development popular these days for which I see little opportunity for private companies. I mean systems for converting municipal waste into energy. In the past I have been in positions where I had to carefully investigate two systems for converting garbage into saleable products. Both were economic disasters. As a nation we must figure out ways of disposing of our huge outpouring of garbage, but I suspect that this will always have to be an activity subsidized by government.

The disastrous garbage-reclamation projects offer a lesson: don't assume or go along with notions that a new venture is a "natural" or "can't miss." One was a whopping success in Europe but failed in the United States because no one realized that European garbage is quite different (or was back in the early 1960s) from American garbage. The former is mostly organic, while the latter contains a high proportion of metals, plastics, and paper.

OPPORTUNITIES FOR NEW SERVICES

Creativity isn't limited to products. The times will generate opportunities for new services as well. In fact, one such service, the

American Load Pool, is detailed in Chapter 11. I am sure that others will come. For example, during the 12 months after the imposition of the Arab oil embargo, over 20,000 service stations were abandoned in the United States. Some have been converted to other useful tasks, such as offices for opticians, veterinarians, and other health practitioners who moved from locations that lacked parking spaces for their patients and clients. I have come up with one more possibility: conversion to facilities in which car owners rent time and tools to service and repair their own vehicles and also buy grease and oil at the same time. This would not require a great investment since the facilities would be the same as those for a service station. And with the great rise in the cost of auto repairs, more and more Americans than ever will be servicing their own cars, particularly if there is a trend to simpler cars with fewer options. Obviously, no one would undertake to service his own car during the warranty period. However, I suspect that Americans will be keeping their more expensive cars longer so that there will be a long period of ownership for cars after the comparatively short warranty period ends. Facilities such as these would also cut down on pollution since fluids drained from cars would be dumped or pumped into special reservoirs instead of down some nearby sewer, which is where those people who change their own oil get rid of the discarded fluid.

REVIVAL IN DOOR-TO-DOOR DELIVERY

A great shortage of gasoline could stimulate a revival in door-to-door delivery services, which have been on the decline for decades. (Perhaps they could use flywheel-powered vehicles?) When I was a child, my parents purchased all dairy products and eggs from the milkman and all carbonated beverages from another door-to-door supplier. Produce dealers used to tour the neighborhoods; their wagons were horse-drawn. Today, about the only touring produce dealers are in Manhattan's ghettos.

Just as you have to investigate all new products carefully before committing yourself to a full effort, new services for an age of shortages must be tested for market acceptance too. For example, after the Arabs imposed their oil embargo, several consulting firms offered "energy conservation" services to industry and to operators of commercial buildings. One service was launched with much publicity while the other advertised regularly in the business pages of important newspapers. The latter drew a complete lack of interest while the former struggled mightily for business.

COPYING FROM THE PAST

In seeking to create products and services, one should also consider reviving a useful product from the past, such as the anti-syphoning coil discussed in Chapter 1. The coils were not the only revival. Companies that had been selling heating units that burned wood or coal suddenly were inundated with orders, and used, old-fashioned stoves that burned coal or wood suddenly increased tenfold in value. Here are some other examples of revived or supposedly obsolete products that have found a new niche in the market:

1. Stokers that feed coal into large utility boilers are once more in demand. One beneficiary is the Laclede Stoker Company in St. Louis, which now offers a line of coal stokers that was purchased from the Babcock and Wilcox Company in 1970 for $250,000. Laclede, which is now a subsidiary of Michigan General Corp., had abandoned its own line of stokers the previous year. The original notion was that Laclede would simply make and sell parts for Babcock & Wilcox coal-fired boilers still in service. From 1970 through 1973, not a single order was received for a new stoker. Then, after the Arab oil embargo was imposed, orders for new stokers poured in. (President Ford's urging that more utilities convert to coal should further stimulate business.) Some of the utilities ordering stokers are continuing to burn oil or natural gas; they want the stokers on hand in case they are forced to shift to coal because of a shortage of oil or gas. Ira G. Corn, Jr., vice-chairman of Michigan General, claims that the $250,000 investment has now long since paid for itself; he expects the stoker business to remain strong for several more years.

A service by which companies can find out about products and product lines available for sale or license is discussed in Chapter 7.

2. Down blankets. When my mother was married, her mother included a down comforter in her trousseau. Decades later, I inherited the little-used comforter for emergency use in case I had to put up too many guests. In fact, I didn't discard it until several years ago when the outer covering had deteriorated beyond repair. In the fall of 1973, a number of department stores began to offer the "Dyne" comforter, which is made in Denmark and stuffed with down and

feathers just like my mother's. The Dyne comforter, which was advertised as an antidote to the energy crisis, retailed for $100.

3. Decades ago Honeywell sold thermostats with built-in clocks that could be adjusted to automatically raise or lower temperature (nighttime set-back). The clocks were of the wind-up kind since the electric clock had not yet been invented. After the electric clock came into being, it was designed into thermostats in place of the wind-up units. In 1974 Honeywell revived the thermostat with wind-up clock. It sells for $25 and has the advantage that it can be installed in place of a present thermostat that is not mounted convenient to an electrical outlet.

4. Retreads. Although retreaded tires are universally accepted for trucks, their use on the cars of the affluent was minimal if not nonexistent. Now I tell my friends to buy retreads when they need replacement tires (see Chap. 10).

5. Airships. In September, 1974, a conference on the airship was held at Monterey, California, under the sponsorship of a gaggle of federal agencies and hosted by the Massachusetts Institute of Technology. John Wood, director of Aerospace Developments, Ltd., London, described a "supertanker of the air" filled with natural gas which it would transport from the Middle East, where it is nearly all flared uselessly. The natural gas would both support the airship and also provide fuel for its turboprop engines. Presumably once the tanker had delivered its load and was deflated, it would have to be transported back to Arabia on the deck of a freighter or one of the supertankers that transport oil from Arabia.

There's one product that I doubt could be revived in today's sexually free society, even though it is a great energy conserver. I mean the bundling bed.

Where do you look for ideas for revived products? How about those facsimile reissues of old Sears, Roebuck catalogs? Crown Publishers, Inc., New York, brought out the 1902 and 1927 catalogs. They sell for $6.98 in hard cover and $3.98 in paperback. Back issues of old magazines, such as the *National Geographic* and the *Saturday Evening Post* should also provide examples.[5] Another good source of ideas might be your parents or grandparents.

---

[5] A mail-order source of old magazines is Everybody's Bookshop, 317 West 6th St., Los Angeles, Calif. 90014.

"REMANUFACTURING" AS A CURRENT OPPORTUNITY

Two forms of "remanufactured" products are discussed in Chapter 10 as opportunities to save dollars. They are "rerefined" lube oil and retreaded tires. The concept of remanufacturing should also be considered by companies as a touchstone to new sales and profits in this age of shortages and inflation.

Remanufacturing is, of course, nothing new. Rebuilt starters, generators, transmissions, and even whole motors have long been available to car and truck operators. The "glider kit," a new cab to fit over an older motor, transmission, and axles, has long been available for the powerful tractors that haul trailers. Rebuilt machine tools are in high demand whenever deliveries on new tools stretch into years, which happens every few years, and as indicated in Chapter 3, when a company rents a computer from one of the computer-makers, it has no assurance that the central processing unit, CPU, is brand-new.

Are there any opportunities in your industry to offer a useful remanufactured product? Even if you don't remain in the remanufacturing business for decades, there's nothing wrong with dabbling in rebuilding for a few years during an era of shortages. It could be an efficient way to maintain sound relations with good customers when you can't supply them with new capital goods because of extremely long lead times. Are you reluctant to offer remanufactured products because it is "bad for the image?" If so, consider that IBM is not too proud to install remanufactured CPUs on customers' premises.

GOOD IDEAS ARE WHERE YOU FIND THEM

This chapter was originally entitled "How the Engineering Department Helps Overcome the Crisis." When I got to writing the chapter, I remembered that good ideas are where you find them. The notion that creative solutions to a company's problems and opportunities can only come from those specially trained to create is nonsense. In fact, a formally organized "creative" department may become so locked into concepts in which it has a big stake or has invested a lot of time that all competing notions, no matter how attractive, are rejected. The greatest example of such rigid thinking is the rejection nearly 100 years ago by the management of the Western

Union Telegraph Company of a one-third share in Alexander Graham Bell's telephone patent for a paltry $10,000.

There's not much use in offering a long prescription on how to stimulate your employees and how to welcome outsiders with ideas. Volumes have been written on the stimulation of creativity and how to operate a suggestion system profitably. If you can't find ways to stimulate your employees, all employees, to contribute ideas, you're most likely beyond redemption.

chapter 9

Cutting costs in paperwork

THE GREAT PAPER SHORTAGE OF 1974, like the great energy crisis that ended earlier in the same year, was also beneficial—if individuals and organizations responded intelligently.

Hopefully, the conservative practices developed to cope with the paper shortage will remain in effect because the price of paper has not dropped much if at all as demand has slackened. There are other sound reasons for extending conservative practices in specification, purchase, and use of paper:

1. Because postal rates are up and are sure to continue to climb, it makes sense to reduce the weight of company mail or use techniques in mailing that cut this ever-growing cost of doing business.
2. Intelligent practices in paper handling can cut the bulk of paper that must be stored on company premises, thus freeing space for other more productive uses.
3. Paper may be in short supply again with any upturn in business because not much new papermaking capacity is being added, and the new capacity always seems to be late in coming on stream. And whenever demand exceeds capacity, lower-cost grades disappear first.

With any upturn in business which should result in sharply increased demand for paper, the scrap price should be attractive enough to make collection and sale of waste paper a small source of revenue. So don't dismantle your procedures for collecting scrap paper.

But by far the most important reason for taking a close look at the way paper is used in your company is to revise paper-handling methods and thus gain dramatic savings in clerical labor, increase customer satisfaction, and reduce errors and the amount of money and space devoted to filing of documents. For example, one small woodworking plant in the southeast by shifting to a new multipart form not only cut its use of paper in order-preparation by one quarter but cut the period required to ship a customer's order by two days. And employee morale actually improved because the new form was easier to work with than the older forms it replaced.

This chapter will begin with the opportunity for greatest savings, new forms, then cover the generally lesser aspects of paper savings, which are computer forms, in-house printing, promotional printing and office procedures.

OTHER BENEFITS OUTWEIGH SAVINGS IN PAPER FORMS

The technology of forms is advancing just as other technologies are making strides. If your company is employing forms that were designed ten or even five years ago, a common situation, they are most likely obsolete. You may not even realize that your forms are obsolete because you believe they were "designed" recently. However, study of the "new" forms will show that they are merely adaptations of forms designed many years prior.

Creating new forms is a real art, one that few office managers can claim they have mastered. How do you take advantage of new technology and "smarts" in forms? Either by working with a manufacturer of forms or one of the brokers in these forms, both categories lumped together in your classified phone book under "Business Forms & Systems." If you deal with a manufacturer of forms, his representatives can only supply those forms that his company has the capacity to print and assemble. Brokers,[1] on the other hand, are

_____

[1] Many of the more knowledgeable brokers or independent forms experts are members of the National Business Forms Association.

familiar with the capabilities of many printers and manufactuerers of forms and should select the one that can do the best job at the best price.

Here are some of the new ideas that you should be utilizing in your forms to cut clerical labor and errors and to speed paperwork: multipart forms that utilize the initial writing or typing of an order to create simultaneously an order to the production department; an invoice (typing the address so that the invoice can go into an envelope with a window) ; a packing slip for the shipping department; a shipping label; an order-taker's copy (if that is necessary— see below) ; a "second-notice of payment due"; and perhaps a copy to the sales department for sales analysis. Despite the fact that multipart forms have been around for decades, too many companies still waste a lot of time and money rewriting or retyping the same information a second or even third time. Even within the same multipart form, there is unnecessary retyping; double typing of the same address for the "Charge To" and "Ship to" portions. If both addresses are the same, all that's needed is writing or typing "same" in the space for the second address or, if there is an indication that no address means both are the same, leaving it blank.

In many companies, hole-punching devices are provided for those people who file certain copies of multipart forms. For a small extra charge, these steps (and purchase of the hole-punchers) can be avoided by ordering punching of the holes as the forms are manufactured.

Some office managers have the mistaken belief that a multipart form for their needs cannot be created because it would be too thick to fit into the company's typewriters. They are not aware that newer techniques permit the creation of thinner forms that can be processed on any electric typewriter. These techniques include carbonless paper, now much thinner than the earlier versions, and gluing machines. In the past, the inclusion of a gummed label as part of a multipart form meant a thicker form. Many do not realize those labels can be applied with the aid of a small gluing machine. (One supplier of small label gluers, Glue-Fast Equipment Co., charges less than $30 for the machine.) No extra steps are involved because extra-thick gummed paper requires a moistening step, now eliminated. (An alternative is a self-adhering label, but they are extra-thick too.)

If you bring in an expert to redesign your forms, here are some of the other clever things he will do:

Arrange spaces to be filled in horizontally instead of in stacked fashion so that they are completed much quicker on a typewriter. Make the forms' spacings match the spacing on typewriters.

Design forms so that they fit into standard window envelopes. Time-saving and error-avoiding window envelopes are often overlooked either because no one seems to know how to do it or because it seems that the window would have to be custom cut in an unfamiliar, awkward, or "illegal" place on the envelope instead of near the center. Some companies have gotten away with windows cut in such odd spots as the upper left-hand corner, which means that the return address has to go on the back. But forms experts warn not to ask permission from your local postmaster before approving such ostensibly unacceptable envelopes. The postmaster will most likely refuse prior permission but raise no objection if presented with a fait accompli.

Eliminate parts and associated carbons. For example, is it absolutely essential that the order-taker retain a copy, especially if he is in the same building as the accounting department? If customers rarely go back to the order-taker to change or question their orders, then there is no reason why he should retain a copy. If he has to check an order he has taken, he can refer to the copy in the accounting department. (If order-takers do retain copies for good reason, these copies should only be retained until the goods in question are shipped, and then the copies can be sold for scrap or destroyed.)

The above discussion, of course, assumes that paper is available. Even if paper is in good supply, most of the above recommendations should be applied to save money. However, what if there is another paper shortage? Here are some ways to cope:

Order in greater quantities to insure cooperation from printers and suppliers of forms. Instead of buying a six-months' or one-year's supply, with the supplier retaining much of the order in inventory, to be delivered as you need it, order an 18-months' or even two-year's supply, and store all of it on your premises. The nuisance of storing it plus the money tied up in extra inventory will be balanced some what by the lower per unit cost and by the usual inflation in paper costs.

Now there is an obvious danger in ordering so much in advance. What if your requirements change and the form becomes obsolete, a common occurrence? One way to salvage ostensibly obsolete forms is to use "crash printing," according to forms expert Seymour Kramer, president of Revere Business Graphics, Inc. In crash printing an old address or some headings no longer relevant are overprinted by heavy lines or crosshatching. Simultaneously, the new address or heading is printed in some blank space on the form with enough force to imprint on every one of the parts. A less-desirable alternative is to print the new address or heading on self-adhering (i.e., pressure-sensitive) labels and apply these over the obsolete data on the forms. This labor-intensive step can either be taken as the forms are used or, more efficiently, in batches before the forms are used.

Cut down on form consumption in one small way by not charging industrial customers for low-value spare parts or hardware. Instead, just drop the requested parts in a small bag, address, and ship at no charge. Stanley J. Fenvessy, a consultant, has been telling his clients to do this for years, pointing out that preparation of an invoice costs more than the parts plus mailing. And the customer should be doubly grateful because he has also saved himself the cost of preparing a small check.

To cut the size of new forms, leave out all promotional copy in the heading, such as the company logo, "Established in 18 . . . ," "A Division of the ABC Company," "The Most Complete Line in the Industry," etc. Those who receive parts of this form outside your own company are rarely buying influences. By removing such gratuitous copy, you may be able to save an inch of paper, which adds up to a lot of paper in an 11-part form with carbon paper interleaved and ordered in the tens of thousands.

In many companies, however, the real problem during the paper scarcity was not the general shortage of paper but shortages in specific grades and colors to which the company and its employees had been accustomed. If many clerks who sort, file, and distribute parts of forms have learned to work by color coding and shape, the losses in terms of retraining and errors and delays in filing and distribution far outweigh the cost of the paper involved.

So *making do* is just as important as cutting consumption of paper. Fortunately, there are ways to substitute or modify papers so that a standard form can be kept as close to its familiar format as possible.

For example, to color parts where the original color is no longer offered by paper manufacturers (as this is written there are still shortages in certain colors), that color can be printed on white paper. Obviously, this adds to the cost of the form. However, this extra printing, which adds very little to the cost of the form, may be economically insignificant compared to the potential for errors in *not* adding the color. Another alternative is to print the required color in striping down the margins.

PAPER SAVINGS IN THE COMPUTER ROOM

There are many ways to save paper in the computer room, some of which involve changes in your entire approach to a task. These changes may also be cost-cutting themselves. Here are some possibilities:

Switch from punched-card input to off-line tape input, direct on-line input, or optical input of masses of data. The savings are not only in the elimination of cards but also usually in faster input. If you are not yet prepared or able to switch to tape or on-line input, at least switch to the new "buffered" key-punch machines, which cut down on wasted cards by holding the characters keyed in a small buffer memory until the operator has finished keyboarding the complete record. The operator, if he or she senses that a mistake has been made, can backspace, correct the error, and resume keying in the rest of the record. Only when the next card is advanced to the keying position are the holes punched in the previous card.

As much as possible, avoid making more copies of a given printout than the number of parts in the standard printout forms. For example, if it has been your practice to prepare 13 copies of a given report, necessitating a second run on the line printer because you only have 11-part forms (9 of the 11 parts in the second run are wasted), make a careful examination of the list of those to whom copies are forwarded. Do they all need copies for retention, or could some of them share a circulated copy? Here's another way to avoid wasting parts of a multipart form.

Let's assume that 12 copies are required and your line printer can only handle an 11-part form. Instead of running a second form, prepare the report "two-up" on six-part forms side-by-side in identical fashion. After the form is run through the line printer, it has to be split lengthwise as well as page by page. Your employees should not object to the fact that the report is only half as wide as previously where many copies are truly required on a regular basis, consider computer output microfilm —C.O.M. 252 replacement.

Analyze jam-ups, printing runs in which forms get jammed in the printer—which sometimes results in rerunning the entire job. You may discover that your printer can't handle certain weights or thicknesses of forms; these forms should be avoided, or some repair or modification may be called for on the printer. If your DP manager is planning to print a report on a new form never utilized before, he should first experiment on a few feet of the form to find out if it can work in that printer. And when the new form is accepted, someone should watch the print run carefully to make sure there are no jam-ups. Another way to save on printing is to reink used ribbons instead of discarding them. One re-inking system is supplied by Burroughs Business Forms (see directory) .

Save by cutting down on the frequency of reports. Are daily reports required, or could they be issued every other day or only twice a week? Are weekly reports required, or could they be issued every other week? Or could summaries be issued weekly, with a comprehensive report only once a month?

To further save on stock printout forms, which were difficult to procure during the paper shortage, switch from double spacing to single spacing and change the computer program so that new paragraphs begin on the same sheet instead of jumping to the next sheet, a common extravagance in computer operations.

Reduce the type size on the printer so that it can print eight lines to the inch instead of six or seven. Because such tight printing may make it difficult to track a line of data across the full width of the sheet, consider switching to a new computer printout form from Moore Business Forms, Inc., called "Speediread." It has alternating guidelines of green, white, and beige, for eight-to-the-inch printing. The sheets on this fanfold form are only 8½ inches deep instead of the usual 11 inches, yet they can hold as much information, thus saving 25 percent in paper and mailing costs, which some early users report more than makes up for the considerably higher price of this new form.

Often a report consists of a series of mostly short lines of information. By adjusting the pin feed on your printer to a narrower form and using that form, much paper can be saved. The occasional long line can be split into two or more shorter lines by a small "patch" in the computer program.

Report by exception rather than in toto. Because the computer has the capacity to grind out so much information, there is the ever-present danger to let it spew forth very detailed reports that are beyond the capacity of any executive to absorb. Insist on reporting of differences or trends only.

Use the backside of single-sheet computer printout paper. In many operations, a slow-speed printer, commonly a Teletype, makes a record of all instructions to the computer. At the end of the day, this record is usually discarded, unless something went wrong. Instead of discarding it, turn it over and run it back through before discarding it.

There are also some newer constructions in computer forms which may help you to cut costs, if not in the computer room then in some other aspect of your operations:

Pockets are now available in paper forms. The pocket can be formed of paper or of transparent plastic film if the contents must be viewed. This handy form is much used for storage or shipment of flat items such as prescriptions, negatives, photos, bond coupons or other documents, or even of three-dimensional items such as hardware, small spare parts, semiconductors, or jewelry.

Plastic or aluminum-foil self-adhering identification plates are available on continuous forms so that serial numbers can be imprinted by typewriter or computer printer on the plates at the time an order is received for an instrument or machine, thus saving time on the production floor.

Companies that mail out large numbers of checks to employees, stockholders, or as refunds to customers should investigate check mailers as an effective means of eliminating the manual or machine effort of inserting and sealing a check into an envelope. Check mailers are computer forms with the check already inside the envelope. Obviously, the "signature" is a carbon copy of the signature written by an authorized officer on an outer sheet, which is retained for record purposes. Banks accept such signatures.

How does a smaller company that does not create many checks gain similar benefits? By dealing with a computer service bureau that orders large quantities of checks at substantial discounts. As required, company names and magnetic-ink code numbers can be added to the standard checks by imprinting. Gaining this saving is a good motivation for arranging for preparation of checks by a service, but it should have been your practice in the past since these services usually prepare checks at a lower cost than an in-house work force, even with computers.

INVESTIGATE INDEPENDENT SUPPLIERS

Now that the great paper shortage has eased, companies should investigate new or supplementary sources of computer forms and supplies, such as punched cards. Where the independent form manufacturers differ from the computer makers is not so much in price per 1,000 (which may be a bit less), but in service and other less-evident aspects of cost. For example, the independent may accept smaller minimum orders, in case you are stuck unexpectedly. The independents are also characterized by much lower order charges, or they may not charge at all for order-processing costs if your order is large enough. In addition, they are much more willing to keep stock on their premises and deliver as needed. Finally, if as a result of a change in procedures you are stuck with an oversupply of a given standard form, such as punched cards, they may be willing to accept a return, especially during periods of shortages.

CONSERVATION IN PROMOTIONAL MATERIAL

There are opportunities to save paper and time and money at all three stages of communication: the creation of the document, its distribution, and its disposition.

Let's start from the back. An analysis of the disposition of a document, what happens to it, provides the greatest opportunity for conservation. All of us receive so-called junk mail, letters or promotion pieces that are of little or no interest. Now put yourself in the place of the sender, who has spent a lot of money and effort to deliver that document into your hands. How many of the letters, brochures, and other items mailed out by your company end up in a wastebasket or in a pigeonhole where no one ever again consults them? Plenty!

Keeping your mailing lists up to date is more important than ever these days of rising paper, printing, and mailing costs. No central office can keep a nation-wide mailing list up to date properly, even if it subscribes to services that keep track of changes at the executive level. Branch offices or local sales reps must be asked to share in this job; it's very much to their benefit to see that relevant documents from headquarters, such as announcements of new products or price changes, get into the right hands at the offices of customers. With just a glance, a local person can tell if a given recipient is correctly listed.

Some years ago when I was the chief editor of a technical publishing company I asked the circulation manager to provide me with a computer printout of the names of all subscribers in Manhattan, the borough of New York in which I then resided. I was concerned because the publication in question did not make as much of an impact as projected. I was about to depart for California, and I used the five hours in the air productively to scan the entire list of some 3,000 names one by one. Merely because I read the *New York Times* and *The Wall Street Journal* every day and because I am familiar with the geography of Manhattan, I detected many errors or highly suspect names on the list: These consisted of:

1. Duplications. Because the list was arranged by zip code, neighboring companies were listed on the same sheet or the very next sheet. I found that the same person might be listed two or even three times at the same address, but over differing company names. Obviously, these were situations in which companies, for their own purposes, had set up subsidiary corporations, perhaps to hold the real estate occupied by the company. Sometimes the duplications were for the same company, but with a slight variation in the listing of the customer's name. For example, T. G. Brown and Ted Brown. (Incidentally, if you have a large list, it makes sense to check regularly for "dups" by means of computer programs.)

2. Companies no longer in business or which had located elsewhere. Because relocations, bankruptcies, dissolutions, or acquisitions by large companies always make the new columns, I was aware of many listings for companies that were either no longer in business

or had moved to another city or state. In the last instance, the names should have been listed at their proper address. When first class mail is sent to companies no longer in business or to individuals who are deceased, the Postal Service is supposed to return the envelopes to the sender with an appropriate indication. Apparently this procedure failed, and there are two possible explanations. First of all, the Postal Service may be lax in returning the envelopes. Second, the low-level clerk in your own organization responsible for updating the mailing list may be lazy. So check out your procedures for updating of mailing lists.

3. Deceased recipients. I found several names of prominent businessmen who had been dead for periods ranging from several months to several years. I was aware of these names because I had either noted them on the obituary page or because I had once known them, either directly or as the fathers of acquaintances.

4. Addresses in residential areas. There is nothing wrong with sending technical material to a potential customer at his home rather than his place of business: he most likely gives more attention to reading matter at home than in a busy office. However, your mailing lists may be loaded down with the names of teenagers who "crash" technical exhibitions and then proceed to fill out dozens of cards requesting company literature (there are individuals who feel important when they get a lot of mail, even if the documents involved are of no value to them). Purge your lists of all such noncustomers, but be careful not to eliminate customers who prefer to receive technical literature at home. To indicate the latter situations, their company affiliations could be included on the mailing list.

5. Competitors. I discovered several instances in which competitors were on our mailing lists under alternate company names, but the addresses, of course, were the same. Your local salesmen should be able to detect and eliminate such listings.

6. Soviet-Bloc and other overseas listings. Several listings were addressed to the Amtorg Trading Corp. This is an agency of the Soviet Government. If it is your intention to do business behind the Iron Curtain, then such listings should be welcome. On the other hand, if you do no export business or are not permitted to export to the Soviet Union, there is no reason you should pay to place technical literature in the hands of those whose only purpose may be to copy your products and sell them in overseas markets in competition with yours. How do you spot such unwelcome listings? First of all, the address

is pretty certain to be in Manhattan. So you can limit your search to zip codes from 10001 through 10022 (above 10022 the zip codes for Manhattan are mostly in residential sections or industrial areas in which no foreign government is likely to maintain an office). Next, check suspicious company names under the extensive list of Importers and Exporters in the Manhattan classified phone directory. For example, the Polish American Purchasing Service, Inc. and the Yangtze Trading Corp. are listed under Exporters. Possibly, the latter is an agency of the Red Chinese government.

7. Overkill. Some of the titles on the list were those of top management, which makes sense in smaller companies, but is obviously wasted on giant corporations whose presidents and chief executives do not participate in product specification or purchasing of standard day-in, day-out items. In addition, too many copies went to some companies. There is no need to send copies of your new product announcements, price changes, and catalogs to every engineer and purchasing agent or other buying influence in a company. In particular, to send too many expensive catalogs that may cost several dollars each to print plus another dollar to mail is a great extravagance.

Here in macrocosm you see a situation that is quite likely to be matched in microcosm in your own mailing lists.

Salesmen in branch offices are your principal means for eliminating unproductive names from your mailing lists. It is not too demanding to send them printouts of your mailing list every six months and ask them to weed out unproductive names. There are lots of periods during an employee's workweek when he is merely sitting around waiting to see someone. Checking lists can be accomplished in such odd moments. If your salesmen balk at eliminating any names at all, then assign each one a quota of new names; this should produce some worthwhile eliminations. (Of course, these printouts must be handled with some care, since they are your customer lists.)

In addition, once a year each person on the list should be sent a form postcard with tear-off return half to check if he is still interested in remaining on your mailing list. Most people are honest enough to admit their lack of interest. However, there is a danger that some truly important customer will be too busy to check off the return portion and drop it in the outgoing mail basket. So before eliminating anyone, send lists of those you plan to drop to each sales office for one more check.

INTRACOMPANY MAILINGS

Most of the wasted mailing is to those outside of companies, but there is plenty of waste within companies as well. Although some of the waste involves sending copies of documents to employees who have left, retired, moved to another branch, or died, most of the waste involves sending material to employees for whom the information is of little or no value. The classic example of such waste occurred in government, not too surprisingly. Each month the headquarters of the Army Quartermaster Corps would run off a computer listing of all items in its inventory and send one copy to the top quartermaster attached to each Army district. Each copy entirely filled a corrugated carton. The head of the Quartermaster Corps was quite chagrined to discover on an inspection tour at one Army base dozens of cartons of computer printouts neatly stored up to the ceiling *unopened*.

Does your company send documents, printouts, and brochures to employees who neatly file them away and never refer to them again? A close inspection might reveal filing cabinets full of documents that no one ever looks at (and if there were a rare need to check the information, it could be done by a phone call to headquarters where the originals are kept). Eliminating such waste correspondence would not only save money in the future but empty a lot of filing cabinets as well. (Some years ago I took over a position vacated by a true "squirrel." When I arrived I was asked how many of my predecessor's 22 four-drawer file cabinets I would require. I replied, "One," and as a result that department did not order another file cabinet during the five years I was associated with that company.)

REPORTING BY EXCEPTION

There's another obvious way to cut down on intracompany correspondence: report by exception instead of presenting the "whole picture," which may be confusing (preventing the reader from seeing the trees for the forest). In other words, simply report where significant changes have occurred. Enforcing a policy of reporting by exception may take some doing. Some insecure individuals avoid reporting by exception because it highlights mistakes and deficiencies; they much prefer presenting the whole picture because it's so much harder or takes much longer to tell that something's going wrong.

IS THIS LETTER NECESSARY?

These are the high-volume categories of company mail. There are also some lesser opportunities to conserve that are important because they are more visible to and have a greater impact on employees. These are based on the "write more on less paper" rule.

1. As much as possible return to the World War II practice of answering inquiries on the incoming document, and then returning it immediately to the inquirer. Besides speeding up the process of re-plying, which the inquirer should appreciate, this procedure not only saves stationery and carbon paper or photocopying, but also elimi-nate filing of the original inquiry and a carbon of the reply. To make this procedure as acceptable as possible, those who use it attach a little tab to the returning document with a printed message to the effect: "Instant Reply: Please excuse our informality. We thought you would prefer a speedy reply to a formal letter. Our reply is at the bottom or back of this document."

Speaking of filing, because of recurrent shortages in manila paper, manila file folders are sometimes in short supply. To cope with this minor shortage all you have to do is reuse file folders. On the first reusing, they should be turned inside out. After that, new identifica-tion labels can be pasted over the old ones as long as the folders hold together. Whenever old files are discarded or destroyed, those in charge should be instructed to salvage all the file folders, after which their contents can be sold for scrap either shredded or whole.

2. Cut down on For Your Information (FYI) copies, most of which are ignored. The average cost of creating, dispatching, and filing a single carbon copy is an incredible $2, going up all the time. (This is in addition to the even higher cost of creating the original.)

3. Use informal "From the desk of . . ." notes printed on small sheets of inexpensive paper (perhaps salvaged from some larger sheets) instead of formal letters printed on full-size, fancy water-marked bond paper.

4. Use form letters to reply to inquiries as much as possible. A General Services Administration handbook (Federal Stock No. 7610–117–8777) [2] shows that a form letter on average costs only one-tenth as much to prepare as a reply that is individually dictated and typed (These figures are for a letter with 25 lines; the longer the letter, the

<hr>

[2] Available from the Superintendent of Documents, U.S. Govt. Printing Office, Washington, D.C. 20402

greater the savings.) Form letters also save paper because no carbon copy is required and there is little or no chance for typing errors resulting in waste of paper—all the typist has to do is type in an address. Will your customers be turned off by a form letter? Consider that a carefully composed form letter may do more to satisfy the inquirer than a hurriedly dictated one.

5. Use the phone! Considering the cost of dictating and transcribing a written reply or inquiry, it is often cheaper, and certainly much faster, to use the telephone. Also, the person called has a chance to ask more questions, thus avoiding further correspondence on both sides. The phone is also a better medium of communication than writing because the intonation of the voice of whomever you're talking to can often provide clues to the real state of events. (The handiest way of recording phone messages for those away from their desks is the Phone-O-Gram, a standard book that automatically makes a carbon of all such notes, very useful when the original note is lost— a common occurrence in busy offices. The Phone-O-Gram is available from The Drawing Board, Inc.)

MORE EFFICIENT RESPONSE TO CUSTOMER INQUIRIES

Earlier, in Chapter 7 an updating of the system for dealing with customer inquiries was urged. This is the right place to discuss the mechanics of such a system since paper is the medium of response.

Word processors, of course, should not be limited just to responding to customers, but for all correspondence. With these typewriters with memories, companies can cut a lot of fat out of their office operations. Some companies that have installed word processors have actually achieved lean ratios of five executives to one secretary.

Word processors come in four main categories. The first, stand-alone machines, is the most familiar. The IBM MTST and Mag-Card Selectrics are examples. A few suppliers have created small systems in which a group of typing stations, ranging from three up to eight or more, feed information onto a central memory, which is often a small disk file. In more elaborate versions, many typing stations feed information into a dedicated central computer, and all correspondence is printed out on high-speed line printers. Finally, the typing stations can feed into the company's large central computer which handles word processing simultaneously with many other tasks.

As far as the individual typist is concerned, it doesn't make much difference which variety of word processor she's working at: she types some material, which is recorded; when the associated document has been reviewed and corrected, she calls up the record associated with that document, and merely types in the corrections, presumably leaving the bulk of the document unchanged.

To speed up correspondence, a number of standard paragraphs and salutations may be memorized by the machine or system. The author of the document merely indicates the code numbers for those paragraphs so that the typist has little to do beyond typing in a few codes, plus any original copy.

When word processors were first introduced there was some concern that secretaries and typists would resent them. Surprisingly, there is little opposition from those who use the machines, which in effect upgrade their operators. Instead, the main opposition came from executives who had grown accustomed to individual secretaries. Companies that decide to introduce word processing must do so with caution and concern. Executives should understand that not having an individual secretary actually frees them from the worry of always providing work for her.

Smaller companies that are not yet ready to adopt word processing should raise the level of their responses to customers by following the Letter-Rating Guide that appears at the end of this chapter.

FURTHER SAVINGS IN DISTRIBUTION

Further savings are also possible in the way letters are sent to recipients. As stressed earlier window envelopes should be used as much as possible. In addition, smaller envelopes into which correspondence is folded should be favored over larger envelopes into which documents can be inserted without folding. Envelopes of the common $9\frac{1}{2}$ x 4 inch size are not only cheaper than large manila or white envelopes, but also weigh less. So use of the smaller envelopes might save an additional 10 cents for that extra fraction of an ounce that pushes the sealed envelope over the next ounce mark on the scale. Such envelopes also move through the mail system faster because they can be handled on the Postal Services' semiautomatic machines, while the larger ones cannot.

Here are some other ways to save in distribution:

In intracompany correspondence to save envelopes, emphasize self-mailers, folding nonconfidential documents (the vast majority of all correspondence), and typing or writing the name of the recipient and his department on the back. The folded document can be stapled or held together by cellophane tape. If this simple way of saving envelopes is not acceptable, then multitrip envelopes with places on the front or back for many names and addresses should be used.

Check the costs of any manila-colored paper or envelopes you are buying against the cost of white paper. Because many mills now bleach all of their output, they have to add color to create manila paper, which may make their manila more expensive than white paper, says Leonard B. Schlosser, president of Lindenmeyr Paper Corp., paper merchant.

If much correspondence is sent daily to the same address, such as regional plants or sales offices of major customers, the mail room should set up pigeonholes for these addresses. At the end of the day, all the mail in the pigeonhole can be inserted in a single large envelope on which the correct postage is stamped. Two forms of savings are achieved—the use of quality bond envelopes is avoided (brown interacompany envelopes are satisfactory) and there are considerable savings in postage since the great majority of first-class letters weigh only a fraction of an ounce. In most companies the heavy duty "communal" envelope is made of manila, but an increasing number of companies are using envelopes made of DuPont's "Tyvek," a paper-like material made of fibers of polyethylene. Tyvek is so strong that it can't be torn like paper—it has to be slit open with a knife—yet it weighs only a fraction as much as paper. Large envelopes made of Tyvek cost about three times as much as paper, but much of the extra cost is recouped in lower postage charges—for overseas airmail where each ounce costs 26 cents Tyvek envelopes actually save money. Among the companies using large Tyvek envelopes for bulked mail to a single address are Coca-Cola and 3M. (Tyvek envelopes are available from many manufacturers of envelopes but not directly from Du Pont.)

All handling of personal mail should be eliminated unless your offices are so far from the nearest post office that it is impossible for employees to visit it during their lunch hour.[3] (This rule would most likely work the greater hardship on executives, who are usually the worst abusers of the mailroom.) If personal mail is accepted by your mail room, then strict accounting of the postage involved should be set up—otherwise your postage bill will really jump.

The mailroom must remain open long enough to get out the day's mail, even if this entails some overtime. Conversely, the mailroom should open early enough in the morning to have all mail distributed and on each recipient's desk at the beginning of the work day.

To speed up delivery of important correspondence overseas, executives who travel to foreign countries should be asked to hand carry such mail for delivery to your offices overseas (as long as they are not too burdened with other company property, such as samples). Even if the letters require local postage at that point, there's a big saving over the airmail charges for each letter from the United States. But the main saving will be in reliability of delivery, since most oversees postal systems are even more unreliable than the U.S. Postal Service.

If your company has many vehicles operating interstate, use them to carry letters and packages. To compensate for deficiencies in the Postal Service, more and more big companies are hauling their own mail. After the driver drops the mail off at a branch operation, it is then posted at a local post office for local delivery.

HOW TO SAVE PAPER IN IN-HOUSE PRINTING

Most companies operate some form of in-house printing shop, and in big companies these can be major operations consuming great amounts of paper. They can also be big wasters of paper.

The rule to "write more in less space" applies equally well to in-house print shops. There are some very easy ways to accomplish this: begin by printing on both sides of the sheet, and specifying narrower margins and single spacing.

Examine some recent jobs printed in your "Repro Shop." You will most likely find that few if any are printed on both sides of the sheet,

---

[3] If your company is promoting car pooling, then employees should be permitted to post mail in the company mailroom.

although two-side printing is the norm in commercial printing, such as newspapers, magazines, and books. There are various reasons why one-side printing is specified. One reason may be that it "looks nicer." Another may be due to the quality of the paper you are forced to buy these days: it is subject to "show-through," the intrusion of the printing on the obverse side. The answer to the last is to examine your daily newspaper. Show-through is quite evident, and you are quite tolerant of it.

The extravagantly wide margins and double spacing characteristic of some in-house printing must also be dropped in an era of adversity.

Careful editing is another way to save paper and the time of all those forced to read reports. Most business writing is terribly verbose. It is filled with such unneeded phrases as "in the area of" or "in order to." Retraining all those who write reports is not easy. If your company generates many long internal reports, the simplest answer may be to hire a good copyeditor. With so many magazines and newspapers going out of business, there are loads of expert copyeditors on the market, and they are not afraid to use their blue pencils.

AGAIN EMPHASIZE REPORTING BY EXCEPTION

If you can't afford or don't want to hire a copyeditor, there's that simple rule offered earlier: report by exception. Even if you're not prepared to give up the complete report, insist that all such long reports begin with a summary that highlights significant changes since the last reporting period. After a while you may find that the summary alone is sufficient; if needed, you can always obtain the background data.

AVOIDING EXTRA FORMS

Judicious editing is necessary to avoid the printing of an extra four-page form just to provide an "odd" page. Few report writers are aware of the mechanics of printing. They don't know, for example, that a report that is 17 pages long requires at least 20 sides of paper. (Since most in-house presses are limited to eight-page forms—assuming that the sheets are four pages to a side and the report is printed on both sides of the paper—printing the seventeenth page calls for a separate two-page sheet printed on only one side.)

Report writers should be taken on a tour of your Repro Shop where the printer can explain how he produces reports of various lengths and the opportunities to save paper by simply eliminating one page. Nevertheless, the responsibility for eliminating that last wasteful page should be assigned to the printer, who can usually recommend to the report writer some obvious ways to save just one page. However, this should be done before the report is typed up carefully for lithography.

Specify cheaper grades of paper for internal publications. There is no need to use the glossiest of papers for internal publications, those never seen by outsiders, except for members of employees' families. In particular, the company newspaper could be printed on newsprint which your employees accept in local newspapers.

OTHER OBVIOUS WAYS TO SAVE PAPER

The above represent the priority steps to be taken to save paper in an in-house print shop. Here are some ways that should nevertheless be enforced:

No personal stationery should be printed on company presses. Unfortunately, it is usually the executives of a company who impose themselves on the printer for such favors as personal stationery, directions and maps to parties held at their homes or clubs, bulletins for their clubs or other organizations outside of the company, and even for Christmas cards. This is not only a waste of press time and ink but usually involves dipping into company paper stocks, which can't be tolerated any longer. Once the printers have been informed of this policy, it has to be enforced by an occasional unannounced visit to the Repro Shop. Just glance at what is coming off the presses—you may be shocked. (Years ago I worked for a company whose president was infuriated to discover that the company print shop was taking in work from smaller neighboring companies, naturally for a fee. He fired the print shop supervisor on the spot.) Another way to check on what is going on in the print shop is to examine the discarded paper in the wastebasket after hours.

Eliminate all unsupervised copying machines. In many companies it is the practice to install copying machines in separate rooms because they were considered noisy enough to disturb office workers. This is no longer the case. The latest copying machines make less noise than a typewriter. Now the practice should be to install the copying machine right in the middle of an office area but under the watchful eye of some supervisor, such as the office manager. This obvious move will eliminate much of the common abuse of the copying machine. Of course, the location of copying machines must be accompanied by a public announcement that the machines can only be used for company business. To make sure that the policy is being enforced, check wastebaskets next to copying machines at irregular intervals; you may be surprised by what you find on the discarded copies inside them.

Insist that all short printed announcements, ones not long enough to fill both sides of a standard sheet of paper, be printed, single-space, on half-sheets. The mechanism for this paper saver is simple: when the original announcement is typed for reproduction, a neat carbon copy should be made. The printer then "shoots" the original and the carbon on two litho plates. After the sheet is printed, it is cut in half, creating two copies for each sheet.

All large amounts of scrap paper should be sent to the print shop instead of automatically selling it to scrap dealers. A smart printer can chop out enough white, unprinted portions of scrapped paper to make many "From the desk of . . ." pads.

"FACILITIES MANAGERS" FOR PRINT SHOPS

In the chapter on the responsibilities of the financial officer the concept of the facilities manager for the company computer room is proposed. The same concept, and potential savings, apply to the Repro Shop. A few smaller companies have hired experienced printers to run their shops on a fee basis, sometimes in a sort of joint venture with a neighboring company or one that inhabits the same building or industrial park. The shop is paid for each job, usually with a descending scale of payments as volume rises—so it's to your advantage or to the shop's advantage to take in work from neighboring companies, even from individuals, such as your own employees. In fact, the "leased" facility could also include the company's main, high-speed copiers. Obviously, with such an arrangement, there is no longer a problem of theft of services, such as printing of private stationery.

HOW TO SAVE PAPER IN PROMOTIONAL PRINTING

Most companies spend more on promotional printing, material directed to outsiders, such as catalogs, technical literature, annual reports, house organs (i.e., company-sponsored magazines), and facilities brochures, than they do on internal printing. Although it is usually the responsibility of the printer or whomever arranges for the printing, such as your advertising or public relations agency, to specify the proper grade of paper, intelligent specification of this printing cannot only save you a lot of money directly in the work itself, but subsequently in lower mailing charges if the item is not as bulky as originally planned.

Again, controlling the ego factor may be one of the most direct ways to save paper and money in outside printing. Let's begin with your annual report, if yours is a publically held company. Fancy annual reports are unlikely to have the slightest beneficial effect on present and potential stockholders. In fact, many individual stockholders may be offended by a fancy, four-color, heavily illustrated annual report prepared on the heaviest and glossiest of paper at a time when your company may not be showing much profit. And you can be sure that the institutional investors, the money managers who have been dominating the stock market for the past several years, are not at all impressed by a fancy annual report. In fact, those who read your annual report may be more impressed by a statement on the cover to the effect that: "In view of projected scarcities in paper and chemicals for bleaching them, and also as a contribution to ecology, your company has directed that only recycled paper be used in this annual report."

Take as an example the annual report of the Coca-Cola Company, whose sales in 1973 exceeded $2 billion. The report for that year is only 16 pages long, contains no photos, has only one added color on the cover, and the pages are only six by nine inches in size. The entire report weighs only one and one-half ounces so that mailing costs are low. (In contrast, many smaller companies that do not come close to matching Coca-Cola's 10 percent after-tax profits, issue costly annual reports that weigh three and four ounces or more.) Of course, if you choose a spartan annual report instead of a very fancy one, your company will never win a prize in the annual contest for best-designed annual report. So what? [4] (Another way to save on annual reports is to publish the nitty-gritty financial details of interest mostly to analysts in a separate brochure available on request—few will ask for it.)

WHO SHOULD SPECIFY PROMOTIONAL PRINTING?

One reason it may be difficult for a company to cut down on the costly ego factor in promotional printing is that it has turned over responsibility for such collateral matters to its advertising or public relations agency. Now it is usually in the interest of such agencies to turn out the fanciest and most expensive printing jobs possible. The higher the printing bill, the higher the agency's fee.

There's still another way in which turning the creation of promotional matter over to an agency raises a company's costs. Many years ago I was employed by a leading advertising agency. During that time I discovered that the agency had set up a very subtle means for increasing its profits, which were quite impressive. This agency had hidden arrangements with many of its suppliers whereby it earned a discount if it gave those suppliers certain volumes of business in any given year. The discount, in the form of a cash rebate, was returned at the end of the year. You're not shocked to discover that none of the clients whose work earned that rebate shared in the bonanza? This agency is not the only one with such questionable arrangements with major suppliers.

Your company may be able to save a lot of money on printing and related efforts, such as photography, if it takes over responsibility for placing the jobs, after some intelligent shopping around or solicitation of bids.

Annual reports are not the only category of promotional printing that require deemphasizing. Many companies routinely forward so-called facilities brochures to their customers. How did this questionable practice get started? Perhaps it began during or after World War

---

[4] To aid companies listed on the New York Stock Exchange, the Exchange has published a 16-page brochure called "Recommendations and Comments on Financial Reporting to Shareholders and Related Matters." The recommendations are worth considering by any public company. The brochure is available gratis from the NYSE, 11 Wall St., New York, N.Y. 10005

II when the federal government called for such brochures to help it decide if a contractor had the capability of handling a specific contract.

A natural skeptic, I have never been impressed by facilities brochures, which are patently immodest, self-congratulatory, and biased. I don't believe that anybody is impressed by facilities brochures, except those they laud.

Many technical brochures are similarly overblown. Perhaps your's can be toned down too? Today, what impresses the customer is delivering a good product on time and at a price he can live with.

Company catalogs also offer opportunities for cost-cutting condensation. Now this is a category of printing in which the outside expert will nearly always do a better job than a company man, unless the latter once worked in the catalog-preparation department of Sears, Montgomery Ward, or Spiegel's. An expert can take a mass of material and use X number of pages to present it. An amateur might require twice or even three times that many pages to present the same number of products. Naturally, a skinnier catalog costs a lot less to package and mail.

Consultant Fenvessey is proud of how he helped cut 16 pages out of a client's mail-order catalog that had been planned for 80 pages. This company offers a very broad line of prepackaged goods, each size of which had traditionally been assigned a distinctive code number. Fenvessy realized that the catalog had become a compilation of numbers. His recommendation was to assign the same letter to every package of the same weight for every single product, each of which naturally had a generic code number for the product itself. Thus, Glop was assigned the code number 123, but each half-pound package of Glop and every other half-pound package always included the letter C, which the customer wrote on the bound-in order form. This simple coding system not only saved 16 pages, but greatly improved the appearance of the catalog by eliminating long compilations of numbers.

APPLYING THE WASTE AUDIT TO PAPER SAVINGS

Obviously, it would not be easy to apply the Waste Audit to savings in paper. If most of the paper-saving recommendations here are applied, the volume of paper used would drop off sharply. Nevertheless, the volume of paper consumed and the amount sold to scrap dealers should be measurable. The real effect of paper savings would be on the bottom line of the company financial report.

ANOTHER WAY TO SAVE PAPER

There's another place to save paper that does not fit any of the categories considered above: in the washroom. Suppliers of paper towels for company washrooms report that towel dispensers with timed release can cut consumption of paper towels by as much as three-quarters. The interval between advances of succeeding sheets can be adjusted to provide the best possible savings without annoying users too much.

SELECTED REFERENCE

"Improve Your Annual Report," 24-page brochure available gratis from from Graphics Institute, 42 West 39th St., New York, N.Y. 10018.

APPENDIX: LETTER-RATING GUIDE

Ask your secretary for an extra carbon of all your correspondence for one week. Then rate it with this guide. The results are bound to surprise you. Do this two or three times at one-month intervals, and you won't have to do it again very often. You will be composing more effective letters.

		Yes	No
1.	Count the first 100 words. Are 70 to 80 of them of one-syllable words?		
2.	Are your sentences short? Do they average about 15 words?		
3.	Does each sentence carry one thought and only one?		
4.	Have you eliminated "that" whenever possible —without altering the sense?		
5.	Does your letter talk "you" to the reader instead of "I" or "we?"		
6.	Is the thing that is most important to the reader at the beginning?		
7.	If you are asking the reader to do something, is it quite clear how he is to respond?		
8.	If you have a direct-dial (Centrex) phone number, have you included it so that your reader is encouraged to call directly if he needs more information quickly?		
9.	Is your letter just one page in length?		
10.	Did you *like* your reader while composing the letter to him or her and does it show?		
11.	Do you *believe* what you have written?		

If you can answer "Yes" to all or nearly all of these questions, you have composed an effective letter.

chapter 10

Selecting and operating vehicles at least cost

EIGHTY-THREE CENTS A GALLON! That's the price projected for gasoline in 1980 by an economist associated with the Ford Motor Company.[1] Presumably, the price of diesel fuel won't be much lower. (In some localities, diesel fuel costs more than gasoline.)

With such steep prices for fuel, and just about everything else associated with vehicle operation, including the vehicles themselves, it is very important for companies to exploit every productive means of cutting the cost of fuel and all other costs associated with operation of their trucks and cars.

Fortunately, there are a number of ways in which to conserve fuel and save in general. Some are one-time modifications that merely call for an authorization to purchase by management; others call for continued management scrutiny because they are based on retraining of employees. Taken all together, these measures indicate that U.S. companies can keep essential vehicles running in spite of any shortages of fuel. And even if the fuel is plentiful, the measures should be taken to cut high costs. They not only pay off in lower fuel bills, but

---

[1] This projection was made before Henry Ford II and others urged the imposition of an additional ten cents/gallon tax on gasoline. If an additional federal tax on gasoline is imposed, then the projection would have to be raised by that amount.

often in lower maintenance and longer vehicle life. These energy and cost-saving measures include:

Promoting "conservative" driving habits among all who drive company vehicles (and those who drive their own vehicles on behalf of the company).

Equipping vehicles with devices that cut drag or otherwise conserve fuel (the latter category a subject, unfortunately, for widespread fraud).

Specifying vehicles in a way that promotes fuel economy.

Changing delivery schedules.

Using company trucks to generate income by back-hauling.

Contracting delivery schedules.

THE MANY BENEFITS OF CONSERVATIVE DRIVING

Potentially the quickest way of saving fuel is enforcing a new discipline on drivers, but this is perhaps the most difficult to implement. The proper way to drive a truck has long been recognized and practiced by the operators of long-haul vehicles:

1. No jackrabbit starts.
2. Driving in the highest possible gear for lowest engine speed.
3. Steady pressure on the accelerator.
4. Slower speeds where this is practical, even below the 55-mph speed limit, if the next destination is close enough.
5. Shutting the engine off when standing still or making a delivery (as long as the power gate is not required).
6. Using the engine to brake the vehicle, if it is gasoline-powered.

Drivers of intracity trucks are the worst offenders, and their employers lose the most by their poor driving habits because the vehicles involved are mostly gasoline powered. Gasoline engines suffer uniquely from prolonged idling and wasteful jackrabbit starts. When a gas engine idles too long, the overrich mixture produces carbon deposits on spark plugs and other vital parts. Jackrabbit starts can cause leakage of unvaporized gas down into the pan where it dilutes the oil, lowering its ability to lubricate. In addition, such starts are also wasteful of tire tread.

Failing to use the engine to brake a vehicle at a stop is also wasteful of tire tread, fuel, and brake linings. Too many drivers of intra-city trucks—and cars too—race to every stop light, then slam on the brakes. (New York cab drivers are the worst offenders.) Gasoline-powered vehicles equipped with standard transmissions are per-ceptibly braked by merely taking your foot off the gas, but there is some saving with automatic transmissions as well.

To induce chauffeurs to drive properly one or all of four measures are required. First, reorientation sessions are productive. It does not take drivers much to realize that conservative driving ultimately benefits them by insuring that the company has enough fuel. Insuffi-cient fuel can mean layoffs.

A "Big Brother" device can also be attached to vehicles that re-ports exactly how a machine has been driven. The tachograph has been used for years on long-haul vehicles. Comparatively inexpen-sive, it is mounted on the dashboard and driven by the speedometer cable. Depending on the model chosen, it can report the results of the preceding 24 hours or seven or eight days (the latter model was de-signed for crosscountry hauls).

There is still also a simple way to force drivers to shut off the en-gine while making deliveries: the locks to the ignition and cargo compartment can be keyed alike, forcing the driver to remove the key from ignition to open the doors to the cargo.

Since the energy crisis, I have become aware that many chauffeurs leave motors running while making deliveries, sometimes prolonged deliveries lasting a half hour and more. Several times I've approached these chauffeurs and asked them why they leave the motors running (no power gates were involved). In all but one instance they re-ported that the engines were so poorly maintained that they couldn't get them started again once they were shut off. I find this a highly questionable response. After all, how were the engines started that morning? The usual reply to this question is "extra batteries are available at the terminal to start cold engines in the morning."

Is there any substance to the claim that the engines can't be re-started easily? According to one expert, gasoline and, especially, diesel engines remain hot for hours after they are thoroughly warmed up. Because of their bulk and the amount of cooling water they con-tain, truck engines remain hot far longer than car engines. There-fore, even a poorly maintained engine should start easily, even in winter, after it remains shut off for a short delivery of 30 minutes or less. And if it is equipped with the special starting equipment discussed on the following pages, it should restart easily on the coldest day.

However, to completely dissipate the notion that trucks won't restart, they should be maintained well, and the resulting ease of starting and restarting demonstrated for all drivers.

AUTOMATIC TRANSMISSIONS TO CUT COSTS?

To cope with poorly trained or poorly motivated chauffeurs some big-city fleets are testing medium-size delivery trucks with automatic transmissions—and not suffering a penalty in fuel economy.

Here's the concept behind buying automatic transmissions, which cost about $900 more than a manual transmission for a 24,000-pound GVW truck. If you are losing clutches at the rate of two per year because of heavy-footed chauffeurs, the cost is $300 per vehicle, plus the day or two required for the replacement of the clutch. (This assumes that the vehicles do not break down on the streets, necessitating the expense of hauling them in.)

Let's grant the claim of a spokesman for the Allison Division of General Motors Corp. that its automatic truck transmissions will stand up for the usual five-year life of a medium-weight truck without replacement and that the transmission will retain about a quarter of its original retail value on resale. On this basis, a company that lays out an extra $900 initially for an automatic transmission will gain over five years $1,500 (avoidance of clutch replacement) plus $225 (residual value of the automatic transmission) minus $900, or $825 net.

Is this possible? Barry Berger, director of maintenance for REA's 4,000 trucks, was so encouraged by the performance of two trucks with automatic transmissions in service since 1969, that he endorsed the purchase of 200 more in 1973. The two original trucks have now each travelled over 80,000 miles in intracity traffic without any maintenance on the automatic transmissions other than three routine changes of fluid.

Is there any penalty in fuel economy with automatic truck transmissions? The same GMC spokesman claims that an unskilled driver will either "overspeed" the engine or "lug" it (fail to downshift when required) enough to make a truck with a standard transmission no more economical and perhaps less economical in mileage than the same truck with automatic transmission. In addition, the unskilled driver with standard transmission can indulge in jackrabbit starts that are also more wearing on the engine and tires.

FAST STARTING IN COLD CLIMATES

In the very coldest parts of our nation and Canada, top-notch maintenance may not be sufficient to insure fast and repeated starts in the dead of winter, particularly if the vehicle has been sitting outdoors all night long. (To make sure their big diesels are operable each day, operators in some of the coldest regions actually left the motor turning over steadily from late fall until spring. Obviously, this practice is no longer acceptable, not only because of the high price and questionable availability of fuel, but because some communities refuse to accept the added air pollution. In addition, unmanned vehicles with the motors running require extra security.)

There are three devices used to insure starts in very cold climates (aside from parking vehicles in heated garages) :

1. Air starters.
2. Preheaters, electric or propane.
3. Ether dispenser.

Air starters, which unlike batteries are not affected by the cold, are now favored by many operators of diesel-powered vehicles because the vehicle's payload is increased by the removal of batteries for starting (one battery is still needed for lights). Batteries lose as much as half their power when it gets very cold. (Remember all those TV commercials of cars starting in Alaska in the dead of winter?) Air starters receive their power from the same compressor that pressurizes the air brakes (so they can only be used on machines with air brakes unless a supplemental air pump is also added). When ordered with a new machine as an option, air starters are about the same price as electric starters. However, if air starters are added to existing machines, the cost is about $500.

Preheaters can be used on both diesel and gasoline-powered machines, including cars. Propane preheaters can be used any place, while electric preheaters require a nearby power outlet. In many northern communities, truck stops, terminals, and even parking lots are now equipped with a network of power outlets for electric preheaters. A dipstick heater requires little or no installation but may not work as effectively as an engine-block or radiator preheater, which have higher wattage ratings. However, the latter require some installation effort. In general, a connection to the preheater is brought out to some accessible point, such as the grill. An extension cord brings power from the nearest outlet to this plug. For safety's sake, the extension cord should contain three wires, one grounded.

Although preheaters usually run all night (a timer could be connected to one to energize it a few hours before a planned trip), the amount of energy consumed is small compared to the amount of fuel required for prolonged idling or to warm up an engine (in many cold regions, car owners rush out before breakfast to start their cars and leave them running for from 5 to 15 minutes while they eat). In addition, the preheater insures that the car will start and also lowers wear and tear on the engine and battery.

Some drivers and chauffeurs will leave engines idling not because they can't start easily, but to keep the passenger compartment warm. Avoiding this waste of fuel is difficult, but not impossible. For chauffeurs of trucks, the answer is to key the ignition and cargo compartment alike. Also, they should be encouraged to wear extrawarm clothing, or even given a special clothing allowance for winter (thermal underwear is not very expensive).

When it gets really cold, many over-the-road drivers sleep in the cabs with the diesel engine idling all night to provide heat. To cut down on such extravagant use of fuel, cabs can be equipped with heaters that run on diesel fuel. While a diesel engine will consume from one to one and one-half gallons of fuel each hour while idling, the cab heater made by one manufacturer, Hunter, consumes only one sixth of a gallon. The company's cab heaters range in price from about $350 to $460 and take from two to four hours to install.

Drivers of passenger cars can avoid the need for such prolonged idling, and also avoid running out in the cold before breakfast, by installing an electric compartment warmer in their cars. These warmers, which draw about 750 watts, should be energized by a timer (about $8) several hours before the first trip of the day. They can be connected to the same power outlet as the engine preheater. Compartment warmers cost about $30.

If a diesel truck is often parked where no electric outlet is available for its preheater (and it is not equipped with a proper heater), then a supplementary ether dispenser should be installed on the engine. These systems, which cost about $35 and take an hour to install, usually start an engine after one "shot" of ether. However, sometimes a second shot is required. The dispensers, which cost about $3.50, contain about 150 shots. This method of injecting ether is favored over squirting ether into the manifold from an aerosol can. If too much ether is squirted in, the engine can be damaged or even destroyed. With the mounted dispensers, the engine has to be cranked over before another shot of ether can be dispensed.

"MIRACLE" THERMAL BLANKET

One device not recommended for cold starts is the "miracle" thermal blanket. Supposed to keep your car engine warm in winter for instant starts, it appears to be a variation on the "miracle" gas savers to be discussed later in this chapter. Like many of the gas savers, these aluminized blankets, which are supposed to be spread over the car motor after one stops for the night, are a revival from the past. And just like the gas savers, they are of questionable value. Although the insulation, if effective, might tend to keep the top of the block warm, what about the other five sides? In other words, on a cold night the heat retained in the block will still radiate out the bottom, sides, front, and back. The blankets are also a nuisance to use: opening up the hood, spreading the blanket, then removing it each morning. Instead of wasting close to $7 on a miracle blanket, invest in a dipstick heater at $8.

The best way to make sure a vehicle starts each morning in the cold is to garage it, which also protects the finish from the weather. Too many Americans use their garages as warehouses and leave their cars outdoors all the time. Instead, they should either throw away some of the things in the garage or construct storage racks in the garage that permit them to garage their cars and still store a lot. The various home-improvement guides contain plans for constructing such useful racks in the air space over the cars. Another storage alternative is to build a little tool shed for your mower and other bulky garden tools and supplies.

PROPER MAINTENANCE PAYS OFF

If driver discipline is not completely amenable to management control, proper vehicle maintenance certainly should be. The payoff in good maintenance practices goes beyond fuel savings to such important factors as extending the life of vehicles and all their vital parts. Replacing present machines is costly both because of inflation and because of the government's requirements for new brakes and anti-skid controls on new tractors and trailers—soon to be applied to other big trucks. As this is written the huge backlogs for trucks have evaporated.

The manufacturers of engines for trucks recommend certain procedures for keeping their products running efficiently for as long as possible. As a rule, these procedures should be followed to the letter. I have had occasion to question several major manufacturers of diesels for trucks about the synthetic lubrication oils that have been attracting so much attention lately. They all gave the same reply: no reason seen for switching from the high-quality lube oils they have been recommending for years.

Synthetic lube oils are not new. Some were developed as long ago as the 1920s, and the Germans were forced to develop synthetics during World War II because they were cut off from sources of natural oil. The U.S. Army has stimulated the development of lube oils that withstand temperatures far higher than those at which natural oils can survive. All of the jet engines flying today require synthetic lube oils to withstand the extremely low temperatures encountered at high altitudes. For the same reason, synthetics are also popular with owners of snowmobiles and operators of chain saws.

The synthetics differ from natural lube oils in one important respect: they exhibit little or no change in viscosity with temperature changes. In contrast, natural oils get much thicker as the temperature drops, which is the main reason why it's so hard to start an engine in winter (batteries also lose power as they get colder). Also, synthetics retain their lubricating properties at much higher temperatures, while natural oils get too thin at high temperatures, and then quickly jell at temperatures above their normal operating range.

Synthetics have one more advantage over natural oils: some of them can retain more "garbage" without losing their lubricating quality than can natural oils, which do a progressively poorer job as they get "dirtier."

In view of all these advantages, it's not surprising that users of synthetics report some very impressive results: 30,000 to 50,000 miles between oil changes; little or no evidence of wear when engines lubricated by synthetics were disassembled at 250,000 miles; no lost engines in fleets that usually lose a few each year.

There are of course, some disadvantages to synthetics. First of all, they are very expensive. Even when purchased in large quantities, they cost from five to ten times as much as natural oils purchased in the same volumes. This means that if you purchase them in quantity much closer security is required for all stored oil. A mechanic who pumps ten quarts of natural oil into his car is dissipating only $3 of company assets. But if that same mechanic takes five quarts of synthetics, the company is out from $15 to $25 (of course, he won't have to steal oil as frequently).

The other disadvantage is more subtle. All vehicles eventually require some additions of lube oil or other essential fluids. At the present cost and limited use of synthetics, truck stops and other service facilities remote from company garages are hardly likely to stock the exact grade required—or any synthetics at all. To maintain the proper level of fluid, some natural oil may have to be added. Depending on the proportion of natural oil to synthetics, the performance of the mixture, if the two fluids blend at all, is downgraded, and all of the fluid may have to be replaced much sooner than usual. (Of course, intracity trucks that return each night to the company garage do not face this problem.)

One of the three kinds of synthetic oils, the polyglycols, does not blend at all with natural oils. This means that if there is a chance that some fluid must be added, the extra fluid has to go along with the vehicle. What a nuisance!

In time, the price of synthetics should drop, and they should become much more widely available. In the meantime, proper maintenance should make the most of the truly excellent natural oils in use. This means replacing all oil filters as required and keeping all seals tight. The latter point is particularly significant.

Ethylene glycol-based antifreezes that leak into the oil can greatly lower its lubricating properties to the point where it no longer functions and a $5,000 engine "blows up." Transmissions or universals that lose too much fluid can also be destroyed, resulting in losses in the thousands.

So far, procedures for relatively normal, noncrisis times have been discussed. What if there is a return to the conditions of the energy crisis of 1973–74 or worse? At the height of the energy crisis the main concern was the availability of fuel. That crisis did not last long enough for really serious shortages to develop in other petroleum-based products such as hydraulic and transmission fluids and antifreeze.

How do you continue to operate vehicles in the face of severe shortages of these secondary but highly necessary fluids? Three "conservative" procedures which also make sense under normal conditions should be followed:

1. When vehicles are brought in for repairs, all fluids should be drained and retained if they have not been in service for the usual period and retain enough of their desirable qualities to make them worth saving. Some bus fleets have made a practice of draining antifreeze from all engines and storing it for the following winter.
2. When fluids have done their job they should be drained into separate tanks for possible rerefining and reuse.
3. Proprietary chemicals that "revive" old antifreeze can be added.

With regard to used fluids, companies no longer need to pay the operators of the "honeycarts" that collect discarded lube oils and hydraulic and transmission fluids. At the very least, they should now haul the used fluids away at no charge. And if enough fluid is collected, some nominal payment, such as one or two cents per gallon is due your company. Or you can trade the fluids for similar fluids properly centrifuged to remove dirt and metal particles and burn the semiprocessed fluids in your furnaces. Many car owners change their own crankcase oil rather than pay a service station to do this for them. Employees should be encouraged to bring in their discarded fluids and dump them in the company waste drums for two reasons. First of all, the added quantity of fluid may be enough to make the total volume interesting to a collector of waste fluids. Far more importantly, those fluids will not pollute local streams and eventually the oceans if they are disposed of properly. Most of those who change their own crankcase oil simply allow the waste oil to run into the gutter or nearby sewer. (Less pollution is created if the waste fluids are allowed to drain into the ground where they can be attacked by bacteria that eventually break them down.) There is evidence that some of the lumps of oil discovered floating far at sea should be blamed on individuals draining waste crankcase oil and not just to tankers cleaning out their bilges at sea.

The companies that rerefine waste oils actually claim that their product is superior to "virgin" lubricating oil. Naturally, the petroleum companies dispute this claim. What is clear is that vehicles, especially cars, are not going to suffer irreparable damage if they are lubricated with rerefined once-used oil (in which the usual detergents have been replenished) . Rerefined oil, which is widely available, costs about half as much as virgin oil.

"FEEDBACK" SYSTEM FOR MAKING GOOD USE OF WASTE MOTOR OIL

There's another way to dispose of waste motor oil and save energy. For years some big fleets have been filtering used motor oil (but not from gasoline engines) and adding it to their diesel fuel, but in proportions no greater than 5 percent. The Cummins Engine Company has reportedly checked and found that the addition of the filtered motor oil has no detrimental effects on its engines after long usage. In fact, exhaust pollution actually decreased.

A pump with filtration is supplied for this purpose by Racor Industries. It sucks out the waste oil from the engine, filters it, and then pumps it back into the fuel tanks of the same vehicle. This takes less time than letting the oil stand so that the sediments can settle out. And a mechanic can check the condition of the engine by examining the sediment bowls of the filtration unit, which costs $845.

SAVE ON DE-ICER FLUID TOO

Savings are also possible in purchases of so-called de-icers used in winter to remove water from gas tanks and fuel lines. The main component in some of the packaged water-removal compounds is nothing but methanol—wood alcohol. (The mechanism by which methanol and the other hydrocarbons used in de-icers remove water is quite simple. Water, which does not combine with gasoline, does combine readily with methanol, which also goes into solution in gasoline. The water dissolved in the alcohol-gasoline solution passes through the fuel line and carburetor easily without freezing and out the exhaust system.)

Instead of buying de-icer in small eight-ounce cans at up to 75 cents per can, buy methanol in larger containers—such as one-gallon or five-gallon cans or even 55-gallon drums if you operate many vehicles—and save. Most paint outlets stock methanol in sizes up to five gallons.

Methanol mixed with gasoline in amounts up to no more than a third makes a good fuel, as auto racers know. Some researchers claim the mixture is a better fuel than pure gasoline because it does not require any leading and causes less pollution. Some engineers at Goodyear have obtained a patent on a fuel containing methanol and about 2 percent water. In California, some proposals have been offered to convert organic garbage into methanol for use as fuel to ease the energy crisis.

During the Great Depression, farmers were encouraged to deliver their great glut of unsold corn and other grains for conversion into alcohol, which could then be used to drive their tractors and other vehicles. Before World War II in Czechoslovakia various kinds of surplus alcohol were routinely mixed into gasoline, according to Ernest Woolish, a retired chemist now residing in Bloomfield, N.J. The alcohol was mainly made from the waste organic material left after sugar is extracted from beets. Huge quantities of sugar beets are of course produced in the United States, but what remains is fed to livestock. Methanol can also be produced from saw dust, wood chips, and a great variety of other organic material.

GOOD MECHANICS ESSENTIAL

With so much invested in trucks and an obvious advantage these days in keeping them running long, good mechanics are essential. Unfortunately, there is a shortage of mechanics in the United States, and this is one shortage that won't be alleviated soon.

Periods of recession, when the trucking industry usually goes into a decline as well, are good times to hire skilled mechanics. However, when business picks up again, mechanics are again scarce.

One way to obtain mechanics quickly is to rent them. Watkins System, Inc., an organization that also rents union chauffeurs, will provide extra mechanics for peak periods at the going union rate plus a fee. These mechanics do not go on your payroll; they are paid directly by the contractor. When you don't need them any more, or if you are not satisfied with a given man, there is no trauma of firing.

An unusual, and time-consuming, way of obtaining excellent mechanics is to "import" them. Since 1967 some fleets have been "sponsoring" mechanics brought over from England and Scotland as permanent immigrants. The main problem has been defections to other companies who hire away these hard-working craftsmen. Several operators of large fleets have brought in diesel mechanics from South Korea trained by Greyhound under a program of upgrading the nation's bus lines. Barry Berger, director of maintenance for REA, Inc., reports that the Koreans are excellent mechanics who work hard ("they don't even take coffee breaks") . If you are desperate for diesel mechanics and willing to bring them over the Pacific, here's the procedure to follow. First, contact the Minister, Health and Social Affairs, 77 Sejong-Ro, Chongro-Ku, Seoul, Korea. If he reports that the required number of men are available, you next contact the nearest Alien Employment Certification Office of the U.S. Department of Labor. After this office verifies with the local state employment office that there is indeed a shortage that no Americans can fill, a certification will be issued. What if your shop is unionized? Before the Koreans can go to work, they must join the International Machinists Union which usually raises no objection during periods of heavy demand when jobs for mechanics go begging.

TIRE AND WHEEL MAINTENANCE TOO

For safety's sake and not just to save rubber and therefore dollars, tires and wheels require careful maintenance too. Such care goes beyond the obvious injunction to inflate tires to the recommended pressures—when they are cold. (To make sure that tires are inflated properly, your maintenance shop should be equipped with a master gauge to check the accuracy of the air gauges that should be carried by each man. Nor are the air pumps in service stations to be trusted. A survey of "air tower pressure gauges" revealed that an error of ± 4 psi was found in 32 percent of those checked.[2])

For example, in mounting dual tires at one end of a large truck's axle, it is important that their diameters be as close to each other as possible so that they wear evenly. Because tires are made of flexible material, units of the same size from the same manufacturer may vary somewhat in diameter. There is considerable variation from manufacturer to manufacturer. For tires of size 9.00 and up, mated tires should be within one-half inch in outside diameter, with the smaller tire on the inside. (Another recommendation: when tires are replaced for wear, also replace the inner tubes, even if they appear sound.)

This need for carefully mating tires implies that companies operating only a few large trucks should select tires, retreaded or new,

---

[2] B. G. Simson and R. W. Radlinski, *The Accuracy of Air Tower Pressure Gauges in Suburban Washington, D.C.,* U.S. Department of Commerce, National Bureau of Standards Technical Note 512, December 1969, 10 pp.

at the dealer's rather than from their own stock: there's less likelihood of a proper mating when there are only a few tires from which to make a match.

"MIRACLE" FUEL AND ENGINE SAVERS

Shortly after the motor car was invented confidence men dropped their snake oil cures and began to peddle various miracle gas savers to the proud owners of the early autos. There is even a possibly apocryphal story to the effect that Henry Ford was taken for $100,000 by an "inventor" who sold him the exclusive rights to a potion that could convert water into gasoline.[3]

Over the years the activities of these miracle workers has hardly flagged. The energy crisis gave them a real shot in the arm. Suddenly, the newspapers began to carry ads for various potions, pills, and gadgets that were supposed to extend mileage from 10 to 50 percent.

The catalogs of J. C. Whitney & Co., the leading mail-order suppliers of auto parts, began to emphasize gas savers to the extent that one issued at the height of the crisis carried a tabulation of 15 "gas savers" on the front cover. (Most were gimmicks that Whitney has offered for years.)

Some of the gas savers are based on the well-known phenomenon of smoother engine performance on damp days. At one point I was asked by one of the leading advertising agencies to advise them on a client's proposal to market a "wonderful" new gas saver based on adding a water-based fluid to the gas reaching the carburetor. Without checking into the merits of the gadget (which I was sure was useless), I advised the agency not to get involved in what had for years been a major area of consumer fraud. The product never reached the marketplace, most likely because the first energy crisis abated as suddenly as it developed.

Every promoter of a miracle gas saver can come up with reams of testimonial letters from honestly satisfied customers supporting all his claims and more. Nevertheless, companies and individuals are well-advised to avoid buying all so-called gas and engine savers no matter how strongly endorsed. To a man, professionals in vehicle

---

[3] The Ford Motor Company could not corroborate this story and claims that many of the anecdotes associated with the senior Henry Ford have no basis in fact. They even deny the famous reference to the color of the Model T ascribed to Ford: "They can have any color they want as long as it's black."

operation and maintenance as well as technical experts reject all claims of miracles as phantasy, wish-fulfillment, or outright fraud. Although they admit that under certain circumstances gas mileage can be improved slightly, none of the gas savers work over the full range of usage—and consistently.

To lay the matter to rest, a group of technical experts at the University of Michigan, under the sponsorship of *Popular Science* magazine, tested over a dozen of the most widely promoted gas savers on a scientifically instrumented engine attached to a dynamometer. The gasoline fed to the engine, a popular V-8 used in one of the "Big Three" automobiles, was carefully measured before and after each test run. The results of the extensive tests published under the title "Those Gas-Saving Gadgets . . . do they or don't they?", published in the August, 1974, issue of *Popular Science,* makes good reading. Although some of the gadgets, which ranged in price up to $25 apiece, produced some small improvements on the order of several percent, none was consistent.[4] In other words, if some gas was saved at 40 mph, it was lost at 60 mph, and vice versa. Most of the gadgets offered no improvement at all; some lowered mileage by several percent. The results are consistent with what some who fell for the claims report. None had anything good to say for the gimmicks; one couldn't start his Buick consistently after he installed a "revolutionary" substitute for spark plugs.

BEWARE OF ADDITIVES TOO

Most of the gas savers are mechanical attachments to engines. In addition, a variety of additives to either the gas tank or oil sump are promoted as gas or engine savers. Again, I couldn't find an unbiased expert who would endorse any of the additives, although I did interview some fleet operators who reported fuel savings plus lower emissions. Since I don't put very much mileage on my car, I induced one of my neighbors, who drives a consistent 40 miles each day to work and back, to test one particular additive, which goes into the gas tank. We followed the manufacturer's directions to the letter, first

---

[4] Consumers Union has also tested so-called gas savers, and its careful tests, also performed with the aid of a dynamometer, confirm those reported in *Popular Science* (see "Four 'Gas-Saving' Gadgets," *Consumer Reports,* Oct. 1974, pp. 732 and 733). Consumers Union engineers disassembled one $60 gadget filled with electronic components and found that most of them were dummies.

checking mileage before adding several ounces of the preparation. To our surprise, my neighbor experienced a 5-percent drop in mileage on his Volkswagen after adding the gunk. When I reported these disappointing results to the manufacturer's representative, he came up with several excuses, none of which were very convincing.

Most of the gimmicks and additives are harmless. However, there is a good possibility that they may harm an engine, increase undesirable emissions, or provide an excuse for the engine manufacturer to void his warranty. For this last reason alone, companies are well advised not to use "miracle" additives.

FUEL-SAVING RETROFITS

Various legitimate fuel-saving attachments are on the market, some introduced in the last few years. These should be considered seriously by operators of big trucks and tractors, in particular those operating long hauls on interstate highways. These attachments are:

1. Special fans.
2. Drag-reducers.
3. Radiator covers for winter use.

If you've ever owned certain brands of small foreign cars, you would be aware that the cooling fans on these machines are controllable. In other words, in winter when little or no cooling of the radiator is required, the fans can be shut off, either automatically by means of a thermostat control, or manually by the driver. There are three benefits: the main one is fuel saving, since the fan can absorb as much as 10 percent of the engine's output at high speed; a second advantage is that the engine reaches its proper operating temperature much faster in winter and can therefore warm the passenger compartment better; a lesser advantage is less engine noise. (American-made cars equipped with air conditioning have thermostatically controlled fans.)

Fans that pull in less cooling air as running speed increases are now available for all sizes of trucks. They are made in two general categories: thermostatically controlled fans that either shut off completely or turn much slower when less cooling is needed as indicated by a thermostat; or fans made of some lightweight flexible material —stainless steel, aluminum, or fiberglass—that pull in less air as they turn faster due to an aerodynamic effect. In effect, the latter category of fans are self-feathering.

In general, the thermostatically controlled fans, which cost several hundred dollars, plus installation, are used on the largest of engines, while the self-feathering fans are employed on smaller trucks and cars too. Self-feathering fans cost about one tenth as much as the thermostatically controlled fans (installation takes only minutes). Increasingly, truckers are ordering the fans as original equipment. The Mack (series 300) engines come with the self-feathering fans as standard equipment. However, most of the fans are added to tractors and trucks now in service. (Thermostatically controlled fans can't be added to some older vehicles because there isn't enough clearance between the engine block and the radiator.)

Truckers that use the new fans are very enthusiastic. In addition to savings on fuel, they also report more power available when needed, such as in climbing a steep hill or passing on a hill. When the thermostatically controlled fans stop, there is a noticeable surge in power; conversely, when the fans kick in, there is a noticeable dip in power, which has made some truckers apprehensive about using them. Companies operating trucks in very mountainous country should favor the thermostatically controlled fans over the self-feathering type because the latter may not deliver enough cooling air in long climbs.

An important advantage of the new fans is much less noise. This is a double advantage in that less engine noise makes vehicles much less objectionable to communities along major highways and also means less driver fatigue. Some National Highway Safety Administration tests showed that drivers subjected to high noise tend to drift within their traffic lanes. This is not only dangerous but also wasteful of fuel and tires.

Other advantages are reported for the lightweight, self-feathering fans:

Quicker acceleration because the fan creates a much lower fly-wheel effect.

Longer fanbelt life and fewer adjustments for wear of the belt.

Where the fan blade is mounted on the water pump shaft, longer pump life. Also less likelihood of a broken shaft.

Less likelihood of radiator damage from broken shafts and fan blades.

To compensate for the added cost of the fans, their manufacturers claim that shutters are no longer needed on vehicles equipped with the thermostatically controlled fans. However, in those regions where extremely low temperatures are encountered it makes sense to retain the shutters (or use "winter fronts") in addition to the controllable fans.

If you decide not to equip your vehicles with controlled fans, then it definitely makes sense to add shutters or wintertime coverings over radiators if your trucks operate in a very cold climate. In fact, your chauffeurs will most likely demand these devices to make sure that the radiator gets hot enough to warm up the cab. There's an advantage to the company as well: engines that operate below the proper temperature are less efficient.

To add shutters to an engine costs about $100. A winter front, which is simply a piece of rubberized canvas, costs as little as $8.

STREAMLINERS

Fuel savings with controllable fans as high as 10 percent have been reported. This is in the same range as savings reported with quite different attachments for large trucks, tractors, and van trailers, the drag reducers.

No one has to be convinced that a streamlined object moves through the atmosphere with much less effort (especially as speed builds up) than an box-shaped object with a flat front. The drag reducers in effect compensate for the very poor aerodynamics of large trucks and tractor-trailer combinations.

The only drag reducer with any history of usage is the Airshield, which is mounted on top of the cab of tractors or trucks with high bodies. It takes only a few hours to mount this lightweight device on the special brackets added to the roof of the cab. It can go behind or over an air conditioner if the cab is equipped with the latter. Including installation, an Airshield costs $175 for a truck and $176 for a tractor, plus $39 for a roof bracket kit. However, it only makes sense to add it to vehicles that are driven most of the time over 40 mph. Depending on how long a machine is driven at speeds over 40 mph., the cost of the device can be recouped in as little as three months. As the price of fuel goes up, the Airshield makes more economic sense. Rudkin-Wiley Corp., the manufacturer, has projected that some 40,000 trucks and tractors will be equipped with Airshields by the end of 1975.

Rudkin-Wiley also makes the Vortex Stabilizer, which is mounted on the front of trailers. Because there are so many more trailers than tractors, it costs much more to equip an entire fleet with the stabilizers, so there are fewer Vortex Stabilizers in use (10,000 projected by the end of 1975). These drag-reducing devices can also be leased.

A tractor equipped with an Airshield will gain up to 75 percent of the effect of an Airshield-Vortex Stabilizer combination, while a stabilizer by itself will only gain 25 to 50 percent of the fuel savings of the combination. However, a Vortex Stabilizer costs only $90.

Back in early 1973 when diesel fuel was still below 30 cents per gallon, Rudkin-Wiley claimed that use of its streamliners could save between $250 and $500 per rig. This in effect confirmed reports from users such as P.I.E., Associated Transport, Ryder, and Eastern Express. Since the total for an Airshield-Vortex Stabilizer combination as of September 1, 1974, was only $305, it is obvious that the investment can be recouped in less than a year at current fuel prices for vehicles in heavy service.

However, it is important to remember that the Airshield alone decreases in effect as the gap between tractor and van increases and has little effect if the gap is greater than 60 inches. For rigs with big gaps, the stabilizer is also required. Conversely, these streamliners are more effective the shorter the gap. The Airshield only works with van trailers or with open trailers that are covered with tarps.

Crosswinds also reduce the effectiveness of the Airshield, which is why it is rarely if ever used by common carriers with north-south runs, yet is quite popular with western carriers with east-west runs that parallel the prevailing winds.

There are other ways to streamline vehicles, but these are associated with the design of the vehicles and cannot be added to existing machines. Bull noses, rounded windshields, and fewer flat surfaces on truck fronts and tractors cut wind resistance. Making the gap between the tractor and trailer as small as possible helps, especially in crosswinds. Smooth-side construction in trailers cuts wind resistance a bit, especially over trailers with vertical exterior ribs. (Horizontal ribs create less drag than vertical ones.) Smooth-side trailers are also noticeably quieter at high speed than trailers with ribs.

However, there are several fuel-saving options available to those with an existing fleet. The new urethane-based paints are smoother than older types of paints and also resist damage from rocks thrown up by other vehicles. They also stand up to the sun, weather, and any corrosive substances carried in trucks or in the atmosphere.

Mudflaps should be mounted as close as possible behind wheels (four or five inches). On the other hand, bug deflectors add to wind resistance and should be removed if possible.

If all of these drag-reducing measures, including Airshields and Vortex Stabilizers are employed, Shelden Saunders, who developed the two products in collaboration with his father, A. T. Saunders, recommends that the tractor's engine be derated by 25 or 30 horsepower. He claims that these measures will cut fuel consumption as much as 10 percent. (If you order a new rig with these features, you can specify a slightly smaller engine as well.)

NEW WAYS TO STREAMLINE

As this is written the Rudkin-Wiley products for streamlining trucks and tractors are the only ones that have been on the market long. However, there is considerable effort going on to develop and market other products or systems for reducing wasteful drag. John Tatom, formerly of Vanderbilt University, now at Georgia Tech, has been working on a new approach since 1971. His "Aerovane" is mounted on the back of the tractor. It is a collapsible device that opens automtically to cover the gap between tractor and van as wind pressure builds up with speed. A prototype of the Aerovane was tested for 40,000 miles on regular runs between Nashville, Atlanta, and Memphis. On the Nashville–Atlanta run it saved 6.4 percent of the fuel, while on the less hilly Memphis run 7 percent of the fuel was saved.

For closely coupled rigs, Dr. Tatom conceded that the Airshield is the way to go. However, he claims that for rigs with a big gap between tractor and van, quite common in the West, his Aerovane should be more effective. Even though the Aerovane, if and when it is available, will cost about $400, Dr. Tatom points out that it would be competitive in price with the Airshield-Vortex Stabilizer combination. For the latter, there is an average of two stabilizers required per Airshield. The Aerovane has the advantage of only being required on the tractor.

A company called Aero Vane, Inc., has been set up in Nashville to produce the Aerovane. Hopefully, it will soon offer production models for evaluation by the nation's truckers. If you decide to evaluate either the Aerovane, the Rudkin-Wiley products, or any drag-reducing device, it's important to make sure that the test vehicles are driven in the usual manner. Either assign responsible drivers who follow instructions and observe speed limits or equip the test vehicles with tachographs. Otherwise, the drivers will take advantage of the devices to drive faster but take longer coffee breaks, thus eliminating most of the fuel savings and producing false test results. And if the favorable results of the tests induce you to equip vehicles with drag-reducers, you must make sure that company chauffeurs do not take advantage of them to simply drive faster.

Drag-reducing devices mounted only on the van trailer have been under investigation at Systems, Science and Software, Inc., for several years under a National Science Foundation grant. The devices, called S^3 Airvanes, are available from Truck & Tractor Components, Inc., in kits that cost $100. Robert Shaw of Truck & Tractor claims that a single device mounted across the front of the van will improve fuel economy by six to eight percent. If a second set of devices are mounted at the vertical front edges of the van, fuel economy improves up to 15 percent. The effect of the vanes, which do not protrude above or beyond the sides of the van so that no governmental regulations on size are violated, is to smooth out the usual turbulence of the airflow around vans at high speed.

The developers of the S^3 Airvane also claim that it reduces the noise and could possibly cut down on the spray thrown off by trailers moving at high speed. If this last effect is confirmed, it would be safer and much easier for cars to pass trailers during rain or snow storms or when the highways are wet.

Shaw of Truck & Tractor Components claims that the device is much easier to market and install than either the Airshield or Aerovane. It is shipped in two parts inside a carton only $48 \times 14 \times 10$ inches and takes about an hour to install. The same two-part unit fits the top or sides of a van trailer.

N. C. Wiley, Jr., president of Rudkin-Wiley, has reported that his company is planning to introduce some new energy-saving devices in 1975. Wiley believes that there are means to reduce drag by about another 10 percent, which translates into a further reduction in fuel consumption of 5 percent.

Another new drag-reducer that is much closer in concept to the Airshield is the "Air Flo." Like the former, it is mounted on the roof of the tractor; it also works best with the shortest possible gap between tractor and van. The Air Flo, which is made by Air Flo Company, comes in two models: the TT1 is for cab-over-engine tractors and costs $210; the TT2 is for the other tractors, which are not as high, and it costs $235. A company spokesman claimed 500 installations, mostly in the Midwest, as of January 1975.

THE REAL ADVANTAGE TO RADIAL TIRES

By now everyone should be familiar with the energy conserving advantage of radial tires. Claims of savings from 5 to 10 percent have been made but may be exaggerated because those claims are based on odometer readings that are higher because the radials used had smaller diameters than the conventional tires they replaced (so the wheels make more revolutions to cover the same distance).

Consumers Union reports that radial tires save about 4 percent on mileage. There are other, perhaps more significant, advantages to radials. For the passenger-car operator, the great advantage is safety. Radial tires are less likely to blow out or be punctured than conventional tires and also provide better traction, important in dangerous or emergency situations. They are also slightly less noisy than conventional tires, significant in those localities and states with tough regulations on noise.

For the operator of trucks, one advantage of radials is that they can be retreaded four and perhaps five times. In contrast, conventional truck tires usually can't be retreaded more than three times. If you do mount radials, make sure that the special inner tubes for radials are used.

Retreading is also a viable concept for passenger cars. During World War II retreading was mandatory as a means of conserving scarce rubber. There wasn't much concern about safety because the speed limit was 35 mph (so don't complain about today's maximum of 55 mph). Retreading has remained a substantial business—about 20 percent of the more than 100 million replacement tires sold each year are retreads. Their great advantage is dollars saved: on the average they cost about half as much as new tires, and much less excise tax is exacted on retreads than conventional tires of the same size. Retreads are sold most commonly to farmers and to used-car dealers. The latter place them on older cars to add the appeal of "new tires" (most car buyers can't tell the difference between fully retreaded and brand-new tires).

Today's retreads must meet strict federal safety standards. In addition, the tire dealers have banded together to sponsor a certifying group that inspects and approves retreading facilities. Tires retreaded in such facilities carry a sticker with the initials of the Tire Retreaders Institute.[5] Companies that operate large fleets of cars or small vans are well-advised to investigate retreads as a simple means of saving money.

However, some cautions must be kept in mind in using retreaded radials on trucks. If the remaining tires are of conventional construction, radials—retreads, or brand-new—cannot be mixed on the same axle. In other words, both front or both rear tires must be radials. Conversely, if all the tires are radials, you can't save money by buying one replacement of conventional design. Most older cars, whose suspensions are not "tuned" for radials, are now out of fleet service. However, if you still operate a pre-1970 vehicle, it most likely can't accept radials.

BUYING VEHICLES THAT CONSUME LESS ENERGY

It should now be apparent that companies buying new vehicles have many opportunities to specify features in them that produce sizeable energy savings and other substantial benefits as well.

To review, these are diesel instead of gas engines; controllable fans and shutters on engines; drag-reducing devices on trucks, tractors, and van trailers; smooth-side construction for trailers; air starters and other aids for vehicles operated in very cold regions; radial tires; and automatic transmissions on intracity trucks (very few long-haul trucks and tractors are ordered with costly automatic transmissions).

Taking advantage of every short-term and long-term means of reducing the cost of operating vehicles is very important because there has never been a tougher time in which to specify and buy trucks. First, there's the high and steadily rising cost of buying and financing vehicles. On top of high prices, the federal and some state and city governments are imposing various new restrictions or mandates on vehicles. For example:

The federal government is insisting on antiskid controls on all tractors and trailers built since March 1, 1975. Depending on

---

[5] To satisfy myself on the matter of retreading, I obeserved the operations at a retreading shop certified by T.R.I. The shop, Daley's Tire Service in Monsey, N.Y., represented an investment in inspection and retreading equipment of about a half-million dollars. What was most impressive was the rejection of six out of ten casings as unfit for retreading.

the number of power axles on a tractor, the cost of these controls ranges between about $1,200 and $1,800 per vehicle.

Certain states, such as Connecticut and Nebraska, are imposing even more stringent noise limits for vehicles than the federal government.

Some cities, such as New York, have also set very tough noise limitations.

One way to cut the noise emitted by trucks is to add more sound absorbers to the underside of the hood. Therefore, the effect of meeting these new regulations on noise and safety is to add more weight to the vehicles, which cuts down on payload and adds somewhat to fuel consumption.

DIESELS—THE INEVITABLE TREND

There's no need to urge diesels on operators of long-haul tractors and large trucks: over 98 percent of these vehicles are now powered by diesels and presumably nearly all gasoline powered vehicles in that kind of service will be retired soon. Some of the diesel engines go 500,000 miles before they are rebuilt or retired.

More and more intracity trucks are now powered by diesels to gain the same advantages as those enjoyed by long-haul truckers. Leaders of the automotive industry are predicting that even comparatively small trucks will be powered by diesels. And there is even a good chance that taxis in large cities will be diesel powered (diesels are the standard in London cabs). Diesels are desirable in such service because big-city cabs are subject to prolonged idling.

Many truck owners are prejudiced against diesels for smaller intracity vehicles because of poor prior experience. Over a decade ago smaller foreign-made diesels were introduced in the United States for intracity service and, unfortunately, they were not powerful enough for the job because most U.S. cities are bisected by interstate highways on which trucks can travel at high speed. The smaller diesels were designed for European cities in which they are never driven at high speed.

Today diesels for intracity use are powerful enough for the job and are gaining wide acceptance.

Improvement in diesel design is resulting in engines with ever higher horsepower-to-weight ratios. This, of course, means less energy needed to haul a given load and more load capacity in long-haul vehicles that have reached the gross weight limits imposed by all states.

There's one hidden cost to keep in mind before purchasing any of the European diesels manufactured to metric measurements: metric wrenches are required. If you do your own maintenance on such engines, an extra investment of several hundred dollars may be required for each additional set of wrenches. (At this time it is hardly fair to require mechanics, who usually own their own tools, to buy metric tools as well.)

FIVE SPEEDS OR TEN?

Another way to hold down the costs of big over-the-road vehicles is to specify one of the so-called constant-torque or constant-horsepower diesels. These big engines develop high torques much quicker than conventional diesels, as low as 1,200 rpm. In addition, the torque remains constant from 1,200 to about 1,800 rpm. As a result, there is less need to shift to increase torque or to downshift. For example, if the vehicle is slowing down for a red light and the light changes to green, the driver merely presses down on the gas pedal: there is no need to shift to gain speed. Thus, fewer gears are needed. In fact, Mack Truck only offers five-speed transmissions with its Maxidyne diesels. A five-speed transmission is not only less expensive and weighs less than a ten-speed, but it is also easier to learn to drive a five-speed and less tiring.

ONE POWER AXLE OR TWO?

Good judgment should also be applied in selecting the number of power axles on a given vehicle. If a vehicle must carry a large load, there is no question but two power axles must be specified to handle the load. However, for lesser loads, a single power axle may be all that's required—and is preferable in terms of energy conservation. A single axle working at full capacity wastes less energy than two axles working at much less than full capacity delivering the same driving force.

ALUMINUM BODIES FOR DELIVERY TRUCKS

After World War II several of the aircraft builders skilled in working with aluminum turned to the manufacture of all-aluminum bodies for smaller delivery trucks. The advantages of aluminum over steel or wood were higher load capacity as well as long life and resistance to rusting and other forms of deterioration. (Some aluminum bodies installed 25 years ago are still in service—on new chassis, of course.) These advantages were enough to attract many fleet operators to aluminum in spite of its higher initial cost. Another but lesser advantage was fuel savings, not too significant decades ago when fuel was cheap.

Here is an actual analysis of the advantages of aluminum over steel van bodies. Chevrolet makes a line of delivery trucks called Step-Vans. Since vehicles of the same dimensions are offered with both aluminum and steel bodies, it is easy to make the comparison, presented here for the smallest and largest vehicles in the line. Model P10 has a curb weight of 3,873 pounds in aluminum and 4,325 in steel, for a 452-pound difference, or 11.7 percent. The largest model, the P30 Series, has a curb weight of 5,423 pounds in aluminum and 6,309 in steel, both with the same V-8 gasoline engine, for a 16.4 percent difference in weight.

In aluminum, the 1975 P10 van is $665 more expensive than in steel. For the P30 Series, the difference is $1,004. (The prices are as of September 16, 1974.)

Let's assume that both of these delivery vehicles travel 100 miles per working day, or about 24,000 miles per year and that the smaller averages ten mpg while the larger averages eight mpg.[6] If the price of gasoline averages out to 80 cents per gallon over the next decade, which is most likely low, then annual fuel costs are $1,920 for the small van and $2,400 for the large van. Assuming that the lower weight of the aluminum body results in a modest fuel saving of only 5 percent, then the annual savings in fuel for aluminum over steel is $96 for the small van and $120 for the large model. This means that over the expected life of steel body on a van, which a Chevrolet spokesman informed me is "seven to eight years," that the aluminum body pays for itself in fuel savings alone for both small and large vans. And then the aluminum body can be moved onto another chassis and function for another 8 years (the same spokesman estimates that the aluminum bodies on average last 16 years), during

---

[6] If these mileage rates appear high, it is because the assumption has been made that when gasoline costs 80 cents per gallon companies will enforce the conservative driving urged earlier in this chapter, especially turning off the engine while deliveries are being made.

which additional fuel savings accrue. These calculations ignore two other advantages of the aluminum body: vans with aluminum bodies can handle a larger payload and the tires on the vans with aluminum bodies should last longer because of the lower weight when returning unloaded.

MORE PAYLOAD FOR TRACTOR-TRAILERS

By taking advantage of various options, those who specify big over-the-road tractors can lower the weight of a vehicle by many hundreds of pounds. In other words, on a tractor that weighs 10,000 pounds, the removal of 500 pounds cuts its weight by 5 percent.

The motivation, of course, is more payload. The weight-reducing options, such as magnesium wheels, do not come cheap. On average, they cost about $2 per pound. Therefore, to strip off 500 pounds means an added investment of $1,000. A vehicle has to cover a lot of miles to justify such an investment. That's why the weight-reducing options are rarely specified on vehicles used east of the Mississippi. In fact, the options are popularly known as the California package. In addition to increasing payload, the options should also result in some fuel economies when the vehicles are not hauling a full load or deadheading.

SELECTING COMPANY CARS

Although not as difficult as specifying trucks, the selection of fleet cars is a real challenge these days. On the one hand, the company wants to keep its investment in cars down as much as possible. In the past, lowering the "holding cost" (i.e., the difference between the purchase and sale price) meant selecting a flashy, standard-size sedan "loaded" with many options which would be expected to remain popular with used-car buyers two years hence.

On the other hand, it is important to hold down the operating costs of cars, particularly if there is another shortage of gasoline or if much higher taxes are imposed on fuels for vehicles. Lower operating costs and higher fuel economy obviously mean fewer power-consuming options. If operating economy indeed becomes even more significant, it is also reasonable to assume that the economical cars will be more desirable to used-car buyers.

Operating economy should also be favored if you adopt the

trendy rule of keeping fleet cars for three instead of for two years or until 70,000 miles have been accumulated instead of 50,000. The holding cost rises per vehicle with longer service but drops on a per-year basis.

In view of these considerations, it is not surprising that a major leaser of cars is recommending to its customers that they select compact cars for employees.

AVOIDING THE EGO-FLATTERING OPTIONS

There are several options that companies are wise to avoid: seat belts that match upholstery in color; metallic paints; and V-8 engines. Seat belts other than the usual black are unnecessary. If you don't specifically ask for black, you may end up paying an extra $15 or so per car for light-colored seat belts that show dirt and stains more than black ones.

Metallic paints are to be avoided because it is difficult to match them in case the car sustains body damage and requires some re-painting or touching up.

What about vinyl roofs? Assuming that vinyl roof coverings are still popular or available in the future (new safety problems in producing the monomer from which polyvinyl chloride is made could restrict production or greatly raise costs), do you need them? At a time when there is so much effort devoted to developing drag-reducers for trucks, it is anomolous that this *drag-inducer* is added to so many cars, and at a cost to the buyer that ranges up to an incredible $385 for certain "landau" treatments.

On the other hand, the vinyl roof makes it much easier to dispose of a used car. To avoid the penalties of possessing a vinyl roof (vinyl roofs of cars routinely parked in inner-city areas are subject to vandalism) yet gain their saleability, some companies arrange for the wholesale addition of vinyl roofs just before selling; the cost is more than recouped. However, I just can't endorse such profligacy in materials.

If you follow the trend to compact cars, there is little need to order V-8s. Although all require more fuel than six-cylinder engines in the same car, certain V-8s are particularly uneconomical. While the usual penalty ranges between one and two miles per gallon, the penalty rises to a depressing four miles per gallon for certain models touted for "economy," according to road tests performed by *Popular*

Science (see October 1974, issue, pp. 90–93) . So check very carefully before ordering a V-8!

Some companies may be seduced away from economical cars by the current barrage of newspaper and TV advertising in which claims are offered that certain brands of big cars were able to travel 14 or 16 or 18 miles on a gallon of gas. Hogwash! Don't believe those claims. They have been challenged by governmental agencies. The cars that performed such miracles were carefully broken in, maintained perfectly, and driven by professional drivers who know how to get the most out of a gallon of gas. I know that none of my friends who own Cadillacs are able to achieve more than ten mpg.

Various arguments are offered by the advocates of big cars, both those who sell them and those who drive them. One is that the passengers are much safer in a big car, one that weighs at least 3,000 pounds. Is this a valid argument? Now I am the first to concede that in a head-on collision between a VW bug or a Pinto with a Cadillac there isn't much chance that the passengers in the small car will survive. However, is this situation typical or even common? It's true that on average drivers in small cars suffer more injuries and accidents than those in big cars. However, analysis of the statistics shows that far more of the drivers in small cars are young people, especially males under 25 years of age, who are traditionally the most reckless of all drivers. Conversely, there is a far higher proportion of drivers of big cars who are older and who drive much more conservatively. What is suggested is that if all the small cars were driven by conservative drivers that the accident rate for these cars would drop sharply. In other words, the chances of an accident have a lot more to do with the driver (and the amount of booze in him or her) than the size of the car.

What about the fatigue factor? Salesmen who switched to smaller cars claimed they were more tired after putting a lot of miles on their cars in a given day. Obviously, small cars don't compare with big cars in comfort. But that's just one of the pleasures we may have to give up. And if your salesmen learn how to manage their time and territories more efficiently, they will be spending less time driving great distances.

Once you and your employees accept the notion of driving smaller company cars, it's obvious how to achieve even greater savings in selection of cars. First of all, smaller cars are so much narrower than big cars that electric window lifts are not required. Now with across-the-shoulder seat belts, it is very difficult to reach across the front seat of a big car to open the right-hand window without unbuckling. But this is no problem with compact or small cars. Even when I am strapped down in my 1974 Chevy Nova I can stretch across and crank down the right-hand window. So scratch electric window lifts. (If you've ever had to pay to have the motor on an electric window opener repaired or replaced, you'd never buy them again.)

How about air conditioning? In order to drive a more economical six-cylinder car, I had to give up the option of air conditioning (some compacts, but not the Chevy Nova, can handle air conditioning without two extra cylinders). There were about a dozen days during the summer of 1974 when I really needed air conditioning. Otherwise, I found that I could survive without it. And I suspect that there are lots of drivers in the northern states who could be induced to give up air conditioning and the four-mpg penalty paid for it. Radial tires are generally worth the extra cost, particularly if fleet cars are retained for three years.

Some company executives and salesmen will argue, and without advancing their own egos, that smaller, un-airconditioned steel-roofed cars might make important customers or visitors, such as security analysts, think less of the company (I don't go along with these arguments). If this is truly an important consideration, then you might consider the approach taken by a major supplier of machine tools to the automotive industry. This company owned (or leased) three top-of-the-line cars, one from each of the Big Three carmakers. When a salesman or executive had to visit a Ford plant, he took the Lincoln Continental; when a visit to a General Motors plant was required, a Cadillac was driven; and, of course, a visit to a Chrysler plant called for the Imperial. So you might consider owning one "show" car that meets all such requirements for image.

What about stick shifts? In city traffic cars with stick shifts get almost two miles more per gallon than equivalent cars with automatic transmissions and one and two-tenths miles more per gallon at 70 mph, according to Chrysler. At the height of the energy crisis, sales of cars with stick shifts were up about 50 percent (from a very small base). Should your company provide cars with stick shifts for its employees? This is a tough question. Not too many younger Americans know how to drive a car without an automatic transmission. Even if one of your employees can drive with a stick shift efficiently (not everyone knows how to shift properly), will his family be able to use the car?

Cars with stick shifts may also be more difficult to dispose of when turned in for new company cars, although I venture that the difference in resale value between cars with and without automatic transmissions is less than the initial added cost of the automatic transmission. Over the two or three years that the car is used, an automatic transmission incurs added costs in terms of changes in fluid. Replacing an automatic transmission runs into the hundreds of dollars, while replacement clutches rarely cost more than $100. On the other hand, there's evidence that today's automatic transmissions stand up better than clutches. In a survey of its members, Consumers Union found that in general automatic transmissions were superior on the question of "frequency of repair" than clutches in the same models of cars. Perhaps Detroit has lost the knack of making clutches for cars because it makes so few?

If any of your salesmen or others to whom cars are assigned prefer cars with stick shifts, they should certainly be accommodated. However, general use of stick shifts should most likely be avoided, unless we are faced with a much more serious energy crisis.

IMPROVED DRIVING HABITS

Just as drivers of company trucks may have to be retrained in conservative driving habits, drivers of company cars may require such retraining as well. In addition to the recommended driving procedures on page 138, there are two other recommendations that apply to operating cars. First, is the removal of detachable roof racks when they are not required. I am amazed to observe cars in summer with ski racks mounted on them. These racks are sure to add at least several and perhaps as much as 10 percent to the wind resistance of cars, a big penalty at high speeds. They may also scratch or otherwise damage the finish on the roof. So remove racks for skis when not required and certainly after the ski season ends.

Extra weight also cuts down on fuel consumption. Yet many car owners drive around with a truckload of weighty objects, such as golf clubs, gardening supplies, beach gear, etc. In addition to the lowered gas mileage, about 2 percent per 100 pounds, there's also a small penalty in tire wear.

WHAT ABOUT DIESEL CARS?

Since the energy crisis, one French manufacturer, Peugot, has introduced a diesel-powered car in the United States. So now there are two sources of diesel cars. Mercedes has sold tens of thousands of diesel-powered cars in the United States since the first one was brought in over 20 years ago, and Mercedes can apparently sell every one it imports.

Do diesels make any sense as company cars? Diesels, as indicated earlier, have some distinct advantages: they are more economical on fuel; they require less maintenance; and they last much longer. On the other hand, they also have some distinct performance disadvantages; whereas it is advisable to permit a gasoline-powered car to warm up, it is mandatory with diesels, which require a good 60 seconds. In addition, there are two other significant disadvantages: fuel is only available where trucks also take on fuel; and there are fewer mechanics who know how to repair diesels.

The two latter points suggest that a diesel-powered car makes sense when the car is operated mostly on local streets and not very far from headquarters—in other words, a car used for messenger purposes and to transport company personnel between facilities in some large city. Nevertheless, some individuals who drive a great deal use diesels,[7] and a few fleet sales have been made.

I suggest that before most companies consider diesels, they wait for some of the other energy-saving improvements[8] in internal-combustion engines to go into production. Right now the high price of diesel-powered cars is enough to turn most off.

DISCOUNTS FOR SMALL FLEETS

One of the inducements to leasing cars on a "finance" basis rather than on the more costly "full-service" basis, which includes maintenance, is that large fleets can obtain substantial discounts on replacement parts and maintenance. The "Big Five" tiremakers all offer such national purchasing programs through their thousands of

---

[7] Some years ago a salesman associated with a firm at which I also worked bought a Mercedes diesel; he boasted that he diverted heating oil from his tank at home into his car (it's practically the same as diesel fuel). Since heating oil then cost ten cents per gallon, his fuel costs were below a half-cent per mile. This is of course illegal but is reportedly quite common.

[8] The next really big change in internal-combustion engines is likely to be computer control. A tiny microprocessor will direct the engine to perform most efficiently and with least pollution. The electronic technology is available now; what is not available at low cost are the transducers, sensitive devices that would inform the microprocessor of what is happening. For example, there is a need in the words of a General Motors expert for a "small, reliable tailpipe emissions sensor."

dealers, and for trucks as well as cars. These dealers not only offer tires, but such maintenance services as front-end alignments, brake jobs, and tune-ups. Some also replace mufflers.

Unfortunately, smaller fleets can't participate in these programs because of their high annual minimum-dollar levels. For instance, for a fleet to qualify for Firestone's national purchasing plan, it must do a minimum each year with Firestone's many dealers of $50,000.

Some regional fleet purchase plans seek out smaller fleets, and there is one national purchasing program that does handle fleets with as few as 30 or 40 cars. It is offered by an affiliate of a Chicago-based tire dealer and is known as Consolidated Service Corp. Discounts from "off-the-street" prices are offered through the same dealers of all Big Five tiremakers and other sources on just about everything except major engine overhauls and body work.

This is how Consolidated Service handles its customers, according to Al Adams, vice president. A batch of Consolidated Service purchase orders are issued to clients. Whenever a distant employee needs work done on a company car, a purchase order is forwarded to him. If the work can be done by a tire dealer, the employee selects a nearby supplier. For replacement of windshields or transmission repairs, Consolidated Service selects a local source and mails a P.O. to your employee. Consolidated also offers a program under which your employees carry its credit cards for use at those same dealers. All prices are predetermined and uniform, and only one bill is presented to customers each month.

DISPOSAL OF COMPANY CARS

How company-owned cars are disposed of after use can influence the holding cost. Disposition is handled in these ways: to the new-car dealer who supplies their replacements in a "net cash difference bid"; through used-car dealers; through wholesalers; by auction; and to employees.

The last is likely to secure the best price for the company and a bargain for the employee. In other words, the company can gain several hundred dollars more per car by selling to employees than by the other methods of disposal, while the employee also saves over what he would pay for the same car from a dealer. On the other hand, there are fleet administrators who believe that it is improper to profit from sales of used cars to employees and who only charge the wholesale price. Then, the purchase of the car becomes a desirable fringe benefit to the purchaser.

There are some risks in selling used cars to employees. What if the car breaks down shortly after sale, a growing risk if the company decides to keep fleet cars for 70,000 miles instead of 50,000 miles? For this reason, some companies refuse to sell used cars to employees, at least to those other than the ones who have been using them.

Employees can also take advantage of the company if they know that they can purchase the cars they drive. How? By arranging for the purchase of new tires and other expensive replacement items at company expense just before the vehicle is offered to them for sale. If you can't control such extravagant purchases, you can protect your investment by simply adding all or a high percentage of the cost of such purchases to the price of the car. This is still a bargain for the purchaser, since he is not likely to be able to buy tires at the fleet discount price, which can range as high as 40 percent.

DO YOU NEED A FULL-TIME FLEET ADMINISTRATOR?

Companies with large fleets of cars usually have a full-time administrator, and he is not responsible for trucks. At what point does it make sense to engage a full-time executive for this purpose? If all your cars are leased and the leasor provides useful administrative reports by computer, a full-time administrator may not be needed for fleets under 300 or 500 cars. On the other hand, if you have company-owned cars, an administrator may be needed for a fleet with only 200 cars.

The National Association of Fleet Administrators offers useful educational programs for such executives. For example, two-day seminars that cost $50 ($75 to nonmembers) include such pertinent subjects as "How to Improve Your Fleet Cars' Fuel Consumption."

APPLYING THE WASTE AUDIT TO VEHICLE OPERATION

It should be obvious that the Waste Audit can be applied to vehicle operation. Much of the record keeping essential for a Waste Audit should be standard operating practice: amount of fuel purchased; mileage; number of miles between overhauls; number of "blown" engines per year; number of vehicle breakdowns; number of tires and retreads purchased; number of trips; amount of goods or tonnage hauled; and total value of replacement parts (adjusted for inflation). Even the accident record could be part of the survey. Unlike other operations where no base data are available and must be gathered, it should be possible to quickly make a Waste Audit in vehicle operation and demonstrate savings in a number of important cost aspects. If your people are not maintaining such careful records, they should.

SELECTED REFERENCES

"How to Establish a Fleet Safety Program," National Association of Fleet Administrators, 60 East 42nd St., New York, N.Y. 10017, 120 pp.

"Tire Inflation and the Consumer," A Program to Improve Safety and Economy, Report of the Sub-Council on Product Safety of the National Business Council for Consumer Affairs, September 1972. Superintendent of Documents, U.S. Govt. Printing Office, Washington, D.C. 20402, 12 pp.

"Standards for the Advertising, Selling, Rental and Leasing of Automobiles and Trucks," Council of Better Business Bureaus, Inc., July 1974. (Available from your local Better Business Bureau), 18 pp, gratis.

chapter 11

Cutting delivery and shipping costs

EARLY in the energy crisis, the independent owner-operators of tractor-trailer rigs went on "strike" to protest the high prices and poor availability of fuel and the 55-mph speed limit. The truckers aren't demonstrating any more, but now that problem has been replaced by a continuing nationwide shortage of boxcars. Shipping goods to customers in a disruptive era is a trial.

Fortunately, there are many ways to intelligently cut the cost of shipping without delaying delivery or other penalties. In fact, the lower-cost approach may be faster and more reliable. The cost-cutting (and fuel-saving) techniques discussed in this chapter are

Proper loading techniques for trucks, trailers, and boxcars.

Route selection to avoid damaging road conditions and/or slow routes.

Revising local delivery schedules.

Ways to avoid deadheading.

Converting to bulk delivery methods.

Contract trucking and owner-operators.

New ways to compensate chauffeurs and contract chauffeurs.

REDUCING DAMAGE IN TRANSIT

These times it is especially important that damage in transit be reduced as much as possible. Even though the dollars involved in the actual damage usually are recouped through insurance (but not all the time wasted in preparing the damage claim), the goods lost may not be replaceable, at least not very quickly, when supplies of raw materials and parts that went into their manufacture are disrupted.

Begin by much closer supervision of loading of trailers and box-cars. Naturally, heavier, denser products should go on the bottom with lighter parcels on top. Proper bracing and dunnage must be set in place to prevent packages from shifting or—much worse—bouncing around in transit. To understand the need for bracing and dunnage, all traffic supervisors should be required to take a trip inside a loaded trailer. I've never done this, but I've seen motion pictures made inside a trailer on a major interstate highway at normal speeds. The parcels begin to shift very quickly as they were subjected to the usual road shocks. The worst shock of all came when the truck passed over an expansion joint in a bridge. Some idea of what goes on inside a moving trailer can be gained by observing it when it is opened after a trip.

Westinghouse's traffic experts have come up with an ingenious but very low-cost way to sharply reduce damage to goods in cartons. Dabs of floor-tile cement are squirted on the corners of the tops of large corrugated containers (for major appliances in this instance). The cartons on top stick to the ones on the bottom. The result is the creation of a monolithic mass with resonant frequencies far below those high-frequency, highly damaging vibrations generated when trailers move down the highway at the usual 60-mph plus. Yet at the receiving end the cartons pop apart easily with no damage to the packaging.

Loading trucks and trailers fully is another way to cut damage in shipping. Cartons shipped in less than full vehicle loads may be handled by loaders as much as five or six times more frequently than cartons that go full truckload.

Containerization also cuts damage sharply—assuming that the container has been braced properly. If you're shipping goods overseas in containers, you can save on the traditional heavyweight packaging required for export and still avoid damage.

No matter how carefully goods are packaged and braced, damage will result. There are two common reasons for such damage: poor maintenance of the suspension systems of trailers and travel over routes with many potholes and construction damage. This means that traffic supervisors must keep much closer track of the damage performance of common carriers. Avoid the ones for which the most damage is recorded. Sometimes it's because they are operating old, poorly maintained trailers. Or they are operating over very badly damaged roads. Or their loaders at trans-shipment points pay no attention to injunctions on your packages not to use hooks.

PICKING THE SMOOTHEST ROUTE

In many instances, it's not the fault of the common carrier when their drivers encounter a stretch of poor highway, but there's a remedy. Traffic supervisors should ask incoming drivers for information on roads or bridges under construction and pass this information on to other drivers before they depart. In addition to reducing damage, the shipments will also get through faster. Road conditions are also reported by AM radio in many localities. Sponsored by International Harvester, manufacturer of International trucks, "Road Condition Radio" nightly warns drivers of weather conditions, detours, and other obstacles along major routes. Of course, trucks have to be equipped with radios to take advantage of this service; most are. (Some owner-operators also use Citizens-Band radios for exchanging information on road conditions—and the presence of unmarked patrol cars.)

CHANGING DELIVERY SCHEDULES TO SAVE FUEL

The escalating costs of trucking should stimulate companies to revise wasteful or inefficient delivery policies. By improving utilization of company trucks, they will not only save fuel and cut down on wear and tear on vehicles, but also avoid paying chauffeurs overtime.

Here are some suggestions on new delivery policies:

To avoid small deliveries at the very limits of your trading zone, set restrictions based on mileage from your warehouses. In other words, no delivery charge (or the standard charge) within say ten miles, with progressive increases the farther away, up to some limit beyond which all small consignments are handled by United Parcel Service, parcel post, or some other common carrier

Turning over as many small parcels as possible to such common carriers or the package services offered by Greyhound and other intercity bus lines.

Raising your minimum order size or quantity to prolong the period between deliveries. In fact, if the order is large enough, it might make up a full truckload, which can be turned over to a common carrier, who may very likely charge less than the round-trip costs of sending one of your own vehicles (because the common carrier can pick up a return load) .

Change from daily to every-other-day or from weekly to every-other-week deliveries, perhaps coupled with increased minimum order quantities. (My milkman has been doing this since the summer of 1974, delivering two half-gallons on Tuesday, instead of one each on Tuesday and Thursday.) Whatever small loss in sales is experienced should be more than made up for by the lower costs of delivery.

Induce customers to accept delivery of your product in larger containers that take less time to load and unload or in larger quantities, thereby also lengthening periods between deliveries. Since such containers or pallet loads presumably save your company some money too, the inducement could be a slight price discount.

If the customer requires a small rush order, ask him to send his truck for it.

Match the size of the truck to the delivery with greater care. For example, it should be obvious that a small load should go in a small truck. What some truck dispatchers may not realize is that a delivery requiring a number of vehicles is best made in the smallest number of large vehicles (or the same large vehicle making the least number of round trips) . This procedure consumes less fuel.

Instead of taking mail and parcel post to the local post office, use local mail pick-up services or the post offices's services to pick up outgoing material. The post office will pick up parcel post as long as there is outgoing first-class mail as well. United Parcel Service picks up packages a few times a week for a small weekly charge on top of its per-package charge. Your company can even avoid taking postage meters down to the local post office. The Postal Service has a service called On-Site Meter Program under which an employee of the Service comes to your premises at a designated hour for your neighborhood and cranks up the meters to full (upon receipt of a check, of course). The charge for this service is $5 for the first meter and $2.50 for each succeeding meter. If you request his services at a nonscheduled time, the charge is $7.50. These charges may be a bargain compared to the true cost of sending an employee to the local post office with a few meters, especially since you can keep all your postage meters operating all day long.

Another way to cut the costs of operating trucks is to buy only enough trucks to take care of *minimum* instead of maximum requirements, then meet the needs of peak periods with vehicles rented by the day, week, or month.

SAVING DOLLARS BY AVOIDING "DEADHEADING"

Too few companies are taking advantage of one important way to cut the cost of operating their trucks and tractor-trailers—by picking up loads on return trips as short as 100 miles. Deadheading, operating a big vehicle empty, represents not only a direct calculable economic loss to the operator, but also entails a less-known loss: vehicles suffer more physical damage and get into more accidents when they run empty. The physical damage is due to the bouncing that naturally results when a vehicle travels down the road at high speed. Big vehicles, but especially tractor-trailers, are more difficult to brake and control when they run empty because there isn't a load in them to hold the tires firmly to the road. And, of course, empty vans are more vulnerable to high crosswinds. Obviously, if all vehicles operated full at all times, the national economy would benefit from lower consumption of fuel and diversion of resources into building trucks.

Big companies have an advantage in eliminating deadheading: they can use one division's trucks to haul goods for another division on the return trip. However, this economic cooperation between divisions does not apply to wholly owned subsidiaries, a strange discrimination in the law.

Smaller companies, and large ones as well, can avoid deadheading by hauling back raw materials used in the manufacture of their finished goods. Obviously, this does not happen very often and is not feasible if the raw materials are in some dense, bulky form, such as coils of steel. Coils of steel are delivered on very strong flatbed trailers. Even if they were strong, van trailers can't be used for this kind of load because they have roofs and the coils are placed on the trailers by crane. However, there must be some categories of raw materials that can be handled without damage to present trailers, or with some slight modification to the trailer, such as specifying stronger floors and axles or perhaps a tarp roof?

Here are some examples of companies using ingenuity to provide backhauls for their big rigs:

Burlington Industries has been using Uniroyal's rubber tanks called Sealdtanks since the late 1960s to haul dyes, motor oil, and other noncorrosive fluids back to its North Carolina mills in the van trailers that bring textiles to distant markets. The rubber tanks are usually earmarked for a single fluid to avoid frequent cleaning. To find out if a given fluid can be transported in a Sealdtank, the company usually sends a sample of it to Uniroyal for testing. Burlington finds that the tanks last from four to five years in this service, which is more than enough to pay for their purchase. (The tanks can be repaired with patches.)

Behlen Manufacturing, a supplier of prefabricated industrial buildings, has equipped 110 flatbed trailers with side panels. Thus, these vehicles can haul from 800 to 850 bushels of grain each. Up until 1970, the trailers, fitted out, of course, with tarps, were often used for this purpose. For example, the income gained for hauling wheat from Columbus, Neb., where Behlen is headquartered, the 585 miles to Chicago, where one steel supplier is located, was 23 cents per bushel. This comes to about $200 per load. Today, Behlen figures that it costs 61 cents per mile to operate those big rigs. So hauling grain in this manner would pay for more than half the cost of sending a rig to pick up steel. At present, Behlen picks up backhauls for rigs delivering prefabricated buildings by arranging for collection of loads of steel at various suppliers as far away as Bethlehem, Pa. However, the company is prepared to resume delivery of grain if conditions warrant this rewarding mode of operation.

A furniture manufacturer with several plants in the Southwest is using Firestone's Fabritanks to provide backhauls for rigs moving between its plants. Instead of deadheading to a plant in

Texas where foam-rubber mattresses and sofa and chair cushions are made, the van trailer now hauls phenolic resins in a rubber tank from the main plant in Arkansas to the smaller plant. After the tank is emptied and rolled up, the van is filled with foam-rubber items.

This cost-cutting ploy could be copied by other companies with interdivisional transfers. For example, instead of ordering smaller volumes of chemicals and other liquids delivered to each of several plants in drums, the main plant could accept delivery in bulk in a 20,000-gallon railroad tanker and then transfer in smaller quantities to subsidiary plants as required. To speed up the transfer, the rubber tanks do not have to be filled on the vehicle in which they move. They can be mounted on large skids, filled before the trailer arrives, and then lifted or shoved onto the trailer.

What kind of loads can a company not primarily in the trucking business pick up, and how does one find out about their availability? Obviously, private carriers can't go into business in competition with the highly regulated common carriers. Yet there is a wide availability of so-called exempt loads that can be picked up and for which fees as high as $3,600 (for bringing refrigerated food from California to the East Coast) can be earned. Most of the exempt loads are unprocessed food, but also include a wide variety of raw materials.

I first became aware of this great opportunity for private carriers back in 1962 when I visited a supplier of building components operating in southern Florida. In spite of the bulk of the product, roof trusses, this company was able to profitably market the product as far away as California. The key to development of this broad national market was the supplier's ability to nearly always pick up loads of perishables on the West Coast and return them to Florida and other eastern states. To qualify for such loads, all the tractors that traveled to the Far West were insulated and equipped with refrigeration. Naturally, the refrigeration was not used on the runs to the West.

Does the extra investment in "reefers" pay off now? Today, a reefer trailer costs about $13,000 more than a standard van of the same dimensions. Assuming that this trailer makes one round-trip every two weeks, and that it is out of service for maintenance for two weeks a year, and that the net on each return trip with produce is $2,000 (after paying for fuel for the refrigeration unit), then it only takes seven trips to pay for the added costs, assuming that interest on the extra $13,000 is 12 percent per year.

In actuality, such fast payoff is rarely achieved. According to one expert it usually takes from 18 months to two years to pay off the added costs because there isn't always a return load. Nevertheless, even if it does take the full two years to pay for the added costs, that refrigeration unit should last 10 years with regular maintenance. If after a few years the company operating the reefer decides not to ship to the West Coast, it can still sell or lease the reefer and recoup all or most of its investment in the refrigeration option.

The greatest opportunities for earning money through return loads are from the West Coast. For some inexplicable reason, a West Coast company can only earn a $1,000 or so bringing a load back from the East Coast. Perhaps the big differential is based on the fact that refrigeration is rarely required for loads that travel West?

There is still one more opportunity to lower the cost of operating your vehicles by picking up return loads. Common carriers may want to lease your vehicle with its driver to bring back a load. The contract covers just the one trip.

HOW TO UNCOVER AVAILABLE LOADS

There are three ways to find out about available loads: at truck stops, through brokers, and through a new service called the American Load Pool.

Truck stop operators post notices of loads available to attract business, mainly from owner-operators. The information is usually obtained from brokers who specialize in matching up available loads with available vehicles. The brokers charge from eight to ten percent of the trucking charge as their fee.

American Load Pool is a service of the Ryder System, a national company primarily in the business of leasing trucks and trailers. Ryder also operates truck stops. American Load Pool does not charge like a broker; in fact, many brokers subscribe to the service and a few have told me that it functions well. There are three different plans under which one can contract for the service: Plan A, for those offering available loads, costs $35 per month for each office registered plus $1 for each call for service (charged even if no match is made); Plan B, for those with available vehicles, costs $20 per month for the first vehicle registered, plus $4 per month for each additional vehicle, plus the usual $1 per referral; Plan C is a combination of Plans A and B (this is beginning to sound like the menu for a Chinese restaurant) in which both available loads and trucks are offered at a ten-percent discount from the combined monthly fees.

To contact the American Load Pool for service, call the nationwide 800–327–777 (800–432–1930 in Florida). To obtain the best results subscribers are urged to call *before* one of their vehicles leaves for its destination.

Incidentally, American Load Pool accepts Canadian customers and does have one who picks up exempt loads in the United States but usually drops them off in the United States and does not cross into Canada with them.

Companies can also use the American Load Pool to ship loads when one of their own vehicles is down for service or not otherwise available.

SAVINGS IN CONTRACTING OUT OF TRUCKING

The next logical step after using the American Load Pool or brokers to find vehicles to haul your products is to contract out the entire task of trucking for your company. Some experts claim that a smaller company can save up to 20 percent of its annual costs of operating trucks by contracting out. The reason is simple: the operator's entire concentration is on getting the best return on his trucks, while yours is making a profit on your primary business. Another positive reason offered is fewer labor headaches.

Faster delivery may be another benefit of contracting out, particularly to owner-operators. Your chauffeurs are not likely to drive more than eight hours a day, unless you pay them overtime. But an owner-operator is less likely to accept such restrictions.

BULK SHIPPING CUTS COSTS

Everyone knows that bulk shipping cuts the cost of delivery per pound or gallon of material very sharply—and also qualifies the customer for lower volume charges on the material itself. However, what if your customer can't handle or afford even the smallest volume shipped in bulk, such as the increasingly rare 4,000-gallon railroad tank car? Perhaps those Sealdtanks and Fabritanks discussed earlier in this chapter has given you an idea?

For a while, Boise Cascade Corporation used 2,000-gallon Fabritanks to cut the costs of shipping phenolic resin to a plant in Singapore so much that it was cheaper than the same resin purchased locally. The rubber tanks were unrolled inside a standard $20 \times 6 \times 8$ foot shipping container, filled, and strapped down. The tanks were sent in groups of 20. After they were emptied in Singapore, they were rolled up and all placed in a single shipping container for the return trip.

Unfortunately, demand for the plywood made in Singapore dropped so sharply that this low-cost method of shipment was suspended after only one trial.

CHANGE METHOD OF REIMBURSING DRIVERS

An obvious way to cut shipping costs is to change the way you pay your chauffeurs. Many companys have made substantial savings by switching from paying on an hourly basis to paying on a mileage basis, according to A. F. Bell of the Watkins System, Inc. For example, one big electronics company was unhappy with the performance of its drivers on a comparatively short run of several hundred miles. Dispatchers figured that the run should take about five hours, but drivers were taking as much as ten hours, which naturally gave them two hours of overtime. Switching to the mileage basis for compensation cut labor costs in half. And, of course, vehicle utilization improved.

By paying on a mileage basis, companies can eliminate long coffee breaks; drivers reaching their destinations so late they have to check into a hotel for the night at their employer's expense; and inexplicable breakdowns of equipment.

APPLYING CONSERVATIVE METHODS TO TRANSPORTATION

The concepts of conservation of assets and the Waste Audit also apply to transportation of goods as much as to warehousing. Losses due to pilferage and sloppy handling on the nation's rail and truck lines are huge. The estimates run as high as $1.5 billion. Just as careful records should be kept of losses in company and public warehouses, loss records should be maintained for each common carrier with whom the company does business. Whenever excessive losses are noted for a carrier, that organization should be dropped. However, don't expect zero losses due to damage on any carrier: no damage losses mean that your company is spending too much on packaging.

chapter 12

Cutting the costs
of packaging

SHORTAGES IN PACKAGING MATERIALS are among the most difficult to counter for a number of reasons:

1. Stockpiling is difficult or very expensive because most packaging materials are bulky and some, such as cellophane, deteriorate unless properly stored.
2. Switching is not simple because substitutes may also be scarce and because selection of a certain material may have resulted in commitment to an expensive and specialized packaging machine—and deliveries of packaging machines that can handle alternate materials can take many months. Also, customers and common carriers may not accept reasonable substitutes.
3. During periods of shortages, prices overseas for packaging materials may be higher, resulting in substantial exports, which makes the materials even scarcer in the United States. (That's what happened to certain popular materials early in 1974.)
4. Quality may be erratic, resulting in poorer appearance, lower "printability," or lower strength.
5. Lower strength is likely to cause higher damage in shipment, which adds still another strain, albeit a small one, to shortages of materials.

6. Health and safety considerations may limit use of popular packaging materials, such as polyvinylchloride (PVC), further exacerbating shortages. (The monomer from which PVC is made has been implicated as carcinogenic. Previously believed inert, vinyl chloride has, of course, been banned as a propellant in aerosol cans.)

On the other hand, there are counterbalancing factors that should be taken advantage of by every company in a position to do so, especially since the prices of packaging materials have not declined much with the decline in scarcities.

1. There are still great opportunities to innovate. Each year exciting new packages are introduced that do an excellent job of protection yet require less material (which also lowers shipping costs), cost less, take up less space in storage, require less labor in handling, and may be easier to dispose of at the receiving end. Companies should be constantly on the lookout for new ideas in packaging, many of which depend on new materials. For example, one class of idea-stimulating new materials is the co-extrusions, sandwiches of plastic films that offer combinations of desirable features. For instance, the strength or stretchability of one film could be combined with the moisture resistance or printability of another.

2. More and more companies are going to reusable bulk containers for shipment or delivery of products. Although the bulk containers must be returned (in some instances they can be collapsed and are therefore treated as dunnage, which is returned free), the overall savings go way beyond the savings in packaging materials. First, shipping charges are lower; second, some processors have been able to lower their costs of manufacture or speed up production by using bulk containers that have to be connected up to process machinery much less frequently than smaller containers. One of the most striking examples of bulk shipment is the delivery of aluminum to die casters in the molten form instead of in ingots. The customer saves the energy required to melt the aluminum in addition to several cents per pound. (Also see Chapter 11 for a discussion of the use of collapsible rubberized-fabric tanks for shipment of liquids.)

3. With the sharp increase in the price of paper and paper-based packaging, scrap corrugated may be worth salvaging and selling to scrap-paper dealers.

4. Suppression of ego can even contribute to greater availability

of packaging materials. For example, one of the major can manufacturers has been trying to induce its customers who can beer and soft drinks to drop all names, trademarks, and other proprietary stampings on the tops of cans. If all canners used the same top, then the canmakers could speed up production and also allocate tinplate inventories with greater ease. (There was a big shortage of tinplate in 1973.) Standardization could also be applied to plastic caps for bottles and cans, which would put less of a strain on supplies of plastic.

5. "Overpackaging" is still common, and its elimination would save much. One manufacturer, Federal-Mogul, substituted open, compartmented trays for small boxes for each bearing inside a larger chipboard container. Although the original objective was to save on materials, the prize-winning redesign has also eliminated about half the different sizes of packages and components required for its line of more than 400 bearings. (Concurrently, the graphics on the packages were also upgraded.)

OVERCOMING SHORTAGES IN MATERIALS

There are some simple rules to follow to not only overcome shortages in packaging materials, but also gain other benefits, such as freeing valuable storage space for other useful purposes, improved product design, and even an enhanced status with customers:

Playing the devil's advocate with all previous packaging.

Tightening up communications between packaging designers and others who influence packaging, such as product designers, purchasing agents, marketers, the shipping department, and suppliers.

Changing manufacturing processes to accept incoming materials in containers of greater bulk so as to lower costs at the supplier end.

To play the devil's advocate in packaging is to question all present packages and techniques. Too many companies, distributors and retailers as well as manufacturers, have settled into a quite passive role in the packaging of their products. Without question, they accept the standard or normal or traditional packages or containers for their industry. Instead, all packages should be reviewed at rather short intervals, at least once a year and perhaps more often. Such questions as these should be posed at the reviews: Can the package be made lighter (in view of few or no reports of damage in shipping)? Can we switch to a lower grade of material without sacrificing appearance and protection, or give up so little in these aspects that substantial savings can be made—or compensate for inflated prices of packaging? In a line of products, can we eliminate a few sizes, especially the smallest one, and thereby save in packaging? Can we utilize a new material to substantially cut packaging costs? Can we redistribute the materials in the package to end up with a stronger package?

Because it usually takes so many months to introduce or upgrade a new package, close communications between all those participating in or influencing package design is essential. In particular, packaging and product designers must be made aware—and quickly—of reports of excessive damage to products shipped. The reports of damage should, of course, indicate the name of the common carrier. If all or most of the damage reported takes place on only one or two common carriers, then the shipping department must ship via other carriers. However, if the damage occurs on all common carriers, and the company's own trucks as well, then the package is most likely at fault. (Not always, because the damage could occur in handling on the company's industrial trucks just prior to shipment—as one of the big computer makers discovered to its embarrassment some years ago.)

In the great majority of instances, the package has to be beefed up. However, sometimes the change can be much more subtle. Instead of adding dollars to the package, which usually means more weight so that shipping charges rise too, consider modifying the product or the manner in which it is shipped in some minor way. For example, if the product contains some delicate elements easily damaged by the rough handling of common carriers, do what some smart suppliers have done: ship the product with the sensitive elements disassembled and packaged separately either inside the product in some void in the same package or even in a completely separate package (although that raises the disquieting possibility that the parts will not arrive together). Of course, proper instructions on reassembling the parts are essential. Product designers may have to modify the parts slightly so that there is no danger of their being reinserted wrong.

Purchasing agents have to maintain a new level of alertness to possible shortages in packaging materials—and then convey information on potential shortages to package designers. An example of this new alertness is practiced at the 3M Company. Its purchasing agents routinely keep tabs on the weather in regions supplying trees for papermakers. When there is too much rain, which slows down felling of trees, a shortage of paper looms.

The marketing department can contribute by keeping a sharp eye on customers and their reactions to new packages. In most instances, the packaging designers will be put out when they discover that the customer does not react at all (in general, customers are much more tolerant of scuffed, bruised, stained, or scratched packages than their manufacturers—as long as the contents are not damaged).

Instead of reacting to a shortage after the fact, which may be too late, there is an approach—albeit demanding—for coping with potential shortages. This is to follow the same system as that urged on product designers in Chapter 4 and indicate alternatives at the time the original package is designed. The alternative does not have to be fully specified, especially since it does not make sense to engage in any extensive testing of the alternatives at that point. But it is surely more efficient to consider alternatives at the time of initial design, especially since such alternatives are usually mulled over in a designer's mind before choosing the most appropriate final design. Instead of discarding the sketches or blueprints for the alternatives, keep them.

CHANGING IN-COMING PACKAGES

Just as you hope your customers will accept changes in your packaging, your employees must be tolerant of changes in the packaging of your suppliers. Since you are in effect paying for that packaging, efforts by your suppliers to combat inflation by modifying their packaging make a great deal of sense.

It makes even more sense for your manufacturing supervisors to initiate changes in packaging of incoming materials that will cut handling costs within the plant. This means swinging along with the big trend to long-lived, reusable containers. Here are some examples:

Stainless-steel containers capacious enough to hold the contents of six or more drums in which liquids, easily pourable powders, or pellets are conventionally delivered. Even though the containers may have to be cleaned prior to shipment back to the supplier (perhaps in the same vehicle that delivers the loaded containers?) and can only be handled by fork-lift trucks, they can generate substantial savings in in-plant handling and help avoid downtime on process equipment. They also take up less in-plant storage space than the equivalent number of drums, which are either returned to the supplier or sold to dealers of reconditioned drums. In particular, these containers and others that replace drums can gain in significance during any steel shortage when the drums become scarce. (To conserve steel, manufacturers of drums are making them of lighter gauge metal, so thin in fact that they can't be reconditioned according to the association of drum reconditioners.)

Giant rubber bladders, the Sealdtanks and Fabritanks discussed in much greater detail in Chapter 11. Since these containers, which hold up to 5,000 gallons, can't be moved while loaded from the vehicles on which they are shipped, some means has to be provided to pump and store their contents until used. So a careful analysis must be made of potential savings.

Large plastic-lined wirebound boxes on pallets for powders or pellets. Of course, they can only be moved about by fork-lift truck.

POTENTIAL ALTERNATIVES IN PACKAGING

Here are some other suggestions on ways to cut down on packaging costs or save materials in short supply:

1. Redistribution of the materials within a package can result in savings in packaging materials, shipping costs, or both. For example, by merely changing the dimensions of a large carton without changing its weight, more cartons can be placed inside a van trailer to take full advantage of the van's dimensions, thus lowering shipping costs per package. Similarly, by substituting chipboard partitions for corrugated partitions, but adding to the weight of the outer carton, less damage may be incurred in shipping.

2. Modern packaging machinery may lower costs. The technology of packaging machinery advances each year in the same manner as for other classes of machinery, perhaps even faster. Your company

may be using an obsolete, fully amortized machine to its detriment. The old machine may do its job as well as ever, but it may not compete with the latest machinery in terms of speed, variety of package sizes it can handle, or least number of operators. It also may be erratic in quality of packaging it performs. Sometimes, all that is needed to substantially upgrade an old machine is a new accessory or attachment. For example, the International Paper Box Machine Company has added a glue-line detector to its machines that triggers a signal to eject a box whose glue line is broken by as little as one eighth of an inch. Such boxes are likely to leak when filled. If as many as ten consecutive boxes are ejected, the detector stops the gluer.

3. Ship the product with little or no packaging by means of special vehicles or an entirely different kind of carrier. For example, the computer makers have long since switched to shipping their big pieces of machinery by padded moving van. Instead of spending a great deal of time and money packaging their delicate machines to withstand road shocks, they select a vehicle with a special air suspension that attenuates those shocks. Similarly, air transportation can be substituted for shipment by rail or truck. Although the former is much more expensive than the two latter categories, the compensating saving in less packaging may be much greater than the added shipping costs.

4. Switch to 20-foot or 40-foot shipping containers for overseas delivery (see Chap. 11). Contents don't have to be packaged in the usual heavy-weight overseas cartons.

5. Use scrap materials generated in production as filler or packaging components. For example, when foamed polystyrene bracing became scarce as a result of the oil embargo, a builder of machinery formed sections of scrap sheet metal into bracing on a brake. The resulting package is naturally somewhat heavier, but the added shipping costs and the loss in return on the bracing as scrap metal is much less than the cost of the replaced plastic bracing. In addition, the foamed bracing takes up a lot of storage space, unless the user has the means to foam in place (see case history below).

6. Unhappy about packaging materials with a finish of diminished or erratic quality? Use bold graphics to compensate or camouflage says Fred Charlton, president of Charlton Lithographing, Inc.

7. Is there a neighboring woodworking plant? Buy the sawdust it generates and use it as protective filler. But remember that dust can

be explosive, so those handling it can't smoke, and warn your customers first, because sawdust is messy.

8. Substitute plastics for paper. With shortages of plastic looming any time there is a shortage of petroleum, how is this possible? The answer is that a very small amount of plastic can be substituted for a lot of corrugated paper, which is likely to be in very short supply again. The best example, according to Joel Frados, the publisher of *Plastics Focus,* is the substitution of clear polyethylene film that is stretched or shrunken around products instead of placing them in a big corrugated box. Obviously, the product can't have any sharp projections that would pierce the film. The contents should be stackable in a cube shape or be made into a cube by the addition of heavy-paper corner posts. If the product does not have a flat bottom, it may have to be mounted in a shallow corrugated tray. However the overall dollar savings in paper and shipping charges are large, even after the purchase of special machines to stretch or wrap the film. (Before committing yourself to shipment in this manner, make sure the package is acceptable to your customers and common carriers. One manufacturer who switched to such shrink wrapping was forced to switch back when a major customer objected, even though disposal of the film wrapping is much less of a burden than disposing of big corrugated boxes.)

Here's another way in which plastics can be substituted for paper with an important side benefit. A processor of pet foods has substituted a shrink-film baler bag for 120-pound (test) kraft bags in which two 25-pound bags of food are shipped. The polyethylene shrink wrap results in a tighter, more compact package less subject to damage. The extra benefit is that the plastic outerwrap does not give way when wet, a problem with the kraft bag.

Plastics are even being substituted for steel. Black nylon strapping is now competing with steel strapping. The strong plastic not only costs less than steel strapping, but is easier to handle and also weighs less, although not enough to generate any great savings in shipping. At the customer end, it is easy to cut—but does not cut fingers—and is much easier to dispose of than steel strapping.

9. Use double-wall instead of triple-wall corrugated paper. If damage reports are rare or nonexistent, such intelligent downgrading makes sense. Similarly, single-layer fiberboard can be substituted for corrugated partitions, and powdered materials can be shipped in multiwall bags with one ply less. You may be forced to make such

switches because the papermakers are dropping some of the thinner grades of paper on which they make less profit because giant paper-making machines run at the same speed for both thin and heavier grades of paper.

10. To compensate for lighter weight or otherwise weaker pack-aging, increase use of dunnage in shipping vehicles. For example, International Paper Corp. makes paper bladders that can be inflated inside a trailer or boxcar to hold packages in place and prevent them from bouncing around en route. The paper pillows are cheap enough to be discarded at the end of a trip. Shipping experts at an appliance plant of the Westinghouse Electric Company have developed a way to use the adhesive used to secure floor tiles so that large corrugated packages form a large mass that is highly resistant to damage during shipment, see Chap. 11).

11. Try to ship full trailer load as much as possible to save on handling costs, as explained in Chapter 11, and to protect packaging.

12. Reuse shipping containers in which your suppliers forward materials to you. This is a much more productive use than selling them to a scrap dealer for pennies apiece. Often, such cartons are in good shape. The big problem is ego: are you willing to let your cus-tomers know you are reusing cartons? Under today's conditions favor your pocketbook over your ego.

13. Increase the standard number of items that go into a box. This recommendation mainly applies to the soft-goods trade. For instance, instead of placing three garments in a box, with four boxes making up the usual dozen, package four garments in a slightly larger box so that only it takes only three boxes to make a dozen. Savings up to twenty-five percent are possible, and retailers are not likely to complain.

CAN YOU PACKAGE IN LARGER, HEAVIER BOXES?

One of the obvious ways to save on paper and other packaging ma-terials is to use larger sizes of boxes which are, however, heavier. Unfortunately, there are four obstacles to such a conservative move. First, can your packaging machinery handle the larger sizes, and if so, will speed of handling drop off sharply? Second, will common car-riers, but especially the parcel post and United Parcel Service, handle the larger package? Third, will the larger package be accepted by distributors and end customers? Finally, and perhaps of greatest significance, will your employees agree to handle the larger container—when organized labor is pushing for smaller packages that are less strain to handle without machinery?

CASE HISTORY: LONG HAIRS REPLACED BY FOAM

A system of European origin is gaining acceptance in the packaging of costly, delicate instruments, especially in the computer industry. Among the users of the Instapak system are IBM, Sanders Associates, and Western Electric. In the past, TRW Data Systems used Instapak to package some computer elements. In one instance, a package based on Instapak that cost $1.55 replaced an earlier largely corrugated container that cost $15.32.

The great appeal of Instapak, which was introduced in 1971, is that it can be foamed in place. This means that it will conform to the shape of whatever is placed next to it. In use, a measured amount of polyurethane plus foaming catalyst is squirted from a dispenser into the bottom of a conventional double-wall carton. As the plastic begins to foam, a thin sheet of polyethylene is laid over it to prevent the product from sticking. Next, the product to be shipped is placed on top of the foamed mass. The next step is to place another sheet of protective polyethylene over the product before another "shot" of foaming plastic is squirted on top. Then, as this added material foams, the carton is closed and sealed so that the foam completely fills it. The result is a package that can literally be bounced without damage. (TRW Data Systems originally chose the Instapak system not to save money in packaging but because its products were suffering costly damage in shipment.)

There are two variations on the above procedure. In one, the product to be packaged is simply placed in a polyethylene "baggie," an approach that is slightly faster than using separate sheets of the film. In the other a mold of the product is made and an upper & lower half of the foamed-in-place package is prepared. The product is then placed in the lower half, the upper foamed element is placed on top, and the package is sealed.

The dispenser for the foam can only be rented and costs $165 per month. Obviously, the greater the number of packages prepared each month, the lower the cost per package of the dispenser. The price of the polyurethane ranges from $50 to $75 per five-gallon drum, depending on quantity discounts.

A current user of the Instapak system is Applied Technology Corp. of Sunnyvale, Calif. In making up a package, this company had been using $6 worth of rubberized hair, a familiar cushioning material. Labor to make up the package was rated at one hour, or $3.50, for a total package cost of $9.50. This package was replaced by a new package based on Instapak that used only $1.60 worth of the foamed plastic and took only ten minutes to make up, for a labor cost of $0.58. Total cost of the new replacement package is $2.18, for a saving of $7.32.

Instapak has a large inventory of the foaming ingredients. In the foamed state, the material weighs only a half pound per cubic foot, yet it has a high compression strength of 2.3 pounds per square inch.

CONCLUSION: MANY OPPORTUNITIES TO SAVE

The Instapak system has been discussed in detail not to recommend it but to show that there are still great opportunities in packaging of products to avoid the use of or save on scarce materials. At the same time, other important side benefits may be gained, such as:

Less damage in shipment, particularly important today when it may be difficult to replace what was lost in shipment.

Less labor required in package set-up or lower level of skill required.

Less storage space required for packaging materials, which are often very bulky, a big gain at a time when storage space may be at a premium.

Lower transportation costs because the new package weighs less or takes up less space.

One possible obstacle to innovation in packaging is rejection by common-carrier trucks because the new package has not been accepted by the National Classification Board of the Motor Carrier Industry. A spokesman for the Board, which is headquartered in Washington, D.C., indicated that it is open-minded about granting temporary six-month permits to test new packages on common carriers. Unlike the hearings before the Interstate Commerce Commission, no trained experts are required to argue before the Board. If the six-month test shows that the new package can stand up to shipping and handling, it will be added to the long listing of packages accepted by the Board.

WASTE AUDIT DIFFICULT TO APPLY TO PACKAGING

Packaging is one aspect of business where it may be difficult if not impossible to apply the concept of the Waste Audit. Particularly if the many recommendations made here to cut the cost or volume of packaging or modify its design are applied, the company's packaging may change so much from one quarter to the next, if not from one month to the next, that comparisons based on the same month in the prior year will not be valid.

However, if a company does utilize substantially the same kind of packaging year-in and year-out, it might make sense to measure the waste in packages. In other words, out of so many containers delivered by your packaging supplier, which is known from invoices, how many were discarded in storage because of deterioration or damage in handling, how many were fouled up on the packaging line or by packaging machinery, and finally what number finally went out your door protecting your products in shipment?

chapter 13

Warehousing: Store more
for less

WHERE SHORTAGES STILL PERSIST, the warehousing function is faced with one great challenge: storing, at least cost in both operating expenses and investment, all the outgoing inventory (for all companies) and incoming inventory and work in progress for manufacturers.

In addition, the warehousing function has an important role to play in conservation of assets: elimination of pilferage of goods for which it is responsible, mainly those in storage but those on the shipping docks as well; reduction in damage due to sloppy handling inside the warehouse or from unprofessional operation of industrial trucks; elimination of aging, loss, or misplacement of stored goods because they were not stored in the correct location or because of sloppy record keeping; aid in selection of the proper fuel for industrial trucks (see p. 213).

THE ROLE OF PUBLIC WAREHOUSING

Public warehousemen have offered their services to business and industry for centuries, going back perhaps to the great trading states of the Mediterranean. If you have to store goods at some city remote from any company facility, the public warehouse is the obvious way to go.

The major users of public warehouses are big companies, those that have the capability and might appear to have the need for operating their own remote warehouses. Why don't they? There are three reasons. First, building of warehouses is not viewed as a smart way to invest company funds, particularly at today's high interest rates. Second, the technology of storing goods is advancing rapidly, in particular the high-rise, high-density concepts detailed later in this chapter; there's a good chance that a company building a warehouse today will pick the wrong technology, one soon made obsolete. The last reason is lower tax liability: with so many states now assessing (with others likely to do the same) property taxes on all commercial property within the state (buildings and goods) one simple way to hold down one's tax liability is to use public warehouses. To further shrink the tax bill, companies make sure that at assessment time there are not much goods within the state. (It is because of California's high property taxes, that Reno, Nevada, just a few miles from the border, has become a major distribution point for goods destined for the big northern California market.)

Public warehouses also offer many other advantages. For example, if you are considering extending distribution to a region in which you have never sold before, it makes sense to store all goods in a public warehouse in that region while testing the market. If the test proves successful, then you can consider the tradeoffs between public warehousing and operating your own warehouse in that region.

During the great energy crisis smaller companies turned to local public warehouses for the first time, mainly to store overflows of incoming raw materials or goods, but also for finished goods and even work in progress in some rare instances. Companies also turned for the first time to the "liquid" equivalent of public warehousing, the tank farm, which is discussed later.

How do you go about picking out a public warehouse? In general, cost is not one of the considerations: they all charge roughly the same in any given region. Their rates, except in a few states, are not subject to regulation. Most charge by the hundredweight and about 15 cents per month. This monthly charge applies to all goods that arrive before the 15th of the month. After the 15th, charges are only half for the remainder of that period.

On top of the monthly charge, there is a one-time handling charge of about 30 cents per hundredweight billed on arrival. In addition, there are other lesser charges called accessorial.

If cost is not a factor in picking one public warehouse over another, what are the factors? They are basically service, but security and limiting of damage are other factors.

For aid in picking a good local warehouse, check with other businessmen, your banker, or truckers with whom you have a good rapport (although truckers are likely to recommend a warehouse with whom they have a favored relationship). For warehousing in remote cities, check with your competition. A handy source of information on warehouses out of town is the national directory, *Distribution Worldwide,* published annually.

One highly experienced manager of distribution offers insights into selection of public warehouses. Clifford F. Lynch of Quaker Oats Company, Chicago, claims that a personal inspection of such facilities is essential. Housekeeping is a reliable index. "Sloppy warehouses are out. I don't want my product, any product, to reach the customer infested with bugs."[1] Lynch also checks out the personnel. Contrary to what is stated in the warehouseman's fanciful "facilities brochure," he finds that too many are only father-and-son operations without enough skilled people to provide quick service. He also favors single-level warehouses because handling charges are generally lower than in multilevel warehouses. In general, a single-level warehouse will be newer and more modern than a multilevel building.

Lynch says it is preferable to deal with a public warehouseman who also operates as a trucker, even though Interstate Commerce Commission regulations require that a separate invoice be submitted for any trucking required. He looks for single responsibility.

Later in this chapter strong efforts to reduce pilferage of and damage to goods stored in company warehouses is urged. The same considerations apply to goods stored in any public warehouse. Keep careful records of losses due to pilferage and damage in handling (if the two can be differentiated). If any public warehouse you deal with shows a record of excessive losses, either in comparison with other public warehouses, or if you don't deal with any other public warehouses, with your own warehouses or those used by other businessmen who are frank enough to reveal this information to you,

---

[1] Infestation is a very real threat. Recent governmental inspections of warehouses operated by food companies show that about half were infested seriously with bugs.

obviously stop doing business with the delinquent warehouseman—and don't hesitate to tell him why he's being dropped.

Incidentally, if you deal with a public warehouse, extend your insurance coverage to all goods stored. Even though the Uniform Commercial Code imposes certain liabilities on public warehousemen, it's not wise to rely on their insurance coverage.

RISKS IN RENTING AN EMPTY BUILDING

One obvious way to temporarily house goods when your own warehouse is stuffed is to rent an empty building. This is risky. Common sense suggests that the closer the building to your facilities, the better. Ideally, the building should be next door or across the street so that company warehousemen can supervise it. If the building is some distance away, there can be little or no supervision, and this low-cost tactic will most likely fail. That's what happened to one manufacturer whose company chauffeurs paid scant attention to instructions on where to place goods inside the building. Soon, the rented warehouse began to resemble the legendary closet of Fibber McGee.

One manufacturer that did have a good experience with a rented warehouse is Southland Paint of Houston, Texas. The reason for the success is simple: the building was quite familiar to employees because the company had occupied it previously. And the cost was a real bargain: 4,000 square feet at $200 per month; that's only 60 cents per square foot per year.

OUTDOOR STORAGE

Few companies have the option of storing anything outdoors, and even those few may find outdoor storage less attractive than believed, even for short periods. Take the case of a manufacturer of materials handling equipment that is used both indoors and out. The production manager reasoned that since the product can stand the weather, certain exposed parts of it could be stored outdoors. Not so! In use these parts are lubricated by the operations of the machine. When standing idle, certain key parts are not lubricated; these deteriorated quickly and required expensive reworking before they could be assembled into completed machines. Outdoor storage in winter is risky because salt used on nearby highways to melt snow somehow works its way under tarps to corrode products underneath.

USING THE SUPPLIERS' WAREHOUSES

Before the age of shortages, one of the most sophisticated concepts in warehousing was to eliminate warehousing of incoming goods—in effect using suppliers' warehouses for this purpose. Obviously, this called for very careful scheduling to make sure that goods needed either for processing or assembly in manufacturing operations or for sale in wholesaling and retailing operations were delivered as required.

Such extremely tight scheduling was impossible to maintain during the period of shortages. Many companies bought and stored all they could lay their hands on. Now that most materials and goods are in greater supply, and their suppliers are once more in a buyer's market, attempts might be made to reestablish such scheduling. Space freed by such efforts could be reassigned to storage of goods and materials in short supply.

"RETIRED" VANS AND SHIPPING CONTAINERS
FOR TEMPORARY STORAGE

In years past when railroads were the dominant means of interstate transportation of goods and boxcars were plentiful, companies often used boxcars for temporary storage of incoming and even outgoing goods. An incoming or outgoing boxcar would sit on the company siding until the goods it contained were required. The daily demurrage charge for boxcars was only $2.50.

Now, this flexible arrangement is a thing of the past: there is little railroad trackage available, and fewer and fewer companies own sidings; boxcars are in very short supply; but most importantly, the daily demurrage charges for boxcars are up sharply ($10 for each of the first two days after delivery; $20 each for the next two days; $30 each for days five and six; and a whopping $50 per day thereafter).

However, there are means of storing goods temporarily in the old manner. "Retired" van trailers, those big steel shipping containers used on railroads, and "containerships" are available for rental at comparatively low rates.

Retired vans are those so worn by bouncing around at high speed that they can't be used for long-distance service. However, they are waterproof. One manufacturer rented several of the old vans, parked them across the street in an empty lot, and used them to store both incoming raw materials and outgoing products at the height of the energy crisis when its warehouse was bulging with raw materials purchased as a hedge against shortages. The daily rate paid now appears too high. It was $12 per day, which is nearly five times the rate quoted by Eagle Leasing Company for a used 40-foot trailer and seven times the rate for a 30-foot trailer, which is $50 per month.

Such vans could be used to transport whatever is stored inside them to another facility or even to a customer, provided he is not too far away.

The "revolution" in overseas shipping via giant containers is providing another means of temporary storage. The sturdy containers, either 20 or 40 feet long, rent for comparatively low rates, especially in view of the inflated demurrage on box cars. The smaller containers, which are eight feet wide and either eight or eight and one-half feet high, rent for $2.50 to $3 per day; the larger containers, which have the same cross-sectional dimensions as the smaller units, rent for $4.75 to $6 per day. Usually, they are rented for a minimum of 30 days.

Unlike the vans, they can be piled up one on top of another, up to nine high. They are either all steel or made with steel frames and aluminum skins. All have wooden floors. (For an excellent description of the various types of containers, request the 48-page "Container Catalogue" published by Interpool—see directory for address.)

Companies with a continuing need for the containers can also buy them. One supplier of used 20-foot containers, Shelter Shed, charges only $995 apiece.

Let's try to compare the cost of renting containers with the cost of public warehousing (obviously, they are not directly competitive in service). Most of the 20-foot containers have a capacity of about 40,000 pounds. Let's assume that your product is bulky and that only 30,000 pounds worth can fit inside the container, whose interior volume runs about 1,050 square feet. At a daily rate of $3, the monthly cost of the container is $90. How much would it cost to keep the same amount of goods in a public warehouse for one month? The storage charges would run to only $40, however the handling charges are $80. So the use of shipping containers compares favorably in cost with public warehousing. And the shipping containers can be set down right in your own backyard. Of course, public warehousing is the only way to go if goods must be stored at some distant point.

The three major leasers of shipping containers are Interpool, Integrated Container Service, and Container Transport International. Other suppliers are listed in the classified phone book under "Cargo & Freight Containers." Before storing anything in shipping containers or vans on your premises, check with your insurance carrier. Present coverage for burglary may not apply to vans and containers.

"IN-TRANSIT" STORAGE

By late 1974 when the full effect of mild conservation and higher oil prices had combined to cut world-wide oil consumption, petroleum storage facilities all over the world were just about fully utilized. Since they did not have any additional storage tanks, the petroleum companies in effect used oil tankers for in-transit storage, either ordering the loaded tankers to slow down en route or anchoring the tankers. (In early October 1974 while crossing the Verrazzano Bridge I noted four large tankers riding low at anchor off Staten Island in the New York's Upper Harbor.)

Not too many companies can utilize the same principle, but it should be kept in mind as an alternative. For example, instead of shipping goods to California from the East Coast via truck, which usually takes five days, shift goods to the railroads, which usually take two to three weeks to move goods to the West Coast. And the railroads charge less. Here's a situation in which the higher speed and dependability of delivery of trucks is no advantage.

MANY WAYS TO STORE FLUIDS

There are many alternatives in storing liquids, which include:
1. Tank farms.
2. Retired tankers and tank barges.
3. Tank cars.
4. Constructing metal or concrete tanks.
5. Flexible tanks.

Tank farms, which are the liquid equivalent of public warehouses, are the traditional place to store liquids off-premises. During the energy crisis and continuing right up to this time, there is little or no available excess capacity in tank farms. In particular, there are few of the smaller tanks available for companies with a need to store comparatively small quantities (10,000 barrels and under). And since these smaller tanks are usually filled with chemicals, the higher "chemical" rate applies, even if petroleum products are pumped in.

Most storage tanks are rented for at least a year, with an option to extend, although on rare occasions an operator of tank farms, such as General American Transportation Corp., may have some capacity available for shorter periods, such as three months. The annual rate for a "small" tank with a 10,000-barrel capacity is about $22,000. In addition, various handling charges are applied each time some liquid is pumped in or out of the tank. And when you finally empty the tank, it may have to be cleaned out at your expense if the next customer's liquid is not the same as yours.

If there is no capacity available in any storage tank and you need to store a large amount of liquids, a truly remote possibility is renting or buying a "retired" small ocean-going tanker or tank barge. But you must have dock space available at your own or some other guarded facility, or some enterprising thief is likely to come alongside in the night and transfer the precious elixir from your tank or barge to his. (This actually happened during the energy crisis.)

Few companies require the huge storage capacity of a tank farm, tanker, or tank barge. They need to store thousands of gallons rather than thousands of barrels. Assuming that the quantity is not so minute that it could be put up in drums and left indoors or outside, there are various alternatives in small liquid storage.

TANK CARS GETTING LARGER

Railroad tank cars are now available in much larger sizes, up to 33,500 gallons. Whereas 8,000- and 10,000-gallon tank cars were standard until recently, the 20,000-gallon tank car is rapidly becoming the standard. Obviously, the larger the capacity, the lower the shipping charge per gallon.

Because of high demurrage charges, tank cars owned by or leased to the railroads cannot be used for temporary storage of liquids beyond a few days. However, tank cars can be leased by companies for temporary storage. The going annual rate for a 10,000-gallon car is about $135 per month.

Of course, this car can also be used for transportation of liquids (many large processors of liquids own and operate big fleets of tank cars). If the tank car is moving about a great deal, the lowered rates charged by the railroads to companies that provide their own tank cars may actually result in the recouping of the rental for the car. For example, a common rebate figure to companies that provide tank cars is 14.9 cents per mile. Thus if a 10,000-gallon tank car is hauled an average of only 900 miles per month, the rebate equals the monthly rental of $135.

During the energy crisis, there was a great shortage of tank cars. As a result, some suppliers of liquids informed their customers that they could only deliver if the customer provided tank cars. (Once the crisis was over, many suppliers of industrial liquids reverted to their old policy and insisted on delivery in their own cars to keep these cars busy.) This situation suggests that in anticipation of a new energy crisis or any other situation that results in a shortage of tank cars that companies dependent on suppliers of liquids in bulk either quickly lease or buy a few tank cars.

Unfortunately, there are few of the older, smaller cars, with capacities as low as 4,000 gallons available. By the time they are ready for retirement they may not be sound enough for safe storage of liquids. Nevertheless, a comparatively small number of older cars do become available. If you have a railroad siding, you can purchase a 10,000-gallon tank car for as little as $4,000. If you don't have a siding, it might make sense to purchase just the tank without the undercarriage. A "ballpark" figure for the 10,000-gallon tank alone is $2,500. Sources for retired tank cars are listed in the classified phone book under "Railroad Cars—Mfrs." and "Railroad Car Leasing."

CONSTRUCTING NEW STORAGE TANKS

If you have a requirement for long-term storage of liquids, you must consider another traditional approach—construction of a conventional metal or concrete tank on your own property. As this is written, backlogs on metal tanks are up to a year. The long delay is caused by the shortage of steel. In fact, in several instances, fabricators of steel tanks have been forced to halt construction and shift their crews to other jobs because the specific grade and thickness of steel plate specified for some jobs was not available.

Costs for big metal tanks run around $20 per gallon. In other words, a 1,000,000-gallon tank in carbon steel would cost about $200,-000. Naturally, the smaller the tank, the higher the cost per gallon. For example, a 100,000-gallon tank would cost about $50,000. If you require stainless steel because the contents attack carbon steel, then costs jump about one third. A good sound metal tank that's well maintained (painted every five years or so depending on proximity to sea air or other airborne corrosives) can last four or five decades.

FASTER DELIVERY ON REINFORCED CONCRETE TANKS

If you can't wait a year for a metal tank, consider reinforced concrete, which is a strong competitor to steel in building construction. If you order a concrete tank today, construction could begin in only three months or so instead of a year. The main advantage of concrete over steel is that it is simple to construct a rectangular tank, whereas steel tanks are nearly always circular in cross section. So if you are cramped for space, concrete may be the way to go. Unfortunately, there are not as many suppliers in concrete. In fact, there is only one listed in the Manhattan classified phone book under "Tanks—Concrete."

If you ask the fabricators of steel tanks about concrete tanks, they will suggest that the concrete tanks sometimes fail due to thermal expansion. One concrete fabricator contacted claimed that this might have happened decades ago to the earlier tanks, but this is no longer the case. The concrete fabricator admits that "little fissures" sometimes develop in the concrete and that they must be patched. On the other hand, concrete does not rust so that concrete tanks don't have to be painted every five to ten years. A major application for concrete tanks is for brewing of beer. There's a good chance your favorite beer, domestic or imported, was brewed in a concrete vat.

COLLAPSIBLE TANKS CAN BE ROLLED UP

In Chapter 11 which deals with shipping, collapsible tanks are discussed as a means of lowering transportation charges. The same rubberized-fabric tanks available in much larger sizes for temporary or long-term storage of fluids. Uniroyal, which claims to be the biggest in this business, makes Static Storage Tanks up to 100,000 gallons in capacity. On special order, Uniroyal will make such Brobdingnagian bladders to hold up to 1,000,000 gallons. Firestone, another supplier, offers its Fabritanks in standard sizes up to 1,000,000 gallons too.

Besides cost, the great advantage of these collapsible tanks is that when they have accomplished a given mission, they can be emptied, rolled up, and either stored or easily moved elsewhere. For example, the 100,000-gallon Static Storage Tank can be rolled up into a crate only 7 × 5 × 2 feet with a shipping weight of only 1,668 pounds, and the 1,000,000-gallon Fabritank can be rolled up into a crate only 14 × 3 × 3 feet with a shipping weight of 4,300 pounds. (When used outdoors, Static Storage Tanks are usually unfolded over a ground cloth that is supposed to prevent any objects in the ground from puncturing the tank when filled. The ground cloth for the 100,000-gallon tank weighs 670 pounds.)

Cost is that other big advantage. In contrast to the $50,000 price tag on a steel tank of 100,000-gallon capacity, a rubber bladder of the same capacity costs under $25,000. Similarly, a 1,000,000-gallon Fabritank costs about $90,000, including site preparation, as compared with the $200,000 price tag on a steel tank of the same capacity.

A minor disadvantage of the rubber tanks is that they take up much more real estate. For instance, when laid out, the 100,000-gallon tank requires an area about 65 × 65 feet, or 4,225 square feet. A steel tank, which rises much higher off the ground, would require only about a tenth as much real estate. On the other hand, the rubber tanks are less obtrusive.

The rubberized fabric tanks are vulnerable to vandalism or sabotage. It would take something close to a bazooka or small cannon to pierce a steel tank, but a high-powered rifle could pop holes in the flexible tanks. If such damage is a concern, the tank could either be laid out indoors (on a sturdy floor) or an embankment could be pushed up by a bulldozer to completely conceal and protect the tank from anyone standing at ground level. In actual installation a dike embankment is normally constructed to contain the contents of the tank in the unlikely event it ruptures. To make sure that the tanks are not ruptured by the pressure of a pump, a pressure-actuated alarm is usually installed on the hardware.

The operational temperature range of the tanks is −40°F to 120°F, which means they can't very well lie outdoors in the Arabian desert or in Alaska in winter. (Special low-temperature versions have been developed for use on Alaska's North Slope.) Usually, the latent heat of the contents and the embankments is sufficient to prevent freezing of the contents. In very cold climates, the contents of the tanks can be pumped through heat exchangers to prevent freezing and also melt any excessive layers of snow.

The rubber containers are also made in more rigid versions for flowable solids. Neoprene-coated Dacron cord with a vulcanized rubber interior are the construction materials used by Uniroyal. Its Sealdbins are available in capacities from 50 up to 300 cubic feet; the latter costs $1,200.

Maintenance is also simpler for rubber tanks. Every five to seven years a few gallons of Hypalon or other sealer has to be spread over the top of the tank. Two men can take care of a 1,000,000-gallon tank in one day, in contrast to the days of work required in sandblasting and painting a steel tank. On the other hand, after interior cleaning a steel tank can be used to store some fluid other than the one previously held, whereas rubber tanks are pretty much dedicated to one fluid for their entire life, which Firestone believes is 20 years.

Delivery is a great attraction of the rubber tanks as this is written. In contrast to long delays on steel tanks, rubber tanks are available in "four to five months," up from the usual "30 to 40 days" because companies that wanted steel tanks have switched to rubber.

NEW WAY TO GO—STORE HIGHER

The ideal solution to the need to store more would be to find some way to cram more into present warehouses. In this way, the problems and expense of public warehousing or renting empty buildings or trailer vans could be avoided. New construction is also worth avoiding, not only because it costs, but also because it takes so long—and you may not need the extra space when the new warehouse is completed a year or two from now.

There are three ways that companies can store more in present warehouses: store higher; compress aisles between storage racks; or go to the latest storage technology based on very narrow aisles and high racks.

New kinds of industrial trucks are enabling companies to stack higher and/or closer together. These are the "sideloaders," fork-lift trucks on which the operator stands rather than sits, and the new "reach" trucks. The sideloaders are just what the name implies: the fork is mounted amidships on the truck and both picks up the load and deposits it on the racks in an action perpendicular to the motion of the vehicle. However, the load can only be carried on one side of the truck, usually the right side. This means that to pick up a load to the left of its travel the sideloader has to move to the end of the aisle, turn around, and approach the load from the opposite direction. Sideloaders are especially handy with very long loads, such as pipes or lumber.

Trucks on which drivers stand rather than sit have been available for years. Although they pick up and drop loads in the direction of their travel, they can operate in narrower aisles, with racks as close as eight feet, because they are several feet shorter than conventional fork-lift trucks.

The latest in industrial trucks are the type that can pivot their forks so that they can pluck out pallet loads perpendicular to their direction of travel. So far, only a few companies offer such "reach" trucks, but more manufacturers of industrial vehicles should enter this market as the storage-expanding concept catches on. I observed a reach truck made by Drexel Industries in action at a Philco-Ford plant near Philadelphia. Ford, the parent company, uses dozens of these trucks in its auto plants. The vehicle, simulating movement in an aisle only five feet wide, grabbed a pallet load out of a rack nearly 30 feet off the floor. The test was quite impressive. The only disadvantage was the vehicle's great weight, which restricted it to operation only on the ground level of the multilevel warehouse.

Another disadvantage to reach trucks is their much higher cost, up to $35,000 with charging accessories (since they usually work indoors, all are electric powered). However, their initial cost can be more than recouped through savings in warehouse space. For example, a small Oakland, California, manufacturer of big valves decided to switch to a Clark reach truck called the Tri-Loader just before authorizing construction of a new warehouse. When management at Pacific Pump figured out that moving the racks about six feet closer together would save a lot of space, they shaved 50 feet off the planned dimensions of the building, which was built 150 feet wide by 200 feet long ($50 \times 200 = 10,000$). At the time the building was put up, warehouse construction costs in that region ran about $10 per square foot, so Pacific Pump came out a whopping $80,000 ahead ($100,000 minus the difference in cost between the reach truck and a conventional fork-lift).

Availability of spare parts is another problem with any new class of machine, and this applies to the reach truck. At one point the Clark Tri-Loader at Pacific Pump was out of service for several weeks because one part was unavailable. This illustrates another problem for smaller companies considering purchasing these new machines. Just like Pacific Pump, you may only need one vehicle to service your warehouse. Should that one machine break down, you may be stuck. Because of the comparatively small population of these machines, it's not likely that a neighbor or dealer can lend or rent a substitute while your machine is being repaired.

HIGH-RISE STORAGE

More and more companies are getting away from industrial trucks altogether, or using them much less by turning to automated or semi-automated storage, the new trend. Because this newer kind of dense storage featuring extremely narrow aisles (far too narrow for any industrial truck) is most effective the higher it is constructed, the most spectacular examples involve new warehouses in which the ceilings are 100 feet or more high. However, some companies have taken advantage of the new technology by converting two-level warehouses to single-level structures by removing one floor. In some instances, campanies have opened up the roofs of older, low warehouses and erected high storage racks straight up from the lowest level. The result is a striking, modernistic tower rising out of a group of humble, old-fashioned warehouses.

If the aisles are too narrow (and the racks too high) for industrial trucks, how are goods stored in and then moved from the racks? The machine that accomplishes this is called a stacker crane. It can best be described as a cross between a monorail and an elevator. In a semi-automatic set-up, an operator called an order-picker rides in the little elevator selecting items from the racks or directing a grabbing mechanism that plucks out large cartons or pallet loads. In a completely automatic set-up, the order-picker is also a machine.

When there is a heavy volume of order-picking, one stacker crane is specified for each aisle, which can be several hundred feet long. However, if the level of order-picking is not high, a single stacker crane could service two or even three aisles, with some sort of switching arrangement at one end of the aisles, similar to a railroad yard, to shuttle the crane from aisle to aisle. It is even conceivable that in a warehouse with many aisles some could be served by single stacker crane, while others with a lower level of activity, could be served by one stacker crane to two or three aisles.

Now this suggests a very capacious warehouse. How does the human or mechanical order-picker know where to look for items desired or where to place incoming goods? Don't be surprised to learn that a computer is required. How else can locations for a great many items be kept track of?

Although the computer (or rather computers, since a back-up unit is the norm) could be one that handles other tasks within the company, the general practice is to dedicate a pair of minicomputers (one for back-up) to the big job of keeping track of all the items *randomly placed* in the stacks.

Randomly placed? Yes, there is no logical order to the placement of items to be stored. A carton or pallet marked for storage is simply stuck into a hole in the stacks known to the computer. The empty space is located by sensors mounted horizontally, and also vertically, at known intervals on the track along which the stacker moves. In effect, the face of the racks simulates a plotting board.

All of this suggests a big investment, and in fact a substantial investment is required. A pair of minicomputers plus disk drives and other "peripherals" plus the necessary programming could represent several hundred thousand dollars. Each stacker crane costs about $10,000, and the rails, sensors, and steel racks can cost between $100,-000 and $200,000 per aisle, depending on length and height.

Does such a big investment pay off? Here's what companies who've switched to high-rise storage report; savings of as much as 75 percent of floor space in warehouses, with lower operating costs and nothing ever lost!

The return on investment on high-rise storage is so great—sometimes these new warehouses pay for themselves in only 18 months—that many larger companies are committing themselves to this new technology. Usually it is most efficient to erect a brand-new building designed as a high-rise warehouse. (There's a special advantage to new construction if a recent Internal Revenue Service ruling holds up. If the roof and other skin of the warehouse are entirely supported by the storage racks and no one works inside—the movement of the stacker cranes is completely automated—then the building can be treated as a machine subject to fast depreciation instead of the long-term depreciation associated with buildings.)

High-rise storage has one other advantage over conventional methods, according to Gregory Schultze, president of the consulting firm of Greg Schultze International: much less damage to goods stored and moved. With fork-lift trucks there is always a certain level of damage running about 2 percent of goods handled due to forks spearing cartons or banging into racks. To reduce this damage, the makers of industrial trucks are adding special features to the vehicles. For narrow-aisle trucks, guide bars are now mounted along the base of the racks, and one manufacturer has added a pushbutton-controlled "automatic shelf-height selector" on trucks that can reach very high up on racks.

AN OPTION FOR SMALLER COMPANIES

Many smaller companies cannot convert to high-rise storage. The big investment may be the main obstacle, but low ceilings in rented quarters may also preclude this cost-cutting move. An alternative is to use order-picking trucks that can operate in very narrow aisles. These trucks can lift the order-picker as much as 20 feet above the floor level. (The same vehicles can also be used to replace light bulbs in high bays.)

TWO CAUTIONS ON HIGH-RISE RACKS

In evaluating the pros and cons of high-rise storage versus use of narrow-aisle trucks (in some high-rise installations, trucks are still required to move loads from the end of the aisles to where needed) companies should be aware of two limitations on high-rise installations. These are fire protection and the problem of obtaining fire insurance on goods stored in high-rise racks; and the ability of the racks to withstand earthquakes. On the first matter, the National Fire Protection Association has issued a standard on fire protection for racks of any height. If your high racks comply with NFPA 231C–1973, you should be able to obtain insurance protection. The matter of resisting seismic forces has not been resolved yet. The Uniform Building Code currently imposes such strength requirements on high racks that it most likely does not make sense to erect them in any "seismic" area such as southern California. However, this could change in the coming months. Despite these limitations, high-rise racks are growing rapidly in popularity and should continue to find ever wide usage.

ANOTHER OPPORTUNITY TO SAVE MONEY

To save dollars, companies should investigate investing in long-lived pallets or switching to one-use pallets of lower cost. There are many situations in which the conventional wooden pallet does not hold up because of the presence of moisture or other contaminants in a warehouse. Those who use large quantities of pallets are switching to long-lived pallets made either of metal or sturdy plastics. Although aluminum or heavy polyethylene pallets cost much more than wooden pallets, they are more *cost effective* because they can outlast wooden pallets by a big factor, perhaps by an order of magnitude.

At the other extreme, where a company delivers its products on pallets that are never returned switching to a lower-cost pallet made of compressed waste paper is a saving. If the product is delivered in company vehicles which otherwise return empty, ask the customer to return pallets. As this is written, the shortage of wood that was so vexing in the early months of 1974 has passed. If wood becomes scarce again, either because of poor weather or a housing boom, viable alternatives to wooden pallets should be considered.

CONSERVATION OF ASSETS IN WAREHOUSING

The goods stored in company warehouses can represent a substantial portion of total company assets. For a distributor, stored goods most likely constitute the greatest part of the company's assets. Therefore, the concepts of conservation of assets and the Waste Audit apply with force to the warehousing function.

Warehouses can suffer losses in three main ways:

Through pilferage by employees and theft by outsiders, such as the crews of common carriers, other visitors, and criminal intruders.

Through damage in handling, such as an industrial truck bumping into racked merchandise.

Through poor record keeping, in which the locations of required goods are not immediately ascertainable, which either forces the company to order more or delays production or shipment while the warehousemen frantically search for the missing items.

In addition, goods may be lost through poor maintenance of the warehouse. If the warehouse is refrigerated and the equipment breaks down, the losses could run the gamut from total to a mere decline in flavor or quality, depending on how soon the refrigeration equipment is returned to service. If the heating system breaks down in winter, water could condense on metal products, rusting or corroding them.

"BUY OR MAKE" IN COMPUTERIZATION

Computerization in warehousing, as exemplified in the mini-computer systems discussed above, can go beyond order-picking. In fact, since the customer order is the basis for computer action, why not go another step farther and create an invoice too?

This is exactly what's happening at a number of distributors which are essentially warehousing operations. Usually, the computer is on the company's premises, but a growing number of distributors are discovering that it makes economic sense to turn all of their EDP over to a service specialist in distributor operations.

Allstate Distributors of St. Louis is an excellent example. This 100-employee outfit distributes about $18 million of liquors in some 2,500 different brands and sizes in one year. Since 1969, all data processing has been performed several hundred miles away in Nashville by a service organization called ADP-Autonet. This subsidiary of Automatic Data Processing charges Allstate about $3,400 per month, which is less than the sum total of salaries for computer-room personnel when Allstate had its own 360/20 computer.

In addition, Allstate employs three clerks to operate four computer terminals at its headquarters and one at another branch operation in the same state. The TC-500 terminals are rented directly from Burroughs for $171 per month each, including maintenance. ADP-Autonet also charges Allstate about $2,000 extra for invoice forms and management reports but makes no extra charge for the phone lines and attendant costs.

This is how the system works. During the day the clerks enter receipts of merchandise from suppliers, cash collections, and orders. Immediately, the remote computer digests the in-coming orders, works out all extensions, totals the amounts and directs the terminal at which the clerk is sitting to print out a complete invoice, which can go out with the order to the customer. This process also immediately updates inventories, accounts receivable and assembles information for reports that are printed on the terminals as needed. These reports include daily registers, stock status, accounts receivable aging, and quota reports for each salesman. The same service may be handling exactly the same vital information for a competitor.

To hold down phone charges, longer reports prepared monthly are printed in Nashville on big, high-speed printers—the TC-500 terminals can only print slowly at 10 characters per second—and then mailed to Allstate. In the event of a strike at the Postal Service or any severe deterioration of its service, these reports could be sent over phone lines to a high-speed printer that Allstate would have to rent on an hourly basis at some local service bureau.

A "reorder list" is another remote service. The list is not put into force automatically. Rather, company buyers use it in conjunction with what they know about upcoming price increases or slow deliveries (liquors originating in Europe are sometimes months late in arrival) to make up the actual purchase orders. The standardized service can't handle such variables.

Fred Croce, the president of Allstate, reports that the switch to the Autonet service has been saving his company about "$50,000 per year." How is this possible? First, the terminal operators are paid at the lowest minimum rate compared to the higher-salaried computer operators and programmers, who often had to work overtime to keep up with the work load. In addition, the in-house computer often ran more than 176 hours per month, so an additional rental fee was incurred.

"Very responsive" is the way Croce described the remote service, which has been extremely reliable aside from a few early breakdowns —none longer than five hours—plus a few short stoppages on the order of 15 minutes due to phone lines downed by storms.

Interestingly enough, Allstate is not completely tied to a remote service. A distant branch operation has retained its own IBM System/3 for all EDP.

HOLDING DOWN COSTS OF INDUSTRIAL TRUCKS

Although the trend is to high-rise storage, the great majority of companies still depend on industrial trucks for materials handling. If your company operates lift trucks, you know that they are a major cost element in warehousing and a big expense in moving heavy items around on the production floor in manufacture of capital goods and many other lines.

The cost of the machines themselves is escalating, and some of the largest ones now cost $50,000. However, if your company has been keeping careful records of all cost elements in industrial trucks you should be aware that your greatest expense is maintenance. Although maintenance is not likely to exceed the first cost of the machine, unless you keep running it too long, maintenance generally exceeds your holding cost (acquisition cost minus trade-in).

Repairs are another big expense because of the relatively high accident rate associated with lift trucks. On average, repairs over the life of a vehicle run about 15 percent of its first cost. (This does not include damage to merchandise dropped or speared or damage to buildings and to trailers being unloaded.)

Energy is becoming an important expense element in operation of lift trucks, particularly if your use of the trucks is intense. In general as all types of energy rise in cost, it becomes more economical to use trucks powered by storage batteries than those fueled with gasoline or propane (LP gas) for the smaller trucks generally used indoors; the big machines used outdoors to move the very largest and bulkiest of loads, such as lumber, are diesels and there is no competition from other forms of power. During the energy crisis of 1973–74, companies that chose lift trucks fueled with propane at 14 cents per gallon found that they had to pay up to 90 cents per gallon. Because their electrical rates did not rise so fast, many are ordering electrically powered machines to replace their propane-powered units. For greater flexibility in case of another energy crisis, companies are also ordering new machines with internal-combustion engines that can operate on either propane or gasoline by merely throwing a switch—concealed under the hood so that the drivers don't throw it accidentally. These conversion features cost about $350 and can also be retrofitted on machines now in service.

Drivers are usually one of the low-cost elements in lift-truck operation, perhaps too low. Most companies pay their drivers the lowest possible wages and get what they pay for. These poorly motivated drivers not only cause too much damage to merchandise and vehicles as well, but may not be diligent in finding loads to be moved and in delivering them. As a result, one large warehouse found that it was much cheaper over the long run to pay its drivers $8 an hour; accidents dropped sharply and "production" was much higher.

Another way to cut down on accidents is to use women drivers. One large appliance manufacturer has been highly successful with women. The women drivers have better accident records than the men drivers. There's no great strength requirement for drivers of lift trucks: the machines all have power steering.

Training is another low-cost or no-cost element that is neglected.

All of the suppliers of lift trucks will help train your drivers at no cost, yet this service is much under-utilized. Drivers who have little education and can barely speak English are given only a few hours of training. Companies that do not train their drivers properly may also be in violation of O.S.H.A. regulations.

PROPER TRAINING SAVES ENERGY TOO

By training drivers properly, companies can not only cut down on accidents but also save energy and extend the life of the machines. All of the manufacturers of lift trucks can provide information on such training. Here are some examples of how to handle machines in the most conservative manner:

The load should be centered on the carriage. Off-center loads cause undue wear on the mast and carriage. Also, the load should be carried as close to the ground as possible.

When a load restricts vision ahead, operate in reverse.

Minimize steering when standing still to reduce wear and tear.

On electrical trucks, when waiting, place the directional control in neutral to deactivate the power-steering motor, thus saving battery power.

Railroad tracks are to be crossed at an angle to reduce shock and avoid knocking the load off the carriage.

Use the power reversing with the hydrostatic transmission to reduce brake wear.

Shut off the motor when leaving the vehicle for any extended break. (To make sure the motor is shut off, a "dead-man" switch can be mounted under the seat of sit-down vehicles. This feature is mandatory on stand-up machines for safety reasons. To add this switch costs from $400 to $500.)

These are just a few of dozens of instructions to drivers; they should convince you that driving a lift truck is much more complicated than driving a car or a truck.

There's still another way in which to cut down on accidents. If your warehouse is not brightly illuminated, perhaps to save energy, headlights should be mounted on lift trucks and on the mast so that the driver can clearly see the spot where he is to pick up or deposit a load.

THE TREND IS TO CONTRACT MAINTENANCE

Maintenance of lift trucks is also much more complicated than maintenance of over-the-road trucks, and the shortage of mechanics qualified to perform on lift trucks is as great if not greater than of mechanics for highway trucks. (As a result, skilled mechanics are also being "imported" to maintain lift trucks.)

Either because of the shortage of mechanics or because they are not aware of what it is costing them, too many users have adopted the rule of running lift trucks until they fail. Ultimately, this turns out to be the most expensive approach. Aside from losses in production and driver wages, this policy usually means that companies must own spare trucks in case a truck fails. And repairs on a truck that's failed may be much more costly than the recommended preventive maintenance. Here's one small example. An item that is replaced at intervals set by experience is the elastomer hose carrying hydraulic fluid for the lifting mechanism. This hose costs about $3. If it is not replaced, it might rupture, with the result that $16 worth of hydraulic fluid spills out on the floor of the warehouse. In addition, it may take a janitor a few hours to wipe up the slippery fluid. Of course an expensive machine is out of service for several hours at least.

To solve the maintenance problem, more and more smaller companies and some large ones too are turning to contract maintenance on owned vehicles or those on lease. The service, provided by local dealers, takes different forms depending on the number of vehicles involved. For instance, if you operate several dozen vehicles, the dealer will provide a "resident" mechanic. If you operate only a few machines, the dealer will send a maintenance truck to your premises equipped with the necessary spare and replacement parts. This work could be done evenings or even on Saturdays to make sure that your trucks are not out of service for maintenance or repair. (That's another advantage of this form of service: there are no spare parts, such as spark plugs, to be pilfered.)

How much does this service cost? It's usually charged on the basis of hours of operation. Every industrial truck is equipped with an engine-hour meter. Rates run from 70 cents per hour for small machines up to $3 per hour for big machines operating in demanding environments.

To make sure that the required number of vehicles are always in operation, the maintenance contract can be written with a provision for spare rental trucks from the dealer to take the place of those machines requiring extensive maintenance.

Usually, contract maintenance is associated with leasing of trucks, another growing trend in this field. Leasing, in addition to offering the known advantage of not tying up capital, has one other advantage to the user: in the event his requirements change, say from wide-aisle to narrow-aisle storage, it's usually easier to change over to another type of industrial truck under leasing. Of course, if you own a number of lift trucks you no longer require and they are in good shape, you should obtain a good trade-in based on the sharp escalation in the prices of new machines. Even electrical trucks, which previously have not enjoyed as high a trade-in value as those powered by internal-combustion engines, are gaining in trade-in value.

WHEN TO SWITCH TO CONTRACT MAINTENANCE

Before deciding to change over to contract maintenance, make sure that you are not stirring up a hornets' nest at the headquarters of your local union. In the past some unions have bitterly opposed contract maintenance, even though it was performed by union labor. The matter is jurisdictional, of course. The mechanics provided by the dealer belong to another union! This is why it makes sense to plan the change for a period of high production when your union may not be able to provide enough skilled mechanics to keep up the lift trucks. On the other hand, during a recessionary period, the union may have an excess of skilled mechanics, and you could take advantage of the situation to hire good men.

NEXT, CONTRACT DRIVERS

Just as you can hire truckers under a contract, it is now possible to hire lift trucks plus their drivers under a scheme quite like contract trucking. Only a few large companies have tried this system, and they are very reticent to talk about it to avoid offending their unions.

AID IN SPECIFICATION

Because industrial trucks come in a great variety of sizes, have different functions, depend on four different forms of energy, and operate in a range of environments, it takes considerable knowledge to specify the right machines for a given situation. To help their customers in specifying, the major suppliers of these vehicles have developed computer programs to aid customers in picking the most efficient, long-lasting, and least costly units for their application. A salesman will come in and make a complete survey of your facilities, including measuring grades (electrical trucks can't make steep grades).

Before making a big investment in new trucks, you should take advantage of such surveys from at least two and preferably three suppliers. If their recommendations vary greatly, you should show the competing recommendations to the others for comments. Then try to make up your own mind.

There's one recommendation on which all suppliers are certain to agree: protection packages. These packages, which can add from $500 to $1,000 to the cost of a unit, are designed to enable the machine to function properly and stand up against such hostile conditions as the extreme cold of an ice-cream warehouse, corrosive liquids or gases in a chemical plant, and the abrasive dust of an engine-block foundry. Unfortunately, some purchasing agents or executives have tried to save the $500 to $1,000 for the protective packages, to their company's ultimate loss.

ACCURATE RECORD KEEPING ESSENTIAL

To achieve the lowest losses and least waste, absolutely accurate record keeping is essential. In fact, poor record keeping could encourage the other forms of loss, pilferage, and sloppy handling. If no one is sure of the exact amount of goods stored in and passing through a warehouse, how can the extent of pilferage or damaged goods be known?

The rule that all entries and withdrawals from the warehouse must be noted down at the time the action is taken must never be broken. Another way to insure accuracy of record keeping is to exclude from the warehouse all employees not assigned to it. During the period of shortages, many companies were forced to return to the wartime practice of "expediting." Energetic young men are assigned to tracking down parts, raw materials, or whatever is needed at the moment to complete some job (so that the next step can be performed). In their enthusiasm, the expediters may grab a box of parts right off the shipping dock and rush it to the production floor.

To deter such actions, warehousemen should be provided with a "hot list," items desperately required for production or reshipment. The hot list, which should be in the form of a blackboard visible to all checkers, should be kept up-to-date by someone with a clear, legible handwriting. To make it easy to spot hot items, their source must also be listed. As soon as a hot item is observed, it should be entered into the inventory record system. Then, and only then, the department that needs it can be informed.

DETERRING PILFERAGE

Here are some ploys that help eliminate "excuses" for outsiders to enter your warehouse:

A washroom for visiting chauffeurs and helpers should be provided right at the loading docks. There should be no door or operable windows between this washroom and the interior of the warehouse.

A telephone should be provided at the dispatcher's window for visiting chauffeurs. It should be right at the dispatcher's elbow so that all conversations can be monitored. Use of the phone for local calls should be extended, but all long-distance calls to remote dispatchers should be placed collect. No other pay or company phone should be installed in the warehouse so that there is no excuse available to an outside driver to enter the building to "call headquarters."

In summertime when the warehouse may become very warm and its occupants naturally want to open doors at the far end of the building to promote natural ventilation those doors should be provided with lockable chain-link or mesh gates that permit air but not people to pass through.

Another conservative practice to institute and enforce: whenever a carton is broken open due to poor handling or because a passing industrial truck gouges it open, the goods inside should be repacked in a fresh carton. Somehow, once a carton is broken open, the contents, if valuable, tend to disappear. (On New York's docks, the longshoremen sometimes deliberately permit a carton or load to topple over, exposing the contents to pilferage.)

THE WASTE AUDIT AND WAREHOUSING

Applying the concept of the Waste Audit to warehousing is not easy. The warehouse does not create anything. Nevertheless, here are some suggestions on developing a meaningful Waste Audit for the warehouse so that employees assigned to it can also be given new goals to achieve:

Develop a "Throughput Ratio," the ratio between items or containers received and those dispatched. This ratio would surely be in the high nineties, which is a more positive and encouraging number for employees to deal with than a percentage of losses, which should be below five percent and hopefully below one percent. However, you may decide that the loss percentage is the one to publicize to employees. Since some employees may also be stockholders, losses, expressed either as a high throughput ratio or as a low percentage, may become public knowledge.

Maintain a ratio of energy consumed in operating industrial trucks to volume of goods moved. This would encourage employees to turn off the motors of trucks when not in use (electric trucks don't draw any power when they stand still).

Keep records on the number of containers damaged and repaired inside the warehouse either while in movement or if struck by a vehicle while on a rack. Since this number would hopefully be very low compared to throughput, it does not appear to be meaningful to record your losses due to damage as a ratio.

chapter 14

Organizing for the next energy crisis

DURING the embargo-induced energy crisis, many large companies assigned a knowledgeable, energetic executive the responsibility for coordinating the organization's efforts toward conserving energy in all its aspects. This "conservation czar," who usually was given the title of director of energy conservation or corporate conservation coordinator, was expected to stimulate others to achieve meaningful savings.

Even though the energy crisis has abated, many companies have wisely retained this function because the opportunity to make further dollar savings in energy is significant. Many companies, especially those dependent on natural gas, are still afflicted with the energy crisis.

Are similar new staff positions required to deal with any continuing shortages of energy or to counter the steady escalation in the cost of some forms of energy? In general, the answer is "No." Instead, all departments must continue to work together more closely and expeditiously. Instead of memos and reports, frequent face-to-face meetings are in order.

The committee approach to coping with continuing energy shortages should be the rule for everyday operations, especially if the company has inaugurated a Waste Audit. However, there are potential crises that call for delegation of special responsibilities. These are those extreme conditions where the company is gravely threatened. Instead of waiting for such conditions to arise before taking action, the smart approach is to delegate one executive to develop emergency plans well in advance. Hopefully, they will never be put to the test. Two levels of emergency are postulated, based on "semicritical" and "critical" shortages.

COPING WITH SEMICRITICAL SHORTAGES

A semicritical emergency is defined as one in which the company can maintain at least 75 percent of its normal level of activity. The shortage could either be in power available, which would affect all categories of companies, manufacturing, wholesaling, retailing, and service, or in some critical raw material which would only affect manufacturing companies.

If the shortage is in key raw materials, manufacturing companies should consider and plan for one of the following alternatives: cutting back to a four-day week or cutting down on the working day, such as closing down the production lines one or two hours earlier. (However, one activity should not be curtailed, and that is the group that processes accounts receivable. During a cutback in production, working capital will be strained, requiring the promptest possible collections. Of course, this also means that the switchboard and mailroom must be manned for the full workweek.)

What if the shortage is in energy, a crisis similar to that induced by the Arab oil embargo? What measures should be written into the emergency plan?

In summer to cut down on the air conditioning load (assuming that companies are permitted to operate their air conditioning), working hours could be shifted to the cooler hours, such as 6 A.M. to 2 P.M. During the late-afternoon power "brownouts" imposed in New York City in the summer of 1972, one manufacturing company in Brooklyn did shift to these supposedly inconvenient hours. To the surprise of management, the employees grew to like the early hours. They offered quite distinct advantages. First, workers were on the road before the heavy commuter traffic. Second, they got home early enough to take advantage of recreational facilities, such as golf courses, tennis courts, or the beach.

To further cope with less or no air conditioning, employees should be permitted to work in loose-fitting, informal clothing, such as shorts and sandals. Of course, ties and jackets would no longer be required for men. If power levels are restored in the evening, when demand is lower, all EDP work should be shifted to those hours, when there are also fewer voltage "perturbations" induced by heavy machinery. In addition, air conditioning might be permitted at night, essential for some computers that can't operate in un-air–conditioned spaces.[1]

If the sharp power cuts occur in winter, then the company has to change its dress standards in the opposite direction: employees permitted to wear heavy sweaters to work, with all women permitted to wear pants (for the few companies that still don't permit pants for women).

Subcontracting of energy-intensive parts to contractors in localities with sufficient electric power or gas should be considered.

If the shortage is gasoline or diesel fuel, the company should consider the following alternatives: relying on common carriers, the Postal Service, United Parcel Service, or courier services, for pick-up and delivery of packages instead of company trucks. Or, use employees who live in the vicinity of customers to drop off small shipments on their way home. Organize car pools and require employees to use them as much as possible. Limit your salesmen's visits to customers who are convenient to public transportation.

Cleaning up during working hours so that after hours the minimum amount of power is consumed as possible.

COPING WITH CRITICAL SHORTAGES

A critical emergency is defined as one in which the company can't maintain more than 50 percent of its normal level of activity. The shortage could be in power available or in key parts or materials. Steps to be taken include:

---

[1] This is another reason companies should favor decentralized EDP based on small local systems rather than one giant computer center tied to branches by phone lines. Most of the small systems can operate in un-air–conditioned rooms.

1. Cut back to a three-day or even to a two-day production work-week.

2. Lay off many if not the majority of your employees, naturally in order of seniority and with the close cooperation of any union. However, the clerks dealing with accounts receivable must be kept on full time along the mailroom and switchboards. (You might investigate providing back-up power for switchboards and PBXs on company premises. Phones connected directly to phone-company exchanges receive their power through the phone lines, but the power for switchboards and lighted pushbuttons is tapped locally. Back-up battery power is available from many local phone companies, but it costs.)

Since few companies are likely to invest in back-up power, it makes sense to have at least one phone on the premises connected directly to the exchange which provides power to it at all times, including during an emergency. (The smart place to install this phone is in the office of your director of security. He may have other reasons for requiring a phone that can't be listened in on by a switchboard operator.)

3. Security measures should be tightened, in particular for fuel or raw materials stored outside. Disgruntled employees who are laid off might resort to vandalism or sabotage. A remote possibility is a community riot with local businesses and factories the butt of riot frustration. Contact should be made with local guard services as to the possibility of hiring additional guards during any emergency. However, make sure that the guards, if unionized, are not members of the Teamsters Union, which means they would not cooperate in the delivery or removal of any machinery or products by non-Teamster drivers in the event of a strike by the Teamsters.

COPING WITH BROWNOUTS

The energy emergency measures recommended deal with the long-term shortages. What about short-term shortages, the brownouts—voltage drops of up to eight percent—that were characteristic only of urban areas with insufficient power capacity to handle all the installed air conditioners operating at a higher capacity? Now brownouts may occur in seasons other than summer because the power companies can't attract enough capital to build sufficient plants. Even worse, some hard-hit areas may be subject to "rolling blackouts" in which all the power is turned off for several hours in succession each day in communities served by a given supplier of electricity.

Brownouts are, of course, preferable, and business and industry can usually cope with them. When they occurred in late afternoon in past summers, some companies took the obvious step of shifting work to hours other than late afternoon. However, those that shifted more work to nighttime reported higher costs if the union demanded the usual night work differential, and employees were not as receptive. Wintertime brownouts may require similar shifts in work hours, with attendant benefits—or higher costs.

THE DISRUPTION OF ROLLING BLACKOUTS

If brownouts are tolerable, the rolling blackouts proposed in some hard-hit states are quite intolerable. Manufacturers whose processes necessarily run 24 hours a day would lose more than the production interrupted during the blackout, which presumably would last only a few hours or one shift. By the nature of many complex processes, once they stop or cool off, they can't be restarted again without special efforts that could take many hours or even days. And the costly equipment used to make solid-state devices would be severely damaged if it were shut down suddenly.

Emergency back-up electric power is no solution, aside from its staggering cost, because it usually requires diesel fuel, which is also scarce.

Hopefully, the spectre of rolling blackouts will never take real form. However, just in case it does, arrange with your local power company for hours of warning so that any electrically operated equipment or process can be shut down in a safe, orderly manner.

THE ROLE OF THE DIRECTOR OF ENERGY CONSERVATION

The executive in the best position to develop necessary emergency plans for short-term or long-term emergencies is the Director of Energy Conservation. That is if one has been designated for this function, which is still needed in spite of the end of the Arab embargo. Another likely choice is your director of security since there is a significant security aspect to any emergency plans. Because some of the emergency measures might conflict with the regulations of the Occupational Safety and Health Administration (OSHA), the executive designated should be familiar with those regulations and might even be the one responsible for their enforcement.

The executive chosen should have a broad knowledge of your entire operation, including any branch plants, warehouses, or offices. Naturally, he should be someone who works well with others, yet can't be induced to compromise his responsibilities. And he should be able to get the ear of top management. (At Itek Corp., the energy coordinator reports directly to the president of this substantial company, which grosses over $200 million per year.)

As soon as a well-motivated director of energy conservation is designated, he should make an energy audit of all facilities and vehicles. Figure that it might take several weeks to a month, depending on the size of your operations for this overview. However, it is an essential step in developing the base data on energy consumption against which all future conservation efforts can be measured.

While making the survey, the new director should be on the lookout for local "assistant directors" to be appointed in outlying facilities not easily reached by the director himself. These assistants need not devote themselves full time to energy conservation, but they should exhibit many of the same characteristics as the director himself.

As soon as your energy conservation effort gets rolling, the director should invite all employees to offer suggestions on how energy can be saved within the company and even in their homes. Employees who are motivated to save energy at home will be well motivated to do the same at work. And they will be protecting their jobs to a certain extent. Remember, in a severe power shortage, residences, schools, and hospitals will be favored over businesses. The less energy used at home, the more left to keep business and industry functioning.

Finally, some overall company goal in conservation of energy should be set and well publicized within the organization. For example, General Electric, in common with many other manufacturers set 20 percent as an overall goal. Although many companies failed to reach such a high level of conservation, some did. Many others got very close, and a small number, such as Raytheon Co. (30 percent drop in fuel-oil consumption) and Wang Laboratories, Inc. (40 percent drop in power and about a 50 percent drop in natural-gas consumption) went way beyond 20 percent. Most had little trouble in saving 10 percent. The goal should be set on a time basis. In other words, 5 percent within one month (easily achieved); 8 percent within two months; 10 percent within three months; and 1 percent per month thereafter until the ultimate goal is achieved or surpassed. If the goal is met, management should find some tangible way of rewarding its employees, such as an extra day off (falling either on a Friday or a Monday so they can have a long weekend).

SPECIAL MEASURES FOR SMALLER COMPANIES

The companies that geared up quickly to cope with the energy crisis and who therefore achieved the most in saving energy (and dollars) were, of course, the giants. They have enough people so that designation of one executive, perhaps with some assistants, as the director of energy conservation does not leave any departments or branch plants shorthanded.

Smaller companies, which usually operate with a much leaner table of organization, rarely can afford a full-time conservation chief. And even if one is designated, he may not have the technical expertise to really accomplish much. Perhaps this is why so many executives of smaller companies responded to surveys on how they were coping with the energy crisis with such expressions of helplessness?

What can smaller companies do? There are several possibilities. First, consultants can be brought in on a temporary basis to prepare recommendations on cutting use of energy. The Office of Energy Programs of the Department of Commerce has prepared a list of experts in energy conservation, some of whom are quoted or referred to in this book. The address of this office is Washington, D.C. 20230. Unfortunately Du Pont's Energy Management Division, one of the long-established and highly successful energy conservation services (see Chap. 15), does not take on small clients, and the same may be true of other consultants. At the very least these consultants will charge $250 per day, plus expenses. Some charge much more.

Another good possibility is borrowing an expert or the director of energy conservation from a large company with whom your company has close ties, such as a customer or favored supplier. Or ask a good neighbor for help. (Incidentally, Itek's Neil Morris has indicated that he is willing to offer advice over the phone to those who request it. His number is (617) 276-2000.)

Some trade associations have hired experts on energy conservation to recommend energy-saving steps in manufacturing, where all the members of the association use the same production methods. If your trade association has not done so, why not recommend this cost-sharing approach to a common problem?

Finally, your local power company may be able to offer some sound advice on how to cut consumption of electricity and natural gas.

THE "ENERGY KIT"

One trade association that responded in a positive manner to the energy crisis is the International Council of Shopping Centers, 445 Park Avenue, New York, N.Y. 10022. An elaborate "energy conservation kit" was prepared by the ICSC and distributed to its 5,000 members early in the energy crisis. The kit included such items as: sample press releases to local newspapers and radio stations on what the shopping center is doing to cope with the crisis; promotion of car pools for shopping; how to sponsor an "energy conservation week"; and examples of posters promoting energy conservation. There's no evidence available on the effectiveness of the program and its implementation at the local level, but the quick response and extensiveness of material offered showed that trade associations can act when crisis strikes.

SELECTED REFERENCE

"Energy Conservation Program Guide for Industry and Commerce," NBS Handbook 115, Catalog No. C13.11:115, Superintendent of Documents, U.S. Government Printing Office, Washington, D.C. 20402, 182 pages.

chapter 15

Conserving energy in manufacturing

MANUFACTURING ORGANIZATIONS must give energy savings in production a high priority. Compared to plant usage, the consumption of energy in offices is low. Turning off electric typewriters when not in use is required for maintaining employee discipline, but the amount of energy saved is minute. Employees if necessary could make do with manual typewriters, but you can't run your plant without energy and lots of it.

A conservation program to sharply reduce consumption of energy should be implemented in three stages. In the first stage are the measures that can be implemented rapidly, such as elimination of waste and more efficient scheduling. In the second stage are the measures requiring some investment and which may take from weeks to months to implement, such as adding insulation. Included in the third stage are those long-term measures with a high payoff in energy savings, but which require a higher investment in both time and money. An example is replacement of present heat-curing processes with radiation curing.

ELIMINATION OF WASTE

That much energy can be saved by eliminating wasteful practices is proven by the record of various consultants in energy conservation.

The Energy Management Service of Du Pont guarantees a "7 to 15 percent saving in power consumption" on all plant jobs that it tackles. Harvey Morris of Fuel Economy Consultants claims that his organization has saved some users as much as 25 percent on their fuel bills.

Before going on to discuss the techniques used by such consultants, the reason that Du Pont's Energy Management Service came into being should be mentioned. This service antedates the energy crisis by some years. It began as an internal service that only took on jobs in Du Pont plants. The objective was to save dollars: long before the oil cartel quadrupled the price of oil, Du Pont realized that energy was becoming a significant cost of processing. Today, of course, all businessmen should be aware that energy is a significant cost.

Here is a review of the areas of waste that every plant manager should use as a checklist of possible savings in his own plant:

Only run machines when they are needed instead of all the time. This applies to most machine tools, except certain high-precision machines that seem to require long warm-up times to perform accurately.

Fuel can be wasted if too much is injected into the furnace space. A furnace can be upgraded to burn more fuel—and therefore deliver a greater output—with the proper burners, according to Harvey Morris. He recommends the recuperative burners that are manufactured overseas. Although they cost several times as much as the simpler burners used on most U.S. furnaces, the difference is quickly recouped in more efficient burning of fuel.

Too many openings in heat-processing equipment wastes energy. Close the unneeded ones and try to reduce the size of the others.

Employees must be trained to close the doors on heat-processing equipment quickly—as soon as whatever task they are engaged in is completed. (This is comparable to training children to close the refrigerator doors quickly after they remove whatever food or beverage they are seeking.)

All cracks in heating equipment, no matter how small, must be sealed.

All leaks in steam lines, usually identified by plumes, must be sealed too. (One expert recommends that the search for steam leaks be conducted after working hours or on weekends when there is no plant noise and steam leaks that are so small they don't create plumes can be detected by ear. The experts are using stethoscopes to detect steam leaks and leaky valves.)

Substantial users of steam are also urged by Morris to consider utilizing the Yarway Steam Conservation Service.

Optimum flame geometry should be maintained, confining the flame to the spot or area needed and not permitting it to flow over a broad area.

All doors warped by heat or over-tightening should be replaced.

Reflective heat shields should be erected to confine heat to a process area.

All heated vats should be covered.

PROPER MAINTENANCE

Maintenance of energy-consuming equipment is essential to its efficiency. The efficiency of a poorly maintained boiler can drop by half if scale accumulates on waterside surfaces. In general, scale should be removed once every year, more often if recommended by the manufacturer or if the water in your locality is particularly hard. Cracked or eroded refractory surfaces should be caulked or the bricking replaced if necessary. Gaskets on boiler doors should be replaced if worn or not able to maintain a tight fit. The interiors of all combustion equipment must be kept clean, from burner surfaces to flues.

Good maintenance also applies to electrical equipment. All connections between power buses and electrical gear, such as motors, reactors, blowers, and any large electrically powered gear should be checked regularly for tightness. A loose connection raises resistance at that point, which is a small energy loss. Many loose connections could add up to a big loss.

MORE EFFICIENT SCHEDULING

By proper scheduling, much energy can be saved. First, preheating of any materials or fluids should be limited to the temperature or time required before further processing. There's no need to preheat steel for many hours before forging if only 20 minutes is sufficient.

Second, short runs should be avoided as much as possible (if more sophisticated inventory and shop controls are applied less-efficient short runs should be avoided in general). Often it takes hours to bring a piece of processing equipment up to the proper operating temperature. Once at this temperature, it should be used productively for as long as possible. In other words, if it takes two hours to bring a reactor up to temperature, it doesn't make sense to process a batch of materials for only one hour. Conversely, once a run is completed and no further loads are scheduled, the reactor should be allowed to cool down to an efficient holding temperature from which it can be brought up to operating temperature without the expenditure of too much energy (of course, if the reactor is well insulated, it will take many hours to cool).

Proper loads should be scheduled for heat-processing equipment. Underloading should be avoided, because this means energy is wasted. Overloading, of course, means that the product under process is not receiving enough heat.

Closely related to proper scheduling is the notion of applying less heat in processing. Is any heat or as much heat really needed in your process? Is it possible that the same result could be achieved with much less heat? By questioning every heat process in your plant, you may find that much energy and time can be saved. For instance, one consultant questioned a client's long-standing practice of cooling a certain intermediate product and then reheating it before further processing. Instead, one batch was processed without the cooling stage and tests of the final product showed no discernable difference.

Better scheduling should also eliminate inefficient cooling off of in-process materials where the materials are permitted to cool off not because this is believed essential to processing but merely because two successive steps involving heated materials are not coordinated.

OVERLAPPING SHIFTS

In Chapter 4, overlapping of successive shifts is urged as a means of reducing scrap. This is also a way to save energy. Instead of permitting machines to stop and cool off, they should be operated continuously for greatest utilization of energy. Continuous operation is, of course, the norm in the processing industries, but could be applied intelligently in metalworking as well.

SOPHISTICATED INSTRUMENTATION PAYS FOR ITSELF

Proper instrumentation for heat-processing equipment and furnaces is widely available, quickly installed, and soon pays for itself. By means of such instruments, the desired temperature, air-to-gas ratios, and pollutants can be held to the most efficient and, in the case of the last, safe levels. No human operator, no matter how experienced, can match instruments in measuring temperature. Some operators, from years of experience, can glance at metal parts inside a processing unit and detect their temperature within 20°F or so. But an optical pyrometer can measure temperature within tenths of degrees. Your product may require processing within plus or minus five degrees, which means that instrumentation is mandatory.

The instrument that measures the air-to-gas ratio is the $300 Bailey meter. This ratio is important because insufficient air means that all the fuel is not being burned, which, of course, also results in pollution. Too much air, on the other hand, is also wasteful. First of all, it takes energy to pump the air into the furnace. Second, the excess air is heated in the combustion process, and this heat is then drawn up the stack and into the atmosphere (unless a heat exchanger or heat-storage unit has been installed) where it can cause undesirable heat pollution. Some excess air is required, but it should be held as close to 20 or 25 percent as possible.

Carbon monoxide is another undesirable product of combustion. OSHA regulations permit no more than a trace of it, and it cannot be detected by humans or animals because it is odorless and colorless. Too much carbon monoxide means incomplete combustion. Kits that detect CO are available from Fyrite, Orsat, and Dunn. These instruments range in price from $50 to several hundred dollars. Fyrite is made by Bacharach Instrument Co.

BEGIN WITH THICKER INSULATION

Many of the above recommendations can be affected with little effort and at low cost. There is another opportunity for elimination of waste that requires more effort and investment, but is well worth it. Most buildings and heat-dependent processes are underinsulated. Even if the building or the equipment was completed only a few years ago, it most likely does not meet the latest standards for insulation. The reason is simple: the optimum thickness of insulation is related to the cost of energy. When the cost of energy is low, the justifiable investment in insulation required to hold losses down is lower. In other words, the amount of energy saved should always cost more than the insulation spread over the number of years the building or equipment is expected to remain in service.

Now that energy costs are so much higher, it makes sense to construct new buildings and processes with much thicker insulation. Not only is there an immediate saving in energy consumption, but the resale value of the building or equipment remains higher. Of course, there is an upper limit to the thickness of insulation specified, otherwise it would be so thick that valuable floor space would be lost. However, in most heating (or chilling) situations, the optimum thickness is still far from the limit of practical construction.

To aid plant designers in specifying the optimum thickness of insulation, the Thermal Insulation Manufacturers Association (TIMA) commissioned the York Research Corporation to aid it in preparing a manual titled *ECON-I: How to Determine Economic Thickness of Thermal Insulation,* published in 1973. In this useful manual, which can be purchased for $15 (but which your supplier of thermal insulation would probably give to you gratis), certain simple assumptions to aid in determining the economically justifiable thickness of insulation for a given situation are made.

The formula on which "economic" thickness is based was first written in 1926 by L. B. McMillan. However, the equations were so complex that they were not applied prior to the availability of computers. It was not until 1960 that West Virginia University published a manual in which the "economic" thickness of insulation for any given situation could be read from tables. These tables were further published by TIMA in 1961 and 1962 (TIMA was then known as the National Insulation Manufacturers Association) and has been further updated in ECON-I.

Here's an example of how the tables are used. Let us assume that the pipe to be insulated has an outside diameter of 4 inches, and that the difference between the temperature of the material flowing in the pipe and the ambient air is 375° F (the tables also provide temperature differences in Fahrenheit), then the "economic" thickness is read off as 5.5 inches. This table provides values up to 12 inches of insulation, which is the thickest specified. The particular table chosen was based on total insulation cost.

In addition to pipe sizes, tables for specifying insulation for flat surfaces are given.

The concept of "economic" thickness should not be limited to new installations of pipe or hot surfaces (insulation is also required for very cold surfaces as well).

In many instances, added insulation can be mounted or sprayed over older insulation with few complications—as long as the original insulation is dry and sound. Plant maintenance personnel can handle straight runs of piping, leaving complicated shapes and valves to the pros. Andrew T. Haas, head of the insulation workers union, told me that his members, about 16,000 strong, don't like to finish such jobs, but insulation contractors have assured me that their unionized craftsmen will accomplish whatever job they are assigned.

Because of increasing costs in both materials and labor, it makes sense to specify insulation carefully. According to insulation contractors, there is much ignorance displayed by plant designers in selecting insulation. Here are some of the common money-wasting and time-wasting errors:

Picking a more costly high-temperature insulation when a less costly grade that can stand the lower operating temperature will do. Insulations are graded by various temperatures, such as up to 1,900° F, 1,500° F, 1,000° F, under 500° F, and so forth. Naturally, the higher the temperature limit, the higher the cost.

Calling for a costly outer wrap on the basis of appearance rather than utility. In too many instances, the outer covering selected, such as stainless steel, costs more than the insulation it protects. (Fortunately, one of the lowest cost and most effective wraps, canvas, which was practically unobtainable for months in early 1974 because of the worldwide shortage of cotton is now available again.)

Not taking advantage of the latest insulations that require far less labor to apply (for most installations, labor makes up 70 percent of the cost). In some instances these newer insulations are also shipped and stored flat, which means they cost less to ship and take up less inventory space in the plant. Example: Preslok, which is made by Keene Corp.

In a situation in which the insulation may become wet, which is destructive of some insulations, not specifying an insulation that regains its full properties after it dries out in place.

Contractors also believe that plant management is not aware of an employee practice that is both dangerous for employees and damaging to insulation. They mean walking on large-diameter, heavily insulated piping to get from one work station to another instead of using catwalks or climbing down to floor level. Traveling via such shortcuts is not only a violation of OSHA rules, but also tends to crush the insulation and make it less effective. It's easy to tell if this is going on—the top of the insulation is covered with footprints!

To gain the high and long-standing payoffs from application of insulation, process designers and mechanical designers for all types of buildings must learn to provide more room for the thicker insulation dictated by the new high cost of energy. When insulation will commonly run to eight inches and more, clearances between adjacent hot pipes will have to be thought of in feet instead of in inches. The same applies to architects. If it becomes the norm to specify, for instance, six inches of insulation in the outer walls of a building, then the interior of that building will be one foot narrower than the uninsulated version. This is an obscure added cost, but one well worth paying for effective energy conservation.

Remounting can sometimes make an older energy-intensive apparatus more efficient. For example, a clever way to save energy—and gain usable floor space too—is to suspend continuously fed annealing and drying ovens in the overhead, loading and unloading them from openings in the bottom. This saves energy, according to consulting engineer Robert E. Lamb, because hot air naturally escapes by convection from conventional end openings. Depending on the size of the product under treatment, the height of suspension can vary. Obviously, the investment in steel mounting structure and materials handling equipment rises sharply with the size of the product. At the same time that it is being raised, insulation should be added to the oven to make it even more efficient. Ovens installed even as late as 1973 are most likely underinsulated by the standards dictated by the new high cost of energy.

SAVING WASTE HEAT FOR USE LATER

Heat recovery—for immediate use—is gaining wider recognition and considerable application through heat exchangers and heat wheels, but heat *storage*—for later use—has received little attention in manufacturing although it is a commonplace in homes in the form of your household hot-water heater). New technology, however, should greatly increase opportunities to economically store heat that would otherwise be lost for later use in processing. The same technology can and already has been applied to create new products with an energy-saving appeal (see Chap. 8).

An R&D firm, Comstock & Wescott, Inc., has pioneered the development of anhydrous sodium hydroxide (plus the addition of small amounts of some unspecified inorganic materials) as the storage medium. The main advantage of $NaOH$ over H_2O is that the same volume of $NaOH$ will hold eight to ten times as much heat.

Once you realize that $NaOH$ is what most of us know as lye, or caustic soda, you may shy away from this technology. "What, keep a tub of hot lye on the factory floor? Not on your life!" Yet extensive testing shows that there is no risk. In the anhydrous, or water-free, form, $NaOH$ is *noncorrosive* and can be contained in a tank of inexpensive mild steel without any rustproofing on the inside. What about a leak caused by rusting through from the outside? This is not very likely because the tank must be heavily insulated, which prevents water condensation.

However, even if a leak should somehow occur, the developers claim that it would plug up automatically as the escaping $NaOH$ recrystallizes. And if some calamity were to rupture the tank, the exposed $NaOH$ would absorb carbon dioxide from the atmosphere and turn into plain baking soda. (Even though sodium hydroxide is an energy-intensive product—it is made by electrolysis—its price has not risen much with the sharp increase in the cost of energy. As this is written it sells for about $120 per ton, which is only about 10 percent more than it cost several years prior.)

Although $NaOH$ is, of course, not as cheap or as widely available as water, it is quite inexpensive and made from common ingredients, all of which are widely available in the United States. A very stable chemical, it does not give off any toxic fumes at the temperatures at which it is stored, which are way below its boiling point of 2,500° F.

In a production application, hot gases that would otherwise escape up a stack are conducted through ducts in contact with the $NaOH$. At some time later, when the heat stored is required, water pumped through the $NaOH$ inside a coil made of steel piping would be converted into steam ($NaOH$) also loses its heat rapidly) and piped to where it's needed.

Unfortunately, heat storage using $NaOH$ has resulted in no practical applications in spite of much advertising and publicity. In late 1974, C. B. Comstock, president of Comstock & Wescott, reported that there was not one industrial application. Apparently, U.S. businessmen were not worried enough about the shortage of energy.

EXHAUSTS CAUSE HIGH LOSSES

Among steps to be taken on the second level of energy conservation is installation of individual controls on each exhaust used to draw off excess heat, fumes, or toxic particles. This investment offers energy savings in plants and laboratories comparable to turning off the lights in offices. Most commonly, all exhausts are controlled from one central location and are turned on at the beginning of the workday, and off at the end. These exhausts, which often run needlessly, also suck away great amounts of cooled air in summer and heated air in winter, putting extra loads on the ventilating system. Individual controls would save much in heating and cooling.

While checking for controls on exhausts make sure that no employees are tapping the plant-wide air-compressor line for local ventilation. In terms of energy, it's a very expensive means of providing ventilation and must be prohibited. This form of waste could be detected quickly by an excess load on the air compressor.

REPLACEMENT OF LESS EFFICIENT EQUIPMENT

Sometimes, there's a limit to what can be done with older equipment in terms of energy conservation. The intelligent, long-term solution may be to replace inefficient, poorly insulated (where it is impossible to add more insulation), poorly instrumented equipment with the very latest in production gear. Not only will much energy be saved, but the newer equipment may not require as much labor.

Continuous, assembly-line heating is not only more efficient than batch heating, but usually requires less labor and is more productive. For instance, at a processor of radioactive chemicals, one continuous-cycle furnace replaced 20 obsolete batch-type ovens. Fuel needs were cut by 20 percent, but more significantly, only two operators were required to man the unit instead of ten. And it takes only one-fourth as much space as the units it replaced.

Older electrical equipment can be replaced too with savings not only in energy consumed but through an improved "power factor."

Too many of the electrical motors in use in industry are merely idling. When a five-horsepower motor is installed for a job that could be done by two-horsepower unit, the waste goes beyond the mere added cost of the larger unit and associated heavier gearing, which is only a one-time charge. The half-loaded larger motor not only uses more power to do the job than a fully loaded smaller motor, but it also results in even more of an undesirable lagging power factor on the power lines. In regions in which heavy industry is concentrated, the power company usually charges a penalty for poor power factor.

Making sure that all future motors installed match the job should not require much discipline. Unfortunately, switching motors in use is not likely to make economic sense, unless the power company has put such severe restrictions on power available or has dropped long-standing discounts for heavy users of electricity (a growing possibility) so that it is the only economic course. As this is written consumer groups are campaigning not only for elimination of volume discounts, but *higher* rates for big users.

If your local electric utility charges a penalty for poor power factor, invest in sufficient power-factor correcting capacitors to bring the power factor on your lines as close to unity ("1") as possible. Smaller companies with many small, yet oversized induction motors are often plagued with very poor power factors, and they may not even be aware of the drain. As the cost of power and associated penalties for poor power factor goes up, the payoff from power-factor–correction capacitors goes up too. Some companies paying a heavy penalty for poor power factor have been able to recoup their investment in less than a year. However, once these capacitors are installed it is necessary to check them frequently to make sure their internal fuses have not blown. The primitive "touch" method is not adequate, since as many as a quarter of the capacitors in a bank may be out, yet the container will feel normally warm. Fortunately, inexpensive and easy-to-use monitors are available from the Capacitor Monitor Co. to check on internal fuses.

NEW TECHNOLOGY TO THE RESCUE

Upgrading present production machinery basically offers only limited (although highly desirable) savings in energy conservation and faster production. For really big savings, the trick may be to switch to an entirely new way of making or processing your product.

"Radiation processing" is one such technique. The concept of using radiation in the form of X-rays or electrons or some other particle of electromagnetic form to process metals, fluids, or food is not new. For years, the preservation of food by means of X-ray bombardment has been investigated by the armed forces, which would obviously gain by a technique for preserving food for long periods without bulky refrigeration. What held back the technology of radiation processing was the lack of reliable, efficient sources of radiation.

Suddenly, in the last few years, radiation processing has taken off. There are two reasons behind this development. Mainly, new machines using solid-state technology have appeared that can do the job with a lower initial investment, yet are highly reliable. Second, the cost of energy has risen to the point where the radiation-producing machines, which require comparatively little energy, have become much more competitive economically with heat processing.

Actually, radiation processing is an old story in some highly specialized industries. Manufacturers of wire and cable have been using electron radiation to strengthen the insulation on their products since 1959. The producers of solid-state devices have found that highly concentrated beams of electrons can modify their products in highly desirable ways impossible to achieve by other means. Now, producers of such prosaic products as printing and paper are finding that ultraviolet radiation can replace heat with big savings.

To understand why radiation processing offers such big savings, consider the following situation. To process a given product by means of heat, a long heat "tunnel" is required. The tunnel may be 200 feet long. Before it can go into operation, it has to be heated for several hours until it reaches the required temperature. Once heat treatment starts, any disruption of the process, such as the discovery that the product is not being "cooked" properly results in high scrap losses—200 feet at a time. Until the end of a run, the heat tunnel has to be maintained at a temperature until the last item has gone through its entire length, which means that it requires full power for an hour with very little product inside. Then it takes hours to cool, keeping the surrounding air hot, an added burden in summertime.

Contrast this inflexible arrangement with radiation processing. As long as the vacuum has been maintained inside the unit (which requires little power), it starts up in seconds. All of the processing takes place within a few inches so that any disruptions or errors results in minute product loss. At the end of a run, the unit can be shut down again in seconds. Obviously, much shorter runs become practical.

Radiation processing has other advantages. Compared with most heat processing, it requires very little floor space because the accelerator, the device that generates the electrons, can be mounted vertically. In addition, radiation processing may generate changes inside materials that cannot be duplicated by heat or any other form of processing. In other words, the product may come out stronger or more flexible or superior in other ways. The accelerator also has a substantial resale value because the same unit has many applications. In contrast, a specialized heat processing unit, if discarded, is not likely to have any value beyond scrap.

Naturally, there are some problems associated with radiation processing. Equipment generating electrons or X-rays has to be enclosed in heavy concrete walls because the rays are deadly to man. Elaborate interlocks have to be set up so that it can't be started while any men are inside the shielding. However, there are enough units now in operation, numbering well over 150, so that these safety precautions are well understood and so far have prevented all injuries. Incidentally, unlike radiation from radioactive sources, such as cobalt, which can't be shut off, there is no radiation from an accelerator after it is shut down. Nor does the irradiated product become radioactive or dangerous.

Ultraviolet reactors also represent a hazard. UV radiation can damage the eyes, so the units have to be light-tight, which is no great problem. In addition, some ozone is generated, and it has to be drawn off and dispersed to the atmosphere.

Accelerators range in price from $30,000 up to $600,000.

The initial investment in a large accelerator including needed shielding, which costs about a fifth as much as the machine, can be large, upwards of a million dollars and more. On the other hand, when the accelerator is fully utilized, the cost of radiation processing is surprisingly low. One manufacturer claims that in the insulation of wire, radiation costs presently run to only 2 cents per pound, compared with 5 to 8 cents by the conventional peroxide-heat crosslinking technique.

ACCELERATORS FOR RENT

To find out if it is possible for your product to be processed by radiation, an accelerator can in effect be rented. Radiation Dynamics, a leading manufacturer, operates two service centers with three accelerators in one center and a single large machine in a nearby center and is planning another for the Midwest. Electronized Chemical, a subsidiary of High Voltage Engineering, another manufacturer of accelerators, and Columbia Research also provide radiation servicing. (I observed the operation of Radiation Dynamics' service facility in Westbury, N.Y. One leading manufacturer of wire and cable has a truck shuttling back and forth with wire—until it sets up its own accelerator. Radiation Dynamics charges about $100 per hour on its machines.)

Here is a summary of how high-voltage radiation processing is being applied:

Irradiation of wood chips to prevent infestation of the chips while stored outside prior to processing into paper. Could eliminate annual loss of chips of about five percent and also result in a higher pulp yield.

Curing of printed circuits for electronic equipment. (One supplier, Dynachem, claims to have received orders for dozens of its DCM MK II system, which reportedly consumes as little as 10 percent of the energy required by infrared or gas-fired ovens. The new system costs about $10,000.)

Polymerization of insulation on wire and cable.

Vulcanization of rubber.

Grinding of specialized lenses.

Curing of coatings and thin films.

Sterilization of microbiological and medical disposables.

Preservation of food.

In addition, two other processing techniques are under study. These are cracking crude oil by radiation and irradiation of waste cellulosic materials to prepare them for hydrolysis and for eventual recovery of valuable by-products such as alcohol or sugars. At present, grinding of the waste materials down to particles only 50 microns in diameter is required before hydrolysis. Irradiation may be cheaper than grinding.

American Can Co. is using ultraviolet light to cure coatings on cans instead of heat. The important fringe benefit is that this also helps meet OSHA requirements and antipollution requirements because the heat curing involves driving out of solvents; no solvents are needed in ultraviolet curing.

In addition, ultraviolet radiation is being employed in printing to dry inks between the application of progressive colors.

Here's a summary of the advantages of radiation processing:

Much less energy required and that energy is electricity, which is generally available while natural gas is under allocation in many localities.

Lower capital investment, particularly when all factors, such as space and no requirement for antipollution equipment are considered.

Higher production rates. (To increase production of a radiation facility might merely call for running the source of radiation at a higher power level or substituting a more powerful source in the same configuration. In contrast, a heat-processing unit may be bound by a certain upper rate that can never be exceeded. To increase production requires costly duplication of the complete, cumbersome system.)

Very little scrap loss.

Much shorter runs feasible.

Much less time required for production.

Wider choice of substrates. In heat processing the substrate must be able to withstand the heat required for curing or processing.

Little or no pollution because no solvents required.

Little or no clean-up of equipment required after a run because the coatings do not contain solvents, so they don't gum up or dry while equipment is shut down. (As a result, operators come to prefer radiation curing over heat processing, especially in the summertime.)

Of course, there are some disadvantages to radiation processing. Radiation processing can only process line-of-sight so that complex shapes with deep valleys may not be suitable, and inks or coating materials may be much more expensive, as much as 100 percent higher. (However, much more mileage can be gotten out of a given amount of ink or coating.)

Because radiation processing is still a very new technology, it should be characterized by important progress. For example, Dr. Kenard H. Morganstern, president of Radiation Dynamics, Inc., has suggested that production rates for shaped plastic parts could approach the high rates of metalstamping if radiation processing is employed. He believes that the shapes, in the form of stamped "prepregs," could be irradiated at rates of 1,000 parts per hour. This is, of course, far faster than the present method of producing such parts by injection moulding.

U.S. manufacturers of electron-beam radiation processing equipment include Energy Sciences, Haimson Research Corp., High Voltage Engineering, and Radiation Dynamics, Inc. Deliveries take a long time. For example, Radiation Dynamics quotes 9 months on its small units, and 15 to 18 months on its large units.

Suppliers of UV radiation systems include Van Vladderen and Radiant Products. In addition, some users have built their own systems using mercury-vapor lamps manufactured by Hanovia.

Excellent sources of information on radiation curing and processing are the papers from the first and second International Conferences on Radiation Curing, sponsored by the Society of Manufacturing Engineers. The first conference was held in April 1974 in Atlanta and the second in May 1975. Complete sets of papers cost $25 each, and individual papers cost $2.50 ($1.75 to SME members). The papers and abstracts of the papers may be obtained from SME, 20501 Ford Rd., Dearborn, Mich. 48128.

ALTERNATIVE METALWORKING PROCEDURES

Metalworking manufacturers have various investment alternatives open to them in the event of energy shortages. If they are rationed on electric power, but not on natural gas, then the following substitution comes to mind: diecasting or forging of metal parts, which depend on gas heat, to replace machining of parts. Conversely, if gas is rationed but electric power is adequate, then machining should be favored over casting.

Unfortunately, it is not easy to substitute processes on a short-term basis. Therefore, the real alternative in the event of rationing of one form or another of power is to subcontract production of the affected parts to a contractor in other parts of the nation, or even to some country overseas, where power is abundant and not likely to be rationed.

However, setting up subcontracting in regions remote from your plant is not easy and is also time-consuming, especially if the metric system prevails. In particular, if you decide to subcontract overseas, negotiations can stretch from months into years. For this reason, it makes sense to initiate such negotiations during periods when you are not threatened—and when competition is not competing with you for the same subcontractors. Thus, the need to anticipate requirements not just months but years in advance becomes apparent.

Subcontracting on the basis of energy availability does not mean assigning all or a large part of the production of the parts or products outside your plant. Only a fraction of the production need be subcontracted. This will also give you a basis for measuring the productivity of your own plant.

BACK-UP ENERGY SOURCES

No matter how successful your program of energy conservation, you may run into trouble, deep trouble, because your local source of either natural gas or electricity puts your company on allocation. This kind of crisis can arise in several ways. First, the local power company's supplier of energy may be forced to allocate its product, most likely natural gas. (Since most power companies are tied into regional electric grids, there is also a possibility that electric power may be allocated in case other companies tied into the grid do not have any spare capacity.)

To cope with such crises, companies are investing in various back-up sources of energy. The power companies are purchasing coal stokers (see p. 107) and laying in emergency supplies of coal. (They are making the reasonable assumption that in an emergency the ban on burning of coal will be lifted temporarily.)

This suggests that manufacturers could do the same, purchasing back-up coal stokers for their space-heating furnaces. (Unfortunately, coal, which sparked the industrial revolution, is now considered too "dirty" a fuel for heat required for manufacturing processes where the hot gases come in contact with the material to be heated, such as metals or glass.)

Some large companies, dependent on natural gas, are erecting back-up propane storage systems. For instance, a $150,000 storage facility at the International Harvester truck plant in Springfield, Ohio, provides enough of this clean-burning fuel to keep the plant running for ten days. The Ford Motor Company has taken long-term leases on ten railroad tank cars which have been pumped full of propane. The cars can be shifted to whichever Ford plant needs an emergency supply of gas.

Unfortunately, manufacturers dependent on electricity can't afford to erect back-up generation units: the cost would be prohibitive. As one plant manager put it, "The cost of providing back-up power for this plant would exceed the cost of all my production machinery." Nevertheless, some manufacturers have purchased small motor-generator units, just big enough to keep lights burning while the plant is evacuated.

However, some steps can be taken to cope with brownouts, those voltage-reducing steps taken by power companies as their total generating capacity is approached (or even exceeded) on hot days in summer when everyone's airconditioner is running full blast. Some useful devices are:

Load-shedding devices that insure critical machines keep running as long as possible by cutting off power to less-critical machinery, such as airconditioners (assuming your process does not depend on airconditioning), exhaust fans, elevators, rechargers for electric industrial trucks, etc. The various sources listed in the directory charge around $6,000 for a basic unit. They are programmable so that it is easy to change the order in which machines are taken off the power line.

Autotransformers that provide the same output voltage over a wide range of input voltages. Because of the comparatively high cost of these electronically controlled units, they can only be attached to critical machines that cannot function when the voltage drops too much. For example, to keep its computers running during the brownouts common in New York City in summer, John Krauss, Inc., of Jamaica in the borough of

Queens, installed a $2,000 autotransformer. One day the input voltage dropped suddenly to 169 volts, yet the computer, which received a steady 208 volts, did not falter.

Under-and-over-voltage protection devices that protect machines that are sensitive to sudden peaks and drops in voltage. The peaks can occur when lightening strikes the line or when some big power consumer, such as a large freight elevator, stops drawing power; conversely, when the elevator starts moving, the sudden dip in line voltage can damage some machines, particularly computers.[1] (To protect sensitive machines and processes during brownouts, some manufacturers suspend use of their big freight elevators late in the afternoon on very hot days.)

COPING WITH THE PETROLEUM-BASED SOLVENT SHORTAGE

At the height of the energy crisis of 1973–74, common solvents used in metalworking and many other industries were practically unobtainable—and if you could buy them the prices in some instances had jumped one thousand percent. The reason was simple: all of these solvents are manufactured from petroleum. In effect, the shortage of solvents was part of the energy crisis.

As this is written, all of the solvents are once more obtainable—except that their prices, in common with most petroleum-based products, have not dropped back to pre-embargo levels. For example, acetone, one of the most common of solvents, was selling for about 6 cents in tank-car quantities; now the price is about 17 cents a pound.

So it makes sense to explore ways to use less solvents or otherwise cut the cost of solvents. And if a new shortage of solvents should arise, you will be in a better position to cope with them. Such approaches include:

---

[1] Because of the growing use of minicomputers in manufacturing, it is important to select units that are as insensitive as possible to the variations in line voltage common in plants. In general, the "slower" the minicomputer, the less sensitive. Even the slowest of minicomputers should be fast enough to handle processing chores. The response time of minicomputers is measured in microseconds so that a doubling of response time to achieve greater insensitivity to voltage spikes is not perceptible to the user even when many steps are executed by the computer.

1. Reusing the same solvent more.
2. Switching to another cheaper or more readily available solvent.
3. Sending "dirty" solvents to a reclaimer for purification.
4. Installing a small solvent reclaimer on your own premises.

The first two alternatives are unhappy solutions for various reasons. Overly dirty solvent or an alternative solvent may not do the job as well or take much longer, which could slow down production. For instance, if a metal part soaked in cutting oil can be cleaned in one hour in a clean, suitable solvent, it might take three hours in a dirty or less-effective solvent. Thus, production is slowed or more careful scheduling is required.

Just as reclaiming of dirty lube oil increased sharply, reclaiming of dirty solvents took on boom proportions during the 1973–74 energy crisis. One New York-based reclaimer reported that his plant's capacity was all booked up for six months, and he was not looking for new customers. Nevertheless, he was not increasing the capacity of his plant because he didn't know how long the boom would last.

The prices for reclaimed solvent are somewhat below those for "virgin" solvents, but not much. The reason is that not all of the discarded material is recoverable: depending on how dirty the solvent has become in use, the percentage of recoverable fluid ranges from a high of 95 percent down to about 55 percent. Solvents that are so dirty that only 50 percent can be recovered are not worth processing. During the energy crisis the percentages of recoverable solvent dropped because manufacturers were reusing their scarce solvents more.

The solvent recoverers obtain much of the material they recover for "inventory" from the suppliers of virgin solvents, who collect drums of dirty solvent at the time they deliver fresh solvent, an efficient use of their trucks. Depending on the market for solvents and the condition of the used solvent, the supplier who picks it up will either credit his customer, charge nothing for picking it up (or just pay for the drums, which can be reused) or charge for disposing of a material that may be flammable, smelly, cruddy, and ecologically sensitive.

All of which suggests that it makes sense to check the arrangements for disposing of your dirty solvents. Perhaps your plant is either giving the dirty solvent away or even paying for its removal when conditions warrant some credit, however small.

To locate a local solvent reclaimer, look for them under "Solvent —Reclaiming" in the local classified phone book. There's a good chance you won't find any. The latest Manhattan yellow pages lists only three, one of whom admitted that he is really not active in reclaiming. Which is why you may be forced to turn to installing your own reclaimer.

The neatest solution of all would be immediate recycling of solvents used in processes. Various manufacturers make small distilling units that occupy only a few square feet of factory floor space (most likely far less than the space now devoted to storage of solvent.) Erie Universal's cost about $8,000. Let us assume that the solvent reclaiming machine distills 500 pounds per day of dirty solvent that costs 17 cents per pound in the virgin state. The recovery rate is assumed to be a conservative 80 percent. This means that each day the unit is in operation it is recovering $68 worth of solvent. If the unit is operated for 220 days per year, assuming periodic shutdown for maintenance, it would pay for itself in about five years. In the meantime, the company would be assured of a ready supply of essential solvent with a very low requirement for virgin solvent (to make up for the 20 percent of unrecoverable solvent).

In actuality, the machines have a much higher capacity than 500 pounds of solvent per day. This capacity suggests that a smaller company with a steady requirement for solvent could arrange to sell time on its reclaiming unit to other local companies with a need for solvents. An obstacle to such an income-generating scheme might be the greater demands placed on whomever is in charge of the unit. As long as it is devoted to reclaiming the same solvent with the same impurities, it is most likely a simple apparatus to operate, as simple as is claimed by the manufacturers of such units. However, if a variety of solvents with a variety of impurities, including water, must be processed on the unit, it may require more chemical expertise than the usual metalworking shop is able to muster.

WASTE AUDIT HAS WIDE APPLICABILITY IN PRODUCTION

In no department is the energy Waste Audit likely to be more illuminating than in manufacturing. Criteria for waste can include:

Consumption of natural gas or other forms of energy for production purposes as related to output, i.e., so many cubic feet of natural gas consumed per unit of production or per pound of end product.

Reduction in pollutants as a result of lower consumption of energy.

Hours of operation of energy-intensive equipment or processes in relation to output (an indication of more efficient scheduling).

chapter 16

Conserving energy in building operation

THE RECENT ENERGY CRISIS showed that the American people were quite adaptable and willing to accept modification of long-accepted standards of heating of buildings in wintertime. In addition, in many buildings, the amount of outside air drawn in was cut down, which also saves energy. In general, we were better off for the lowered temperatures—most buildings are too hot and dry in winter, which is bad for our respiratory systems.

Just about every business lowered the thermostat settings so that the temperature did not rise above 68° F—with attendant savings. Most of the other savings in building operation are also simple to accomplish. These will be discussed here along with some long-range ways to save a lot of energy in building operation. These are in the operation and maintenance of boilers; shifting to cheaper, more abundant fuels; savings in illumination; sophisticated controls for buildings; and savings in hot water.

"NOT FIXING UNTIL THEY STOP RUNNING"

"Too many companies maintain their boilers the way they handle their cars—they don't fix 'em till they stop running." This is how one expert described boiler maintenance in most commercial buildings, and the same level of care seems to apply in most other aspects of building operation. Proper maintenance can play an important role not only in reducing the amount of energy expended on heating, cooling, hot water, and illumination, but in enhancing the resale or mortgage value of buildings—as well as maintaining the comfort of those who work in it.

Proper maintenance applies to every aspect of the building but has the highest payoff in saving energy in the boiler room. All of the measures suggested for heat-processing equipment in the previous chapter (see p. 232) apply to boilers that provide heat for buildings. Proper operation and maintenance procedures for all machines should be posted on or near the machines.

In particular, management should check to make sure that the boilers are not generating steam at too high a pressure for the heating requirements of the building. On surveying buildings, experts have found boilers generating steam at high pressures, when much lower pressures are sufficient. The high-pressure steam does not carry much more heat than the lower-pressure steam. Switching to lower pressure is simple. Usually all it takes is an adjustment on the outlet valve on the boiler.

In addition, all dust, dirt, and oil deposited on the blades of fans and blowers must be removed much more frequently to enable these power consumers to function at their highest efficiency.

RETRAINING HELPS

Just what and how much maintenance is required is not a matter to be left to the discretion of present maintenance personnel. Just as in other aspects of business operations maintenance personnel require retraining and reorientation to upgrade their knowledge and skills. Suppliers of boilers and instrumentation and other equipment for buildings have much valuable information available in booklet form. Maintenance personnel should be required to read such booklets. In addition, suppliers are often prepared to send in their technical experts to help advise maintenance personnel. Another source of training are the energy-conservation consultants.

SHIFTING TO ALTERNATE FUELS

Another way to save money, although not necessarily energy, is to modify your boiler so that it can burn a cheaper grade of fuel. The cheaper grades are always more viscous, which means that they require somewhat more energy for pumping. One way to cut down on the amount of pumping effort is to keep the fuel warmer; the warmer it is, the less viscous it becomes.

Keeping fuel warmer calls for two measures: storing and moving it in insulated tanks and lines and using waste heat to warm it up before it is injected into the boiler. As demonstrated in the previous chapter, added insulation really pays off. Insulation on storage tanks is particularly effective if the tanks are outdoors. Of course, if insulation is applied to outdoor tanks, it must be properly waterproofed.

The conversion to cheaper fuels may also call for replacement of present burners with ones specially designed to properly "atomize" and inject the heavier grades. These burners are more expensive and might cost as much as several thousand dollars. However, this cost, together with that for bigger pumps, insulation, and a heat exchanger to warm the fuel before injection, is a good investment. What it does is free you from dependence on a single grade of fuel, the grade that is most frequently used in homes and would be denied to business and industry if shortages develop. Depending on the usual big difference in price between the lighter distillates and the heavier fuels, the investment is also recouped quickly.

What about conversion to burning of coal? Many utilities now burn coal, and some converted back to coal during the energy crisis. Few buildings can consider reconversion to coal because the manufacture of grates to properly burn coal in smaller boilers (small, that is, compared to the boilers that generate steam for power companies) is a thing of the past. However, a prolonged shortage of petroleum might stimulate some manufacturer to again make smaller equipment for burning coal. Presumably it would be highly automated equipment requiring little human labor or intervention.

MODULAR BOILERS

Before shifting to the burning of coal, companies should investigate a significant way to cut energy consumption. If your boilers need replacement, specify a modular boiler. A modular boiler is really two, three, or even four boilers in one. Depending on the requirements for steam, one or more parts could be fired up. This arrangement is much more conservative of energy because each unit would operate at close to its full efficiency, whereas a single large boiler operating at one quarter or one third of its capacity is highly inefficient. According to one government report,[1] the point at which modular boilers make economic sense is delivery of 1,000,000 Btus per hour. The same report also urges that boilers be specified to deliver no greater than 125 percent of requirements; studies have shown that in many commercial buildings the boilers can deliver from twice to three times the required amount of heat. Oversizing is wasteful in two other ways: in terms of investment it means money wasted in constructing support structure for a boiler that is too large; in operation, money is wasted because an overly large boiler operating at less than one third or one half of its capacity is less efficient than a boiler operating near rated capacity.

USING AND STORING WASTE HEAT

In the previous chapter the advantages of using and storing waste heat were discussed (see p. 235). Waste heat can also be used in buildings as well. An heat exchanger or heat wheel can be installed to capture the heat in air exhausted from the building and transfer it to the cold incoming air in winter. Heat exchangers can also be installed in the uptakes of boilers to capture heat that is wastefully dispersed to the atmosphere and transfer it to either incoming air or to the fuel just prior to injection into the furnace.

Usually there is far more heat lost than can be transferred for immediate use. It would be useful if this heat could be stored for later use, such as in heating the building at night when the boilers are shut down. In Chapter 15 there is a discussion of sodium hydroxide as a medium of storage for heat. This concept has been applied also to storing heat in buildings. In Toronto four large buildings were equipped with sodium hydroxide storage units for "peak shaving," storage of heat generated by electricity in off-hours so that peak demand is lower when requirements for heating are highest. The same compact storage units could be applied in buildings heated by steam.

"Cold" could also be stored in summer to lower peak demands on airconditioning systems and thus permit companies to spend less on such systems, or increase their cooling needs if required. The storage

---

[1] "Report of the Ad Hoc Committee on Energy Efficiency in Large Buildings to the Interdepartmental Fuel and Energy Committee of the State of New York," published on March 7, 1973, p. A–13.

medium would be water, and it would be stored in a large insulated tank at night for use during the peak demand for cooling the following afternoon, when the power company is likely to lower voltages.

WAREHOUSES AMENABLE TO CHANGES

Methods of heating warehouses can also be changed with resultant savings. For example, the gas-fired, forced-air heaters at the Joseph T. Ryerson steel service center in Cleveland were not doing a good job. Not enough heat reached the floor level where metals were stored. As a result, on very cold days water would condense on the cold steel and aluminum, which had to be wiped off hurriedly by all the workers in the building. The old heaters were replaced by highly directional infrared heaters which eliminated the condensation problem. The new heaters also used natural gas, but much less of it. Experts report that use of infrared heaters instead of blowers in warehouses can save from 10 to 30 percent.

In many warehouses there is no need to keep the entire building warm, just those places where the few employees are stationed. Running steam lines or gas lines out to such remote stations is costly. The economic approach is to mount small electric heaters in those areas. Unfortunately, some of the small portable heaters that sit on the floor are dangerous. They tip over too easily, which could set fire to papers and other combustibles. A more satisfactory device is the large radiant panel made by such companies as Aztec. They can be mounted vertically against a wall, taking up very little space. Although they provide a lot of heat, they are not so warm that touching them results in a burn.

Speaking of small electric heaters, management should make sure that no employee brings his or her own electric heater to their workplaces to compensate for lower heating in winter. There are two problems: first, if too many such personal heaters are used, the company's electric bill will jump so high that it will more than outweigh any savings in fuel; second, many of these heaters are poorly constructed and therefore dangerous. There are various sensible alternatives: first, permit employees who complain of cold to dress accordingly; second, apply the weather stripping and storm windows as discussed later in this chapter to cut down on seepage of cold air into the room; third, carpet the cold area; fourth, arrange switches of employees who complain of the cold to other areas where they are more comfortable (this is not easy). If the first four measures are not sufficient, install the radiant panels mentioned in the previous paragraph.

LIMITED OPPORTUNITIES TO ADD INSULATION

Once a building has been erected it is costly and very difficult, if not impossible, to add energy-conserving insulation. The best opportunity may not come for ten years, when a new roof is required, which makes adding insulation comparatively easy. However, there is one situation in which it makes sense to add insulation to an existing building: if for some reason ducts carry cold conditioned air through an un-airconditioned or warm space, these ducts should be insulated with fiberglass or rock-wool sheeting.

MAINTENANCE OF THE BUILDING REQUIRED

Regular maintenance is also required on the building itself. Cracks around windows and their frames should be caulked. Loose-fitting panes require putty (if they get too loose, they are more likely to break, requiring a higher level of expenditure than puttying). The very walls of the building require maintenance. Everyone understands that the roofs of buildings should be watertight. What few realize is that vertical surfaces require waterproofing too. Damaging moisture can penetrate concrete, masonry, and even brick.

If too much moisture penetrates, the damage is apparent to the occupants in the form of peeling paint and plaster. Other damage done by moisture is not so apparent but just as destructive. Insulation loses its properties when wet. "Wet insulation is worse than none at all," according to Joseph F. Cuba, director of research and technical services for the American Society of Heating, Refrigeration and Air-Conditioning Engineers.

Cracks in outer walls are repaired in a variety of ways with patching cement and caulking compounds: the latter are usually of silicone. The compounds used to waterproof complete surfaces come in a great variety of formulations, including silicone. Unfortunately, according to T. C. Lazarr, a leading consultant on waterproofing, silicone compounds do not stand up in the corrosive atmospheres of many of our larger cities and industrial areas. (The level of acidity of the rainfall in larger cities has been rising steadily.) Instead, Lazarr recommends Hydrozo, a comparatively low-cost material that was developed decades ago. It is guaranteed for an unusually long period—ten years. Hydrozo and other waterproofing compounds can also be applied to sidewalks and ramps to prevent seepage that causes unsightly chipping when freezing temperatures are encountered. (Hydrozo also prevents penetration of fluids seeping out of vehicles in garages.)

SIMPLIFIED REROOFING

Waterproofing of the roof remains most significant because heat losses through the roof are highest. Companies are aware that roofs have to be redone about every ten years: patching of damage can't be continued indefinitely.

A sophisticated new technique has been developed to detect leaky roofs. Aerial cameras loaded with infrared film can indicate the exact portion of the roof that must be replaced from an airplane flying hundreds of feet overhead. The damaged portions appear warmer because heat losses are greater.

Traditional methods of reroofing are cumbersome. First, the entire roof has to be removed, which means the work can only be done in good weather; next, the old roof has to be disposed of; flammable materials have to be lifted onto the roof, another disadvantage.

For years roofing suppliers have been attempting to develop reroofing techniques that would involve laying down of a plastic covering directly onto the old roof. Now, several such methods have been commercialized. One of the most highly recommended by companies that have used it is the Trocal approach. Developed in West Germany, the Trocal technique involves the laying down of wide sheets of heavy opaque vinyl sheeting right over the old roof, even when it is still wet. (The moisture underneath permeates upward, but no new moisture enters once the sheets are sealed together.) After the roof has been completely covered, a thin layer of gravel is laid down to prevent the sheeting from lifting and tearing during wind storms. Trocal roofs are guaranteed for five years, with an additional five years offered by the payment of an additional "insurance" charge. No heat is required in laying down a Trocal roof.

A Trocal roof costs about the same as traditional roofing for a new roof, but offers real savings in reroofing. It is supplied by Dynamit Nobel of America, Inc.

REDUCING VENTILATION

One of the simple ways to reduce energy requirements is to reduce the number of times each day that the air is changed inside a building. This saves energy in two ways: less pumping and less energy required to heat or cool incoming air. Experts have found that in most buildings the air is changed more frequently than required by local building codes. So check with local building inspectors or the health department to find out how frequently the air has to be changed and reduce changes accordingly.

Traditionally, certain areas, such as washrooms and locker rooms, have required much more ventilation than the other zones in buildings. An energy-saving alternative is to utilize chemically activated deodorizers to remove odors and therefore cut down on high ventilation.

There are generally only a few days each year in which extremes of temperature—high or low—are encountered. To design and operate a ventilation system to meet these extremes is to add unreasonable cost to ventilation. An alternative is to cut intake of outside air sharply on such days for a few hours when the extremes are encountered.

MINOR MODIFICATIONS TO CUT ENERGY REQUIREMENTS

Everyone knows that storm windows cut heating costs in homes, and the same applies to commercial buildings. What few realize is that storm windows also cut air conditioning costs in summer too. If your buildings are older and/or not equipped with double-paned windows, it makes sense to have storm windows installed. These energy-saving windows can be mounted on the inside of present windows with much less effort; it's actually difficult to mount storm windows on the exteriors of most tall commercial buildings.

Storm doors are also helpful, but deep vestibules and/or revolving doors for busy doors are even more effective in retaining warm air in winter and keeping out cold drafts. Naturally, all doors leading to the outside should be equipped with effective door closers and weather stripping. Weather stripping should also be applied to all windows that require it, including those on which storm windows are mounted.

If you do decide to install storm windows and doors, make sure that you are dealing with an established, reputable local dealer (in storm windows as in other aspects of home improvement there are many fly-by-nighters). Look for the AAMA label of certification. This indicates that the windows and doors have been made to the specs set by the American National Standards Institute and enforced by the Architectural Aluminum Manufacturers Association. Select units made of heavier weight aluminum and glass with neat joints and deep tracks for the sashes and screens. (Naturally, this advice applies to storm windows for your home as well.)

Good storm windows cost money. If you can't afford or would prefer to postpone an investment in storm windows, even though it is a highly cost-effective expenditure, plastic film can be used effectively in their place. Although the film will only last one season at best (polyethylene, the most common plastic used for this purpose, is weakened when exposed to sunlight for a long time), it is cheap. When purchased in bulk, the cost per 3 × 6 foot window may be only ten cents. Hardware stores sell pre-cut film in packages containing enough for two windows for 59 cents. The plastic film may not be suitable for use in an office, but is worth considering for warehouses, garages, and factories. (At the peak of the energy crisis, one promoter tried to sell a heavy-weight plastic film to act as a storm window for the incredible price of $6 per window. Of course, this is close to a fraud.) Instead of storm windows, some plant managers are ordering double-pane, translucent fiberglass glazing in place of glass (see Directory).

Warehouses and factories with loading docks absolutely require weather curtains or air screens for use in the winter and summer (if the building is airconditioned). Weather curtains are made in a variety of forms designed to meet various conditions. Most are simply curtains that fit snugly around the trailer or boxcar. However, some weather curtains can be expanded against the side of the trailer or boxcar by air pressure to make a very close fit. Air screens are simply systems for excluding outside air by a strong vertical flow of interior air.

For factories or warehouses with outside storage requiring frequent entry by fork-lift trucks, traffic doors should be installed. These are sturdy two-part swinging doors that can be knocked open by the movement of the industrial truck without damage.

Installation of storm windows coupled with closing of all cracks around windows and doors will have another beneficial effect: the natural draft of the building will be sharply reduced so that every time an entrance is opened there will be no in-rush of cold air in winter or hot air in summer.

WINDOW COVERINGS

Just as storm windows are mandatory in winter in cold climates and make sense in summer too, shading on windows is mandatory in summer and has a purpose in winter too.

For low-lying structures in suburban or rural settings, trees are effective in blocking the sun's rays and make a building more attractive too. Deciduous trees, those that lose their leaves in winter, should be planted along the east and west exposures. In summer, the leaves block the hot rays of the sun but permit them to strike the building in winter. Evergreen trees should be planted along the northern exposure to break the cold winds of winter. Lawn rather than concrete around a building also helps cut down on reradiation of heat in summer.

If parking lots surround the building, the development of car-pooling arrangements and the switch to smaller cars should permit the company to reassign narrow strips of real estate alongside the building for trees and lawn. Few employees would object. (Some might even prefer to park their cars where they can be shaded during some portion of the day from the summer sun.)

Unfortunately, only a small number of companies can use trees to effectively shield buildings. For the majority, traditional window shadings are required.

Venetian blinds and shades are moderately effective. They reject most of the direct rays of the sun, but the heat they absorb remains inside the building. They also block natural light, which is why they should be drawn up when the sun's rays don't hit them directly. Unfortunately, some decoraters specify other than light, highly reflective surfaces for shades and blinds. If some "decorator" color is selected for the inside surface, a highly reflective color can still be specified for the outer surface. However, a light color is still preferred on the inside for two reasons: a light surface radiates less of the heat it picks up from the outside, and reflects back more interior light.

Those oriental-style shades made up of thin strips of bamboo or wood or synthetics woven together horizontally are not recommended. Although they are attractive, they let too much heat through. Neither blinds nor shades are very good insulators in winter. To prevent the loss of a lot of heat through single-pane windows, especially at night, insulated drapes are highly effective. They are usually aluminized on the inner surface to reflect heat back into the room.

Awnings are most effective because the heat they absorb remains outside the building. Unfortunately, few companies other than those operating small, one or two-story buildings are likely to erect awnings. Awning materials other than the traditional canvas include Dacron, fiberglass, and aluminum. Dacron awnings are about twice as expensive as canvas but should last much longer. Fiberglass and aluminum cost about three times as much as canvas and should also last long—they are usually guaranteed for five to ten years. Awnings require more cleaning than blinds, but they can usually be cleaned with a hose just like a car. A newer equivalent of awnings is a product called Koolshade. It consists of very narrow horizontal strips of aluminum held at a prescribed angle by steel wiring. Koolshade can be mounted in panels that slide aside to permit the cleaning of the windows they cover. The manufacturer of Koolshade claims that it can withstand the winds of winter (it is not taken down in winter). However, some architects claim that the reason Koolshade is not used much if at all outside of the South and Southwest is because there are doubts that it would withstand icing in winter. Koolshade Corp. disputes this assertion.

A new alternative is aluminized plastic film. This largely transparent film rejects about three quarters of the sun's heat. It is used in two ways: applied directly to the inner surface of the window or in the form of shades. In the first form it is usually applied by "dealer-applicators," who charge from $1.50 to $2 per square foot covered depending on the size of the job and local labor rates. Recently, one supplier, Hy-Sil, made the polyester films available in kit form for do-it-yourself application. I tried the films myself and found that they peeled off if the directions were not followed very carefully. The kits, which contain 10.8 square feet of material, have been selling for about $5 in local hardware stores. For shades, the film base is tough DuPont Mylar. They cost about three times as much as conventional shades but offer transparency. Standard Packaging also manufactures this shading material and the polyester films; 3M offers just the films.

One user who is very pleased with the aluminized films is the president of the First National City Bank. His office, high in the bank's tower on Park Avenue in New York, was struck by the sun's rays in the morning. Even with the airconditioning on maximum, the room became too hot. The films cut the maximum temperature by three and a half degrees, making the room much more comfortable. Before using present window-cleaning compounds on these films, check with your supplier.

SAVINGS IN LIGHTING TIE IN WITH SAVINGS IN COOLING

For office buildings, savings on illumination tie in directly with savings in energy expended on cooling. Why? Because from 80 to 95 percent of the electricity consumed by lights is converted into heat. Incandescent lamps are least efficient in converting power into light, but fluorescents, which are about four times as effective as incandescents, convert only 20 percent of the power they consume into light.

Therefore, the injunction to turn off lights when not required is particularly relevant in summer; however, lights should also be turned off in winter: in some large office buildings so much heat is generated by lights that some airconditioning is required in winter to keep the occupants at the core of the building comfortable.

The summer is also the time when the most natural light is available. Architects are once more emphasizing natural light. They are specifying photoelectric controls that automatically dim interior lights when outside light is sufficient. There are some cautions to consider in using natural light, however. Desks and workbenches should be parallel to or facing away from the sun. Because of the glare, no desks should face the sun. Entrance lobbies should also be illuminated by strong light so that those entering and leaving do not face the problem of suddenly adjusting their vision to the contrasting light. One suggested solution is to install two levels of lighting in lobbies, for day and for night.

Begin your program to save energy in illumination by urging all employees to shut off the lights in their work areas when they leave, even for short periods. (The shibboleth against turning off fluorescent lamps for short periods no longer holds true. Because of the rising cost of energy, while longer-lived fluorescents have generally dropped in price in terms of output, it now makes economic sense to turn off fluorescents for periods as short as 15 minutes.)

Unfortunately, the turn-off rule may be difficult or impossible to apply in many modern buildings because they have been constructed with few light switches, sometimes only one to a floor. If there are few light switches in your facilities, you can effect a turn-off policy by the following ploy: remove up to half the overhead fluorescents and install lamps with individual switches on desks or workbenches. Maintenance workers must be ordered to clean light fixtures frequently, particularly in localities with dirty atmospheres. Some lighting fixtures by their very nature collect a lot of dirt. These are the ventilating luminaries that include outlets and intakes for air. Dirt on fixtures and the lamps themselves can cut light output by as much as 50 percent. And the darkening process is so gradual that no one is aware of it. Plastic louvers, prismatic panels, and diffusors should be replaced when they become yellow with age.

Another way to increase light output is to repaint or wash the paint more frequently. Ceilings should, of course, be repainted in light colors with a matte finish to reduce glare. Lighter-colored file cabinets and desks also have the effect of increasing illumination with no expenditure of energy. (However, pure white desktops are a strain on the eyes.)

Energy can also be saved by cutting the level of lighting in areas in which there is little or no concentrated work performed, such as corridors, storage, and filing areas. However, a good level of lighting should be maintained on fire stairs, escalators, and at the entrances to elevators. And to protect employees who work late, illumination should not be cut in parking lots for security reasons. However, there is no need to increase the amount of energy it takes to illuminate parking lots. Instead of using big incandescents outdoors, replace them with long-life, high-intensity mercury, metal halide, or high-pressure sodium lamps.

Companies can also use more efficient lamps indoors. In general, the higher the wattage rating, the more efficient the lamp. For example, General Electric's standard (i.e., lowest cost) 100-watt incandescent is rated "1,750 lumens and 750 hours of life." GE's standard 25-watt lamp is rated "235 lumens and 2,500 hours of life." This means that it takes 7.45 25-watt lamps to equal the output of one 100-watt lamp, yet they cost about the same (the list price of the 100-watt is actually two cents less than that of the 25-watt). Of course, the 25-watt lamp lasts 3.33 times longer. But there is even an advantage to the shorter life of the 100-watt lamp; replacing it provides an opportunity to clean the fixture. (Assuming that the 100-watt lamp is used 50 hours per week, it would last about 15 weeks, which in a city like Chicago would match needed quarterly dusting of the fixture.)

On the other hand, if the fixture is very high in the ceiling or otherwise difficult or dangerous to replace, then a long-lived lamp is preferable. For example, GE's "Extended Service" 100-watt lamp has a life of 2,500 hours, which is over three times the life of the standard lamp. However, to achieve this longer life, light output is sacrificed somewhat—1,490 lumens, which is only 85 percent of that of the standard lamp. The Extended Service lamp also has a list price of 47 cents versus 34 cents for the standard. Because of the lowered output and higher price, long-life lamps should never be used in fixtures where it is easy to replace them.

You also pay a penalty in light output for "color-corrected" fluorescents, which should only be used in situations where their more natural output is highly desirable, such as in cafeterias or over the mirrors in powder rooms. For example, for GE's 30-watt "preheat" fluorescent line, the standard "cool white" lamp delivers 1,875 lumens and costs $1.80, while the "daylight" lamp delivers 1,570 lumens and costs $2, and the "Deluxe Warm White," which delivers 1,250 lumens, costs $2.80. All have the same "approximate" life of 7,500 hours.

There is no great secret in checking the ratings of lamps; by law these ratings are all printed on the package. (The prices given here for the various lamps may be higher by the time you do your "comparison shopping" since they are from GE's Large Lamp Catalog of October 24, 1973. However, the ratios between prices for standard and special lamps will most likely remain the same.)

IMAGE LIGHTING

Now that the 1973–74 energy crisis has abated, many companies are once more bathing their offices or plants in bright lights at night. The only purpose is image building. Is this waste of power and lamps really necessary? If you feel that image lighting is needed, at least program the lights to go off after midnight when there are few passers-by.

SOPHISTICATED CONTROLS ALSO PAY OFF

Many companies are finding that sophisticated controls for heating and ventilating of buildings pays off. What the more advanced controls do is modify the ambient conditions in a given portion of the building to suit the situation in that portion. It is easy to understand that not all portions of a building require the same degree of heating or cooling. In summer, the side of the building exposed to the full effect of the sun's rays is obviously going to require much more cooling than the unexposed sides. In fact, after a cool night, the western side of the building may not require any air conditioning until late in the morning, while the eastern side needs full cooling from 8 A.M. on. Similarly, in winter, the northern portion of a building may require substantial heating, while the southern side, which receives some warmth from the winter sun, needs much less heating. In general, the interior portions of a building require less heating and cooling than the perimeter, which experiences much higher fluctuations in ambient conditions due to heat transfer through the windows and outer walls.

Breaking a building down into various zones and equipping each zone with a sensor is not terribly expensive. The sensor may cost only about $50, plus the cost of running wires. (Obviously, it is less expensive to install these controls when the building is under construction or renovation.) The central controls that direct the proper amount of heat or cooled air to each zone may cost only a few thousand more.

There is still another level of sophistication to consider in such controls. Most climate controls only sense what is going on *inside* a building. Yet what is happening outside obviously has a substantial effect on conditions inside. Newer control systems include the mounting of sensors on the outside. If there is a big change outside, the controls can start to compensate for it earlier than if they depended on interior sensors only. This means that the whole system operates much more smoothly without sudden strains that not only require the expenditure of more energy, but also make the building more comfortable for its occupants. Also, when it becomes cool enough outside, the system simply stops cooling and pulls in outside air for cooling. The system can also be programmed to pull in cold night air to delay the need for air conditioning the following morning.

REMOTE CONTROL SERVICES

The most sophisticated of the climate controls for buildings are organized around minicomputers. Even though a minicomputer itself may cost only $5,000 or $6,000, programming it properly for building control raises the cost of the complete system into the tens of thousands of dollars. Few smaller companies can afford such systems. However, there is a lower-cost way in which a smaller company can obtain computer control without buying or renting a complete system. Both Honeywell and Johnson Service offered a "shared" service in which a single larger central computer controls the climate within a number of buildings that could be as much as 100 miles away. The signals from the sensors and the control signals are carried over leased telephone lines.

Honeywell and Johnson Service both offer central monitoring security services. Their remote building supervision is offered from the same stations. This means that companies can also obtain security services over the same lines. Charges for the supervisory service are similar to those for security services. In other words, you pay a one-time charge for the installation of the sensors plus a monthly charge for supervision. Johnson Service charges an average of $16 per point per month and expects its customers to sign up for three or five years.

WHY HOT WATER SHOULD BE SAVED

Saving hot water in washrooms may not appear to be worth the effort, except that doing it is significant in maintaining a positive attitude among employees towards conservation.

Hot water and the energy used to heat it can be saved in the following ways:

Replace present hot-water faucets with spring-loaded types that shut off the flow after a short period for sinks and a longer period on any showers.

Reduce the temperature of hot water to the lowest level that is acceptable for washing without mixing it with cold water. (I've discovered in visiting many buildings that the hot water is sometimes so hot it is nearly scalding.)

In factories, use pure, hot water discarded in some process in lavatories and company cafeterias. (And hot discarded water that is not pure enough for washing hands could be used for washing of floors.)

Repair all leaks in faucets and lines and insulate hot-water lines where practicable. An easy-to-apply urethane insulation for low-temperature (domestic service) lines comes in a spongy form that can be applied in two ways: preferably, if the line is opened for repairs or replacement, the insulation is simply slipped over the piping whole; or the insulation can be slit open with a knife and snapped over the piping. This insulation does not require an outer wrap.

To avoid operating a large boiler in summer just to provide hot water for cleaning, set up a separate small heating system or use waste heat from processing.

WASTE AUDIT EASY TO IMPLEMENT

Setting up a Waste Audit for a building should be rather easy. Input energy is known from power and fuel bills. The concept could even be applied to consumption of electric lamps, although it would take many months to determine the effect of a turn-off policy on life of lamps because most of the lamps in place were there before the new conservation concepts were applied.

SELECTED REFERENCES

"American National Standard Practice for Office Lighting" (Approved June 21, 1973), Illuminating Engineering Society, 345 East 47 St., New York, N.Y. 10017, 42 pp.

"Standards for Natural and Mechanical Ventilation," American Society of Heating, Refrigerating, and Air-Conditioning Engineers, Inc., 345 East 47th St., New York, N.Y. 10017. 17 pp.

chapter 17

Conserving energy in building construction

AFTER READING the previous chapter it should be apparent that energy conservation measures are simplest to apply to a building *before* it is constructed. If your company is planning a new building or an extensive remodeling or reconstruction of an older building, you have an unparalleled opportunity to add features that not only lower the costs of operation greatly, but also add just as much to the resale or mortgage value of the facility. In fact, with energy costing so much and sure to rise in cost, the savings in operation over the life (assumed to be 50 years) of the building are sure to at least equal and perhaps surpass the original cost or the cost of renovation. (From now on any organization considering the purchase of an existing building should carefully check into the cost of operation and favor those buildings that require much less energy.)

To review, the conservation measures consist of:

Much heavier insulation in walls and roof and for all hot piping.

Control of air conditioning by adjustment of flow.

Smaller, operable double-pane windows with highly efficient shading.

Proper landscaping if there is space for it.

Modular boilers.

Sophisticated instrumentation for control of heating and cooling.

Odor-removal apparatus to permit maximum recirculation of air.

Deep vestibules or revolving doors for all exits leading outdoors; weather curtains for loading docks.

Light switches for each room with photoelectric controls for areas receiving strong sunlight.

Reuse or storage of waste heat.

In addition, other experts urge (for tall buildings) that fan rooms be located on every level instead of being concentrated on special floors at every tenth level or so. In this way, ventilating air has less distance to travel, requiring less energy, and fans can be shut down— for only one floor if unoccupied.

An incinerator that uses the heat generated by burning trash.

THE GSA ENERGY CONSERVATION DEMONSTRATION BUILDING

As a guide to those companies planning new buildings, a new office building has been ordered by the Federal Government, called the GSA Energy Conservation Demonstration Building. It should be finished in early 1976. The nine-level building has seven working floors plus a two-level basement garage.

The building, which is now under construction in Manchester, New Hampshire, occupies a site of 42,437 square feet and encompasses 175,000 square feet of space (131,000 net). Because it contains many unusual and experimental features, its cost is high. Assuming that it costs $7 million (the original estimate was $6.8 million if started in July, 1974), excluding many hundreds of thousands in design and consulting fees, cost per square foot is $40. Obviously, few companies would authorize a building at that price, except in those areas characterized by inflated construction costs, such as Manhattan or California. However, by stimulating the availability of energy-conserving devices, the building should result in lower costs for others.

Here are the features of the new building that make it so interesting in terms of energy conservation:

No windows in the north wall. Windows in the other exposures will be limited to 10 to 15 percent of the wall area.

Core elements (stairs, elevators, toilets, mechanical rooms, and so on) will be located next to the north wall and therefore will not require such close environmental control.

The exterior wall mass will be 100 pounds per square foot compared with the usual 20 to 30 pounds for curtain wall construction. The heat transmissibility value for these walls will be a very low 0.06, compared with the usual 0.4 to 0.2. The roof and the floor directly over the basement will also have heat transmissibility value of 0.06.

The exterior walls will incorporate shading for windows in the form of projecting ledges, which architects call berms.

Each floor will incorporate a different type of heating-cooling arrangement for comparison purposes; however, none will include reheat air conditioning systems. (Very few are aware that the most common type of central air conditioning for commercial buildings controls the degree of cooling by *heating* the cold air entering each space. In other words, the volume of cold air delivered to each outlet remains constant. Obviously, the reheat technique is wasteful of energy and most likely requires more cooling capacity than is actually needed to meet peak requirements. Experts on energy conservation urge that the degree of cooling be controlled by limiting the *volume* of cold air entering any given space. Volume controls are more expensive than reheat controls.)

Waste heat will be used for space heating at night and for domestic hot water.

The central chillers for floors 4 through 7 will be powered by a gas-engine generator that can be disconnected from the chiller and used for emergency power in case of blackouts.

Waste heat will be used and chilled water stored to cut down on the overall size of heating and cooling units. The chillers will be undersized in relation to peak load. At night when the electrical load is light and the building is cooler the chillers continue to operate storing chilled water in a insulated tank for use the next day during the peak load period.

Boilers and pumps of modular type.

Different systems will be installed on different floors for comparison of performance and efficiency. One floor with larger windows will be studied for the effect of natural light on perimeter needs.

SOLAR ENERGY SYSTEM

Collectors of energy from the sun will be mounted on the roof of the building (if funds are available for this purpose). The collectors will be flat plates. The energy they collect will be stored as heat in the same tanks used to store water heated by waste heat.

The operation of the building will also embody concepts of energy conservation. Cleaning will be done during the workday.[1] All ventilation fans may be shut off for ten minutes during each hour of the workday. Temperatures of the corridors, restrooms, equipment and storage rooms will vary from 60°F in winter to 85°F in summer. Temperatures will be set back from five to ten degrees one hour before closing time in the winter. Comfort conditions will not be maintained at night (obviously, the federal government does not expect any of its workers to stay late). During the summer higher temperatures than is current will be accepted. At night, the building will be flushed out with 100 percent night air as cool as 65°F whenever the air gets cool enough in summer.

The architects for the building are Nicholas and Andrew C. Isaak of Manchester. The engineering firm of Dubin-Mindell-Bloome Associates acted as consultants on energy conservation.

LONG-TERM STUDY PLANNED

By means of extensive instrumentation and surveys of the approximately 418 people working in the building, some conclusions as to how well the building "performs" will be sought. Obviously, this evaluation will take at least several years, so all the results will not be available until late in this decade.

However, the building should act to inspire some immediate changes in the design and operation of office buildings. For example, by specifying operable windows, others may pick up this excellent notion. Windows that can be opened easily are useful beyond any

---

[1] Before emulating this energy-conserving measure, take special precautions. First, check with your insurance carrier on sufficient coverage in the event someone, employee or visitor, slips on wet floors. In case someone does fall and injure himself or claim injury, you are less likely to be held liable if there has been a timely effort to clean up the wet floor and its presence has been patently marked by signs and cordoning off.

energy savings on the many days in late spring and early fall when air from the outside is of the proper temperature to eliminate heating or cooling. During blackouts or brownouts it is a definite plus if the windows can be opened, even on very hot days. More importantly, in case of fire, suffocating smoke can escape from open windows (that's why fireman always smash windows when they are fighting a fire) .

The windows for the new building will be made by the Amelco Window Corp. These double-pane windows with blinds sandwiched in-between were invented over 20 years ago and have been available since the late 1950s. To date they have been applied most often in hospitals, most likely because they require little maintenance. I saw an installation of them at the giant Columbia Presbyterian Hospital in Manhattan. At the time the windows had been in place for over six years but showed little or no sign of weathering. I found them quite easy and simple to operate. By means of a hand crank, the blinds, which are less than one inch across, can be tilted, lowered, or raised. Depending on the design, the windows pivot either horizontally or vertically to open for ventilation or cleaning (there is no need for any potentially dangerous cleaning of windows from the outside) . The windows I inspected could only be opened with a special tool in the custody of maintenance people to prevent any suicides by patients in the hospital.

In addition to cutting heat loss through the glass, these windows are made in a way that cuts heat loss through the metal frames. (If you've ever felt the metal frames of single-pane windows on a cold winter's day you can appreciate how much heat can be lost through the frame.) There is insulation between the inner and outer frames.

Because these windows require special frames and mounting, it is basically impractical to specify them except for new construction.

On the other hand, it is practical to specify reflective coatings on glass in the renovation of older buildings. These coatings, which go on the inside of the glass with a hard chromium surface, are far more efficient than heat-absorbing window glass, which only keeps out about 30 percent of the sun's heat. Even though the chromium coating can take a lot of wear, it should not be cleaned with any abrasive compounds. Some experts on energy conservation do not favor the reflective coatings, either of the chromium or plastic variety because they are essentially inflexible. In other words, they can't be taken down in winter when all of the heat and light from the sun is desired.

INSULATION MATERIALS AVAILABLE

Now that building insulation materials are once more readily available due to the current decline in home building there is no reason why these high-return materials are not applied where practical in the renovation of commercial buildings. However, there is a penalty that must be paid if insulation is to be used—in new as well as in old construction. Insulation takes up space. For example, if the usual amount of insulation in curtain-wall construction is raised from three to six inches, then a half-foot of interior space is lost in either direction. However, this loss in useful space should be more than made up for in lower operational costs over the life of the building, which should also have a higher resale value.

Similarly, mechanical designers must leave more clearance between adjacent piping so that more insulation can be specified.

Heavier insulation offers another value that should be brought out; lower noise transmission is significant for buildings in crowded downtown areas or near airports.

THE ADVANTAGES OF REVOLVING DOORS

The document describing the Demonstration Building did not detail entrance doors. However, another government report, that of the Ad Hoc Committee on Energy Efficiency in Large Buildings,[2] does provide some useful guidelines. The infiltration rate through a swinging door is "about 900 cubic feet per person for a single bank entrance, and 550 cubic feet per person for a vestibule-type entrance." Under the same conditions, the filtration rate is "about 60 cubic feet per person for a manually revolving door and 32 cubic feet per person for a motor-driven type."

PEOPLE WHO LIVE IN GLASS HOUSES . . .

By now it should be obvious that one of the most popular architectural styles of the last two decades is doomed. The all-glass exterior buildings introduced by Lever Brothers in the early 1950s makes no sense in an age of energy conservation (all-glass exteriors have sort of gone out of style in an esthetic sense anyway). Glass all by itself is a poor insulator, and glass exteriors that offer no openings

---

[2] See footnote at bottom of p. 253.

to fresh air are too inflexible. In effect, the economics of shortages are stimulating a return to exteriors that are much more masonry than glass. This is all to the good.

Configuration of buildings also has a lot to do with the amount of energy it takes to heat or cool them. In general, it makes sense to keep the outside surface as small as possible in relation to volume. This suggests that a round building is the optimum shape. Since a round building is not too practical for most situations, especially in downtown areas where real estate is at a premium, the next best shape is square. Significantly, the Energy Conservation Demonstration Building now under construction is very close to square in cross section. The upper floors are 135 by 155 feet.

The "slab" buildings so popular with architects are particularly difficult to cool in summer, especially when the long axis runs north-south. On the other hand, if a series of slabs are constructed in parallel and close to each other, those to the east shade the building immediately to the west in the morning, and those to the west shade the ones immediately to the east in the afternoon.

If you are forced to construct a rectangular building, it makes a lot of sense for the long axis to run east-west. According to Fred S. Dubin of Dubin-Mindell-Bloome Associates, a rectangular building with a two-to-five side ratio will use 29 percent less energy for cooling if the short axis faces north and south.

It should also be obvious that a single large building is more efficient than a group of smaller buildings of equal floor space.

chapter 18

How to stimulate and maintain car pools

ONE OF THE BENEFITS of the energy crisis of 1973–74 was expanded car pooling and increased use of public transportation to get to work.

No need to list all the secondary benefits of car pooling and mass transportation, such as reduced pollution. But I would like to emphasize one: reduced wear and tear on private vehicles at a time of burdensome inflation in the cost of buying, operating, insuring,[1] and maintaining a car.

While your employees benefit from reduced commuting costs, you their employer benefit in some distinct ways by promoting car pooling. First, long-term carpoolers claim as one of the big benefits *reduced fatigue.* Not having to drive a car through rush-hour traffic is a great gain. So your employees come to work in a better frame of mind and more likely to do productive work. Next, fewer cars means lower demand for parking space, which can chew up a lot of valuable real estate, areas that may be needed for plant expansion or temporary outdoor storage.

---

[1] State Farm Mutual Automobile Insurance Company is offering reduced premium rates to car owners who cut down on driving by joining car pools or taking public transportation. Savings range between 10 and 35 percent.

How to organize and maintain pools using private cars is the main subject of this chapter, but some related matters will be treated. These are chartering buses for daily commuter runs, either on a club basis or through the company; subsidizing public transportation to provide more commuter bus transportation to a given company; and company provided vans for car pools.

THE KEY INGREDIENTS IN CAR POOLING

The easiest way I know to promote car pooling among employees is to provide each interested person a copy of a brochure entitled "Secrets of a Successful Car Pool." This delightfully illustrated brochure tells it all in 20 pages. Written by Bernie Smith, a veteran car pooler, and distributed free by his employer, the Shell Oil Company, the brochure stresses the key ingrediant—compatability of those in the pool.

A car pool can founder for a number of reasons, such as:

Smoking: the nonsmokers will object, particularly if the smoker is seated in the middle away from a window.

Conversation: some people are talkative in the morning, while others abhor small talk.

Station selection: if the radio is played, everyone has to agree to the choice of music or news.

Good manners: neither the driver nor any of the members of the pool must keep the group waiting—at either end (one of the obvious limitations of a car pool is that those who need to can't work late—or they have to find another way to get home).

Bernie also stresses the need for proper insurance coverage on any car used for pooling. As he put it, "When in doubt, call your agent and attorney for clarification of insurance risks, legal risks."

To obtain free copies of "Secrets of a Successful Car Pool," write to Shell Oil Company, Dept. JH/1, P.O. Box 53083, Houston, Texas 77053. Since the brochure was first offered, over 50,000 copies have been distributed. There is no limit on the number of copies your company can order; one organization distributed 7,000 to its employees.

PROS AND CONS OF PROMOTING CAR POOLS

At the height of the energy crisis, many companies throughout the United States were actively promoting car pools among employees. The prime benefit to the company was obvious: car pooling was one important way to insure that employees got to work. Car pooling also helped reduce tardiness caused by waiting in line for gas. (Many employees were also late at the end of the lunch hour because they used the interval to shop for gasoline.)

To stimulate more car pooling, companies set aside special bulletin boards where those offering and seeking rides could leave their names. Some companies even reserved the best spots in the parking lot for car poolers, which must have been a shock to those executives who relish the perquisite of a favored parking place. In large companies, computers were used to match up riders and drivers.

According to a study funded by the Department of Transportation, manual match-ups of prospective carpoolers are efficient up to 500 names. And beyond 2,500 names, computerization of matching up is just about essential. So if you have between 500 and 2,500 names to match up, you have to decide on your own whether or not to handle the chore via computers.

The same study also suggests a self-service system for promoting car pools. At some central location in your plant or offices, a large map of the area divided by a grid system is posted. The squares created by the grid are numbered and a pigeonhole is assigned to five adjacent squares. Employees seeking to join an existing car pool fill out red 3 × 5 inch cards with all pertinent data. Those seeking to join existing car pools fill out cards of another color. Employees shuffle through the cards placed in the pigeon holes corresponding to their squares. When a match-up is made, the cards are, of course, withdrawn.

Although the system is designed to work with little supervision, a Carpool Supervisor should be assigned to monitor the operation. He or she may find that there aren't enough employees living in a given square to make a car pool. In such instances, the underpopulated square must be combined with an adjacent square or squares until a viable minimum population is achieved.

For more aid in setting up car pools, a 270-page report entitled "Transportation Pooling" is available gratis. Write for a copy to Department of Transportation.

In smaller companies it is obviously more difficult to set up car pools because of the smaller population: How is this disadvantage overcome? Here are some suggestions:

If employees park their cars in the street where employees of neighboring companies can see them, place signs in the windows saying Riders Wanted. The sign should also indicate the locality of the home of the driver and his business and home phone number.

Neighboring companies, those that work the same hours as your company, should be invited to place car pooling notices on your bulletin board. If your company is located in an industrial park, the management of the park should be asked to set up a common bulletin board devoted to car pooling. If the board is outdoors, it should of course be sheltered from rain. (Car pooling should also cut the usual traffic congestion at closing times at the industrial park.)

Local neighborhood newspapers (perhaps of the free Pennysaver variety) should be asked to set aside free "classified" sections for those interested in car pooling.

Supermarkets usually offer free access to bulletin boards which could be utilized for car-pooling notices.

Churches, PTAs, and clubs could be asked to make announcements about car pooling to their members.

To promote car pooling among smaller businesses, the *Phoenix Central News,* a free weekly, carried data input cards in its January 16, 1974, issue. Included in the issue were maps of the county divided into 329 numbered sections. Out of 40,000 cards distributed, about 3,000 responses were received in the first three days and quickly processed by Professional Data Processing Services, Inc., which did the keypunching and processing gratis.

Several hundred match-ups were made via computer, resulting in many car pools. Unfortunately, when the gasoline shortage ended shortly afterwards, the car pools mostly evaporated, according to Ron Hogan, president of the service bureau. (However, there was one permanent effect of the oil embargo. Hogan reported that many residents of Phoenix are taking advantage of bike paths laid down by the city and biking to work and elsewhere. About one out of ten of Hogan's employees now bikes to work, quite feasible all year round in Phoenix's mild weather.)

The good citizenship of Professional Data Processing Services in

Phoenix has been matched elsewhere. Many banks made time available on their computers for those trying to arrange car pools; some universities and state and local governments have done the same. The Department of Transportation offers a car-pooling program free to those organizations who will use it only for noncommercial purposes. Others have to pay $40 for duplicating the tape.

A free car-pooling program called Operation Energy that runs efficiently on only 20K bytes of memory and a manual describing its use are available gratis from one of the major computer makers, Burroughs Corp., Detroit, Mich. 48232.

INCREASED CAFETERIA SERVICE

One possible disadvantage of promoting car pooling is the need for more in-plant food service. When employees don't have cars available, they are less likely to go out for lunch. On the other hand, one way to stimulate car pooling would be to offer better in-plant food service. During the energy crisis, some companies in effect forced employees to eat lunch in the company cafeteria by cutting the lunch period to 30 minutes. The objective was to save gas by eliminating car use to visit outside lunchrooms.

SPECIAL VEHICLES FOR CAR POOLS ONLY

The vast majority of car pools use the private cars of members. For years, however, some highly organized car pools have purchased special vans whose major purpose is car pooling. These vans, which usually accommodate at least 9 passengers, and may take as many as 12, are in effect the property of a small, nonprofit partnership or corporation. I've seen such vans on the streets of New York; they originate in suburban counties such as Westchester, on Long Island, in New Jersey, and even in Connecticut. Even though each member may contribute as much as $60 and more per month, which may be higher than the commuter fare on the nearest railroad, the total cost to the members is still a bargain. First of all, they don't need a station car, or they avoid the nuisance of having to be taken to the station in the morning and picked up each evening by their spouses. Second, the van takes them right to the door of the building in which they work so they avoid paying any fares on public transportation from the railroad station to their place of employment (70 cents per day in New York as this is written and sure to go up).

The concept of the "dedicated" car-pool vehicle has been extended by the 3M Company. Since March, 1973, 12-passenger vans have been purchased, insured, and maintained by the company for those employees signing up for car pools. The driver of the vehicle, who is known as the Pool Coordinator, not only rides free, but retains all fares over the minimum of eight passengers (the program is supposed to pay for itself, and presumably each vehicle pays for itself when it carries eight passengers not including the Pool Coordinator). In addition, the Pool Coordinator or members of his or her family can also use the $6,000-plus vehicle at other than working hours by paying a rather modest mileage fee.

In return, the Pool Coordinator must do the following: provide a garage or place to plug in an engine pre-heater (see Chap. 10) at his residence; recruit passengers (there's an obvious incentive to carry more than eight); collect the fares—based on mileage—and turn them in for the first eight passengers; make sure there is a back-up driver; and arrange for fueling and maintenance of the vehicle, for which he is reimbursed by the company.

The "Commute-A-Van" program has been a great success at 3Ms big St. Paul, Minn., headquarters where it was first tried. Since the end of the energy crisis, more and more vehicles have been purchased, and as of late 1974 there were over 60 in operation. In addition, several other companies in the Twin Cities area have copied the popular program.

The appeal of the program to employees is obvious. First of all, it costs less to ride a van than to operate one's own car. In fact, some employees have been able to dispense with second cars, saving about $1,000 per year. The vans are parked in a special area right at the door of one of the main company buildings; this area is also equipped with power outlets for engine pre-heaters so that the vans start immediately and provide interior heat quickly in winter; passengers are always picked up by a vehicle that is warm inside in winter months, a distinct attraction in the upper Midwest.

All of the "Big Three" carmakers offer vans suitable for this kind of company-sponsored car pooling. In addition, some of the manufacturers of motorhomes are converting to construction of "people-movers" with capacities from 10 to 15 passengers. One motorhome maker charges about $8,000 for a 15-passenger van.

SUBSIDIZED PUBLIC TRANSPORTATION

In addition to its van-pooling program, 3M is also subsidizing several buses that bring employees in from an isolated suburb about 19 miles from headquarters. Many companies and some industrial parks are doing the same. (In one instance in California, the bus has been equipped with a bar—open only on the Friday return run.) Other companies subsidizing buses include Atlantic Richfield and Textron. Other companies have taken a slightly different approach. Instead of subsidizing the bus companies or operating buses themselves, they are simply subsidizing employees directly. For example, the Colorado National Bank reimburses employees half the cost of taking the bus to work. Before the subsidy began only 20 percent took the bus; at the height of the energy crisis, half took buses.

BIKES AND "TRIKES" TOO

In many larger cities companies are also encouraging their employees to use bicycles or motorcycles to come to work instead of cars. If you pass the Time-Life Building at 50th Street and Sixth Avenue in Manhattan, there's a large rack out front with dozens of bikes chained to it during the workday. The city administration in New York has also provided free parking areas for scores of motorbikes at the Bowling Green in downtown Manhattan and at Columbus Circle in midtown. However, these are only "half-year" solutions, since only a few hardy souls ride their bikes to work in winter or when it rains. An unusual bike rack that does not require users to carry heavy chains with them is available from Park-A-Bike (see Directory).

Companies should also consider supplying bikes instead of electric carts or scooters to enable employees such as security guards and messengers to move about large industrial complexes. Aside from the savings in energy, maintenance, and investment, pedaling a bike is good exercise for people who may otherwise lead overly sedentary lives.

One obvious objection to bikes—some people don't know how to ride two-wheelers—is no longer valid. Tricycles for adults are now available from a growing number of manufacturers at prices ranging from about $125 to $175. Some 150,000 were expected to be sold in 1974. Unlike the versions for children, "trikes" have rear-wheel drives. For in-plant use they can be equipped with commodious baskets or even covered baskets for carrying tools, spare parts, or intracompany mail. In selecting a trike, favor those with the least distance between the rear wheels for ease of manueverability through narrow corridors.[2]

SUMMARY

Car pooling and increased use of public transportation is one of the most productive ways to conserve energy, vital materials, and also fight inflation. Companies should really make an effort to promote these alternatives to the one-person-to-a-car syndrome. Some companies have encouraged car pooling by providing a free testimonial dinner. If promotion of pooling means that executives have to give up their reserved space right at the entrance to the company building and move a few rows back, so be it. I think that visitors to your company would be impressed if they saw a line of parking spaces right at the entrance marked "Car Pool 1," "Car Pool 2," etc.

Business should also support municipal efforts to encourage car pooling and increased use of public transportation. For example, in Seattle the city and county governments are offering free parking to car pools under an elevated portion of an expressway in the down-town area.

Some bridge, tunnel, and toll-road authorities have reduced or even eliminated tolls during commuting hours for cars carrying more than one passenger. (Some larcenous commuters tried to take advantage of one bridge authority's magnanimity by trying to pass through the toll booths with dummys as passengers to qualify for the lower toll. After they were caught, they were fined.)

SELECTED REFERENCES AND ADDITIONAL READING

The following booklets may all be obtained gratis from the Federal Highway Administration, Urban Planning Division, U.S. Department of Transportation, Washington, D.C. 20590.
"Organization for Carpooling," 28 pp.

---

[2] Some years ago a neighbor of mine purchased one of the early trikes as a birthday gift for his wife, who was unable to join the rest of the family on bike outings because she couldn't ride a two-wheeler. To his consternation, the rear wheels were too far apart to fit through the front door of the apartment.

"Buspools," 18 pp.

"Vanpools," 13 pp.

"The 3M Commute-A-Van Program, Status Report, May 1974." 50 pp.

"Transit/Taxi Coordination," 26 pp.

"Legal and Institutional Issues of Carpooling," 14 pp.

"Incentives to Carpooling," 24 pp.

"Carpooling Case Studies," 31 pp.

"Car and Bus Pool Matching Guide," 3d td., 31 pp.

"Manual Carpool Matching Methods," 34 pp.

"Program Documentation for the FHWA Carpool Matching Program," 16 pp.

"User Documentation for the FHWA Carpool Matching Program," 51 pp.

"Review of Matching Software and Procedures," 27 pp.

chapter 19

Relocation or restructuring
as the solution

MOST OF THE CONSERVATION MEASURES urged in this book are easily
or quickly implemented or do not require any great investment, and
it's usually recoupable within a short time. By applying those measures that make sense for your company, you will not only conserve a
lot of energy or materials dependent on petroleum, but also put
yourself in a much stronger position to resist the effect of the future
shortages sure to occur in a world with a rapidly exploding population. There are lots of dollars to be saved too.

For the majority of companies these conservation measures should
suffice. However, there are two circumstances in which a minority of
companies will never be able to reduce their appetite for energy
enough. First, if they are young and still in a strong expansion phase
(since allocations of energy or raw materials are usually based on
prior demand, past history dooms them to stagnation). Second, if
the energy demand in the locality is rising faster than the ability of
power companies to supply it. Although nearly all power companies
seem to be facing problems in financing needed expansion, it appears
that some towns, cities, and even whole states are going to face
energy shortages much sooner and more severe than others, California, with its growing population, energy-intensive life style, and

industrial expansion, is expected to be seriously short of electric power during the next ten years. New England especially, but the East in general, are facing shortages of natural gas. And New York City, with the highest rates for electric power in the nation, (over 9 cents/kilowatthour for residents as this is written) appears doomed to ever higher rates and possible shortages of power caused by a variety of reasons. The problem areas are quite predictable. It's foolish not to face up to the fact if your plant is located in a problem area.

To insure future growth, if not survival, the managements of companies in a sharp growth phase or heavily dependent on energy may have to consider three traumatic possibilities:

1. Restructuring.
2. Relocation.
3. Selling out.

INTELLIGENT RESTRUCTURING

Restructuring to cope with predictable crises is the least traumatic approach. Restructuring can mean any of the following: setting up a subsidiary plant in a region with abundant or more abundant energy in which the components, such as castings, that require a lot of energy are fabricated; contracting out the manufacture of a good fraction or all of those components that require a lot of energy; converting to a manufacturing process, such as irradiation (see Chap. 15), or a finishing process, such as powdered paint, that sharply reduces energy requirements.

Restructuring obviously requires much management effort and considerable burning of the midnight oil. If a subsidiary plant is set up, it should be as close to the parent plant as possible to hold down on transportation and communication costs. In selecting a site for such a subsidiary plant, top management should keep in mind the possibility that in time the entire company may have to be moved to that location. That's the next possible and even more traumatic response.

THE TRAUMA OF RELOCATION

A relocation is one of the great traumas faced by companies. Relocating always costs much more than projected—both in terms of money and time (to return to full production). Today, the cost of relocating is even higher than usual because of high interest rates, which are not only a burden on the company, but also on those employees who are forced to buy homes near the new plant. (Because of those high rates, they may not be able to sell their present homes.) This means they may be forced to quit rather than move with the company, or the company has to pay special living costs to employees who are affected.

If a company is relocating to a region because it has more and lower-cost energy, obviously this factor was paramount. Companies that are relocating to help overcome some other problem, such as availability of raw materials, must, of course, consider the cost and availability of energy. Availability does not mean just for now, but for ten years after the move. How do you find out if there is enough energy today and in the future? Also, what is it likely to cost in the future?

Here are some of the tough questions you should direct to real-estate brokers; the local "industrial commission" or whatever group, such as a railroad, that invited you to evaluate the locality as a possible site for a facility; local bankers; local businessmen; and representatives of the power company itself:

1.   What are your current rates for energy (electricity or natural gas)?
2.   How do they compare with the national average and the range of energy costs nationally? (Information on the national average is available from the Edison Electric Institute, 90 Park Ave., New York, N.Y. 10016) The average cost per kilowatthour in 1974 was 2.83 cents for residential service, 2.85 for commercial and only 1.55 cents for industrial service. However, the range of rates in each category is very wide.
3.   What were the same rates in each of the past five years?
4.   What discounts are provided to industry for power?
5.   Are these discounts threatened by any action by consumer or environmental groups before state commissions that set power rates?
6.   How many times was electric service interrupted by failures of equipment in each of the past three years? (Because they are in a cost bind, some power companies are skimping on maintenance of power lines and other equipment.)
7.   How many times was electric voltage reduced (i.e., brownouts) in each of the last three summers because demand exceeded

capacity? If there were many brownouts, what is the power company doing to avoid them in the future?

8. If the power company is heavily dependent on hydroelectric power, check carefully to find out if there is a pattern of recurring droughts that severely limits energy from this source. Can these cutbacks be made up by other sources, such as fossil fuel or nuclear plants? (During the winter of 1972–73, the Pacific Northwest suffered such a shortage of electric energy, due to low waters in rivers, that heavy industrial users were denied power in favor of residences.)

9. Is natural gas under allocation? If your company does not now consume natural gas but should require natural gas at some time in the future, will it be available? Does the power company depend on natural gas suppliers in the same state or is all natural gas piped in from out-of-state? Does the power company have any plans to install a plant to generate gas from coal? If so, when is it scheduled to begin operation, what is its planned output, and how much will it cost? In the event of a natural gas shortage, does the power company have plans to cut off service to industry in favor of residences?

10. Are there any major energy consumers in the neighborhood of planned sites for the company's new plant? Are they planning to expand operations, and if so, what plans has the power company made to expand availability of power and/or natural gas? Do these companies operate any big machines that cause sharp peaks and valleys in voltage? (Check with the plant managers for these companies to find out if they have been experiencing undesirable variations or prolonged drops in output voltage, all of which degrade machine performance, especially that of computers.)

11. Assuming that your company plans to heat the new facility with heating oil, what is the availability of such fuels in the area? Were heating oil and other fuels suitable for use in boilers under allocation during the 1973–74 energy crisis? If the company also equips its boilers with auxiliary coal stokers, would the community permit the burning of coal for short periods during an emergency on days when atmospheric conditions are suitable (i.e., steady winds)?

12. During the energy crisis did the community take active and effective steps to promote car pooling and extend local bus

service? In the event of a new shortage of gasoline, is the municipal mass transportation system in a strong financial condition? Does it operate modern equipment at fair rates? Did some companies subsidize the local bus companies to provide extra service, and if so, how much was required?

13. What was the availability of gasoline during the energy crisis? (This could best be checked by reading past issues of the main local newspaper published during the energy crisis; this would be an excellent investment of one day of a junior executive's time to check this and other pertinent facts.)

Proximity of airports is stressed in the promotion of "industrial commissions" and those groups trying to induce industry to move to their town. An *all-weather* airport is indeed desirable, but you should also check into rail travel as well. The way the cost of air travel is mounting, it's handy to be able to turn to the railroads when time is not of the essence—or the weather is so bad that planes can't land or take off.

SUPPRESS THE EGO FACTOR IN PLANT LOCATION

There's one factor in plant location that must be suppressed in these tough times. In years past, the personal preference of the chief executive or chief stockholder in a company was often the major factor in choosing a site. If the boss was a golfer, somehow the town chosen had at least one if not several great golf courses. If he was a sailor, the plant was erected near a large body of water. Or, if he was a music-lover the town selected had a symphony orchestra.

The ego of the boss must be subordinated to the real needs of the company in selecting a plant site. If the town has plenty of low-cost electricity available, that's more important than a golf course. If it has extensive mass transportation in clean buses, that's more important than great restaurants. If local colleges and universities offer plenty of technical courses, that's a far more important factor than recreational facilities. To solve today's problems, we need brains.

AVAILABILITY OF NATURAL GAS

For companies that are absolutely dependent on natural gas, an important location factor is "guaranteed" availability of this clean-burning fuel. The state of Oklahoma has been advertising steadily that plenty of energy, including natural gas, is available there. Natural gas has been found as far east as Pennsylvania and New York and as far south as Alabama. If this gas is not transported outside the state in which it is found, it is not subject to the pricing regulations of the Federal Power Commission.

Several economically strong companies have actually drilled successfully for natural gas on their own property. In fact, a local geologist urged the management of General Motors Corp. to sink a well right in the middle of a parking lot at one of its Ohio plants.

Striking "gas" on your own property is no guarantee of availability, oddly enough. The state may insist that any natural gas uncovered within its borders be delivered in the conventional manner to a supplier of natural gas. Two of the "Big Three" carmakers have worked out unusual agreements with the Public Utilities Commission of Ohio to insure that they benefit from natural gas discovered on their own property. For example, under such an agreement, the Ford Motor Company delivers to Columbia Gas of Ohio, Inc., 2.3 billion cubic feet of natural gas each year from wells drilled on Ford property in fields in southeastern Ohio.

In turn, Columbia Gas delivers half this volume of gas to Ford's truck plant in Avon Lake. The rest is sold to the public. Since there is no connection between the fields in Morgan County (the gas is delivered to Zanesville via a 26-mile pipeline) and the plant near the shores of Lake Erie, it is obvious that it is not the gas actually pumped on Ford property. It's a swap!

This clever arrangement suggests that smaller companies which may not require as much gas as Ford's 870,000 square foot plant, could drill for natural gas, selling most to the local energy company, perhaps taking in enough to in effect make the smaller volume of gas used by the company "free." To spread the risk of drilling for natural gas, a group of smaller companies could form a joint venture. Those not within pipeline distance of the well could receive an allocation from the energy company to which the gas is sold or swapped. Before entering into such ventures, however, it makes sense to negotiate an allocation agreement with whatever state body has jurisdiction over sale and distribution of natural gas. (In Texas it is the Railroad Commission.)

Even if there's no natural gas to be found in your locality or state, the agreement between Ford and the P.U.C. of Ohio suggests still another approach to guaranteeing supplies of vital gas. A group of smaller companies could cooperatively sponsor a coal-gasification plant. Since such plants using today's technology represent multi-million-dollar investments (at least $15 million, sure to go up with inflation) , half or more of the output could be sold to a power company as a means of justifying the investment. Or the power company could be one of the partners in the joint venture.

In time, new technology in coal gasification may bring down the size and cost of an "economic" plant. The new technology may also reduce the cost of the gas too, which is presently far more costly than any natural gas.

RELOCATION OVERSEAS

After the Arab oil embargo was imposed in 1973, there was much talk of U.S. companies setting up plants overseas in nations with abundant energy. With the end of the embargo, there is naturally much less interest in such relocations. Another reason American companies should be very hesitant about setting up more plants overseas is growing political instability and lowered worker discipline. World-wide inflation hits the low-paid factory worker more than most other segments of the population. Even in West Germany, which has one of the strongest economies in the world, there are new inhibitions to business. By law workers are being given representation on boards of directors—and U.S. companies with plants in the Federal Republic are gagging at the concept.

Transportation costs overseas are also rising sharply, both by sea and air. All of these factors are making investment in the good old U.S.A. the most attractive of all.

THE IMPORTANCE OF TIMING IN SELLING OUT

The greatest trauma of all for a company that's crippled by shortages in energy, by the lack of energy, or by the excessive cost of energy is selling out. Nothing is more pathetic in the business world than a top executive frantically trying to sell his company when it's on the verge of going under. By then it's nearly always too late. The mere fact that he's waited too long before trying to sell out is a strong indication of unrealistic or immature management.

Selling out is a true blow to the egos of many founder-enterpreneurs. Ofttimes, their businesses are more important to them than their wives and children. However, when a long and careful look ahead shows that the company does not have either the internal resources or the necessary standing with its bankers to finance an upgrading into a technically stronger position or to a new location, then selling out is an intelligent and *honorable* course.

Directory of consultants and suppliers

THE HANDIEST DIRECTORY of sources of information, products, and services useful in conservation programs is always your local classified phone book or that of the nearest large city. The limited directory that follows is designed to supplement the classified phone book and other comprehensive directories, such as *Thomas' Register,* particularly for companies located in smaller communities without a substantial classified phone book or other major directories available to them. All the consultants, suppliers and trade associations, as well as those companies identified in case histories and as examples, are listed in the alphabetical section of this directory, Part II. In addition, to further aid those seeking specialized products and services, there is a breakdown by such products and services in Part I, and the full addresses of these companies, many not referred to in the text, are also given in Part II.

PART I. PRODUCTS AND SERVICES

Consultants, Energy
Conservation
Battelle Memorial Institute

Dubin, Mindell, Bloome
  Associates
Du Pont Company

Flack & Kurtz
Fuel Economy Consultants, Inc.
Grumman Aircraft Corp.
Robert E. Lamb, Inc.
Peter E. Loftus Corp.
Yarway Steam Conservation
  Service

Consultants, Inventory Control
Arthur Andersen & Co.
DIY Control Systems
G. W. Plossl & Co., Inc.
Greg Schultze International
VanDeMark Associates
Oliver Wight

Consultants, Waterproofing
ARMM Consultants
Thaddeus Lazarr

**Drag-Reducers for Trucks,
Tractors, and Trailers**
Aerovane, Inc.
Air Flo Co.
Rudkin-Wiley Corp.
Systems, Science and Software
Truck & Tractor Components,
  Inc.

**Energy-Conserving Fans—
Temperature Controlled**
Horton Mfg. Co. Inc.
Rockford Clutch Div.,
  Borg-Warner Corp.
Schwitzer Div., Wallace-Murray
  Corp.

**Energy-Conserving Fans—
Self-Feathering**
Auto Trend Products
Flex-a-Lite Corp.
Kool Klutch Mfg. Co.

Ether Starting Systems for Diesels
Kru Bur, Inc.
Turner Co.

**Fiberglass replacements for
windows**
Kalwall Corp.
New England Pacific Corp.
Sanstruction, Inc.

Heat-Radiating Panels
Aztec International Ltd.
Continental Radiant Glass

**Heat-Reflecting Transparent
Shading Materials**
Hy-Sil Mfg. Co.
Minnesota Mining & Mfg.
Standard Packaging Corp.

**Power-Factor-Correction
Capacitors**
Cornell-Dubilier Electronics
General Electric Co. Industrial
  Power Capacitors Products Div.
McGraw-Edison Co., Edison
  Power Systems Div.
Sprague Electric Co.
Westinghouse Electric Corp.,
  Distribution Apparatus Div.

Rubberized Fabric Tanks
Firestone Coated Fabrics Co.
Uniroyal, Engineered Systems
  Dept.

**"Senior" Alarm Systems for
Trucks**
Babaco Alarm Systems, Inc.
Ever-Guard Alarm Systems

Tachographs
Argo Instrument Corp.
Engler Instrument Co.
Sangamo Electric Co.

**Weather Curtains and Air
Screens (for Loading Docks)**
Frommelt Industries, Inc.
Nieco Products, Inc.

PART II. ALPHABETICAL LISTING

Aerovane, Inc. (drag-reducers)
Box 6310
Vanderbilt Univ.
Station B
Nashville, Tenn. 37235

Air Flo Co. (drag-reducers)
P.O. Box 705
Elkhart, Ind. 46514

American Load Pool (backhaul
  loads)
P.O. Box 816
Miami, Fla. 33152

Allstate Distributors, Inc.
  (case history)
6622 Vernon Ave.
St. Louis, Mo.

American Production and
  Inventory Control Society
2600 Virginia Ave. N.E.
Washington, D.C. 20037

Argo Instrument Corp.
  (tachographs)
36–21 33rd St.
Long Island City, N.Y. 11106

Arthur Anderson & Co.
  (inventory control consultants)
1345 Avenue of the Americas
New York, N.Y. 10020

ARMM Consultants
  (waterproofing consultants)
North King & Warren Sts.
Gloucester City, N.J. 08900

Auto Trend Products
  (energy-conserving fans)
1911 E. 51st St.
Los Angeles, Calif. 90058

Aztec International Ltd.
  (heat-radiating panels)

3434 Girard N.E.
Albuquerque, New Mexico 87110

Babaco Alarm Systems, Inc.
  (truck alarms)
1775 Broadway
New York, N.Y. 10019

Bacharach Instrument Co.
  (carbon monoxide detectors)
Div. of American Bosch Arma
  Corp.
Pittsburgh, Pa. 15238

Battelle Memorial Institute
  (energy conservation
  consultants)
505 King Ave.
Columbus, Ohio 43201

Wm. M. Brobeck & Associates
  (propulsion systems)
1011 Gilman St.
Berkeley, Calif. 94710

Burroughs Corp.
  ribbon re-inkers)
Business Forms & Supplies Group
Rochester, N.Y. 14603

Capacitor Monitor Co.
  (electric power monitors)
21130 West Wager Circle
Cleveland, Ohio 44116

Comstock & Wescott, Inc.
  (heat sinks)
765 Concord Ave.
Cambridge, Mass. 02138

Consolidated Service Corp.
  (fleet discount services)
P.O. Box 4809
Chicago, Ill. 60680

Container Transport
  International, Inc.
  (container leasers)

1 N. Broadway
White Plains, N.Y. 10601

Continental Radiant Glass
  Heating Co.
  (heat-radiating panels)
215 B. Central Ave.
East Farmingdale, N.Y. 11735

Cornell-Dubilier Electronics
  (power-factor-correction
  capacitors)
150 Ave. L
Newark, N.J. 07105

Cummins Engine Company, Inc.
  (diesels)
Columbus, Ind. 47201

Demand Limit Control, Inc.
P.O. Box 960
Bryn Mawr, Pa. 19010

Dill Div., Eaton Corp.
  (master air gauges)
Rt. 501
S. Roxboro, N.C. 27573

Distribution Worldwide
  (publishers)
Chilton Way
Radnor, Pa.

DIY Control Systems
  (inventory control consultants)
102 Janine Drive
La Habra, Calif. 90631

The Drawing Board, Inc.
  (message books with carbons)
256 Regal Row
P.O. Box 505
Dallas, Texas 75221

Drexel Industries, Inc.
  ("reach" trucks)
Horsham, Pa. 19044

Dubin, Mindell, Bloome
  Associates (energy
  conservation consultants)
42 W. 39th St.
New York, N.Y. 10018

E. I. Du Pont de Nemours & Co.,
  Inc. (Energy Management
  Service)
Wilmington, Dela. 19898

Dynamit Nobel of America, Inc.
  (waterproof roofing)
105 Stonehurt Court
Northvale, N.J. 07647

Eagle Leasing Co.
  (trailer leasors)
One Eagle Place
Orange, Conn. 06477

Electric Power Research Institute
  (trade association)
P.O. Box 10412
Palo Alto, Calif. 94304

Rue R. Elston Co., Inc.
  (starting aids)
815 East 79th St.
Minneapolis, Minn. 55420

Engler Instrument Co.
  (tachographs)
248 Culver Ave.
Jersey City, N.J. 07305

Ever-Guard Alarm Systems
  (truck alarms)
512 West 20th St.
New York, N.Y. 10011

Erie Universal Products Co.
  (solvent reclaimer)
311 State St.
Erie, Pa. 16507

Fenvessy Associates, Inc.
(consultant)
745 Fifth Ave.
New York, N.Y. 10022

Fee & Mason Mfg. Co.
(case history)
Manasquan, N.J. 08736

Firestone Tire & Rubber Co.
1200 Firestone Parkway
Akron, Ohio 44317

Flack & Kurtz
(energy conservation
consultants)
29 West 38th St.
New York, N.Y. 10018

Flex-a-Lite Corp.
(energy-conserving
fans)
5915 Lake Grove Ave. S.W.
Tacoma, Washington 98498

Frommelt Industries, Inc.
(weather curtains and air
screens)
Box 1200
Dubuque, Iowa 52001

Fuel Economy Consultants
(energy conservation
consultants)
747 Third Ave.
New York, N.Y. 10017

General Electric Co.
(information service)
Business Growth Services
P.O. Box 43
Schenectady, N.Y. 12301

General Electric Co.
(power-factor-correction
capacitors)

Industrial Power Capacitor Pro-
ducts Div.
John St.
Hudson Falls, New York 12839

Glue-Fast Equipment Co., Inc.
(gluing equipment)
11 White St.
New York, N.Y. 10013

Grumman Aircraft Corp.
(energy conservation
consultants)
Bethpage, N.Y. 11714

Hewlett-Packard Co.
(calculators)
1501 Page Mill Rd.
Palo Alto, Calif. 94304

High Voltage Engineering Corp.
(radiation curing equipment)
Burlington, Mass. 01803

Honeywell Co.
(thermostats)
Commercial Div.
2701 Fourth Ave. South
Minneapolis, Minn. 55408

Horton Mfg. Co., Inc.
(energy-conserving fans)
1181 15th Ave. S.W.
Minneapolis, Minn. 55414

Hunter Mfg. Co.
(truck-cab heaters)
30525 Aurora Rd.
Cleveland, Ohio 44139

Hydrozo Coatings Co.
(waterproofing compounds)
855 W St.
Lincoln, Nebr. 68501

Hy-Sil Mfg. Co.
(heat-reflecting materials)

28 Spring Ave.
Revere, Mass. 02151

Instructional Resources Corp.
    (defensive driving course)
251 E. 50th St.
New York, N.Y. 10022

Integrated Container Service, Inc.
    (container leasers)
522 Fifth Ave.
New York, N.Y. 10017

Intelligence Services Products
    Div., Inc. (truck door seals)
6901 Jericho Turnpike
Syosset, N.Y. 11791

Interlease Services, Inc.
    (container leasors)
420 Lexington Ave.
New York, N.Y. 10017

International Computer
    Programs, Inc. (computer
    program exchange)
1119 Keystone Way
Carmel, Ind. 46032

International Council of
    Shopping Centers (energy
    conservation booklets)
445 Park Ave.
New York, N.Y. 10022

International Paper Company
    (shipping bladders)
220 East 42nd St.
New York, N.Y. 10017

Interpool (container lessors)
630 Third Ave.
New York, N.Y. 10017

Kalwall Corp.
    (fiberglass windows)

1111 Candia Rd.
P.O. Box 237
Manchester, N.H. 03105

Keene Corp.
U.S. Route 1
Princeton, N.J. 08540

Kim Hotstart Mfg. Co.
    (starting aids)
W. 917 Broadway, Box 42
Spokane, Wash. 99210

Kool Klutch Mfg. Co.
    (energy conserving fans)
400 E. Vickery Blvd.
Ft. Worth, Texas 76104

Koolshade Corp. (awnings)
1705 Gardena Ave.
Glendale, Calif. 91204

Kru Bur, Inc.
    (ether starting systems)
900 Pingree Rd.
Algonquin, Ill. 60102

Robert E. Lamb, Inc.
    (energy conservation
    consultants)
Valley Forge, Pa. 19481

Thaddeus Lazarr
    (waterproofing consultant)
51–16 Parsons Blvd.
Flushing, N.Y. 11355

Leeds & Northrup Co.
Sumneytown Pike
North Wales, Pa. 19454

Peter F. Loftus Corp.
    (energy conservation
    consultants)
Chamber of Commerce Bldg.
Pittsburgh, Pa. 15219

Master Specialty Co.
445 West Nixon St.
Savage, Minn. 55378

McGraw-Edison Co.
  (power-factor-correction
  capacitors)
Edison Power Systems Div.
Cannonsburg, Pa. 15317

Mileage Consultants
  (fleet discount service)
21111 Chagrin Blvd.
Cleveland, Ohio 44122

Moore Business Forms, Inc.
  (business forms)
1001 Buffalo Ave.,
Niagara Falls, N.Y. 14302

National Association of Fleet
  Administrators, Inc.
  (educational programs)
60 East 42nd St.
New York, N.Y. 10017

National Business Forms
  Association (business forms)
433 E. Monroe Ave.
Alexandria, Va. 22301

National Safety Council
  (defensive-driving course)
425 North Michigan Ave.
Chicago, Ill. 60611

New England Pacific Corp.
  (fiberglass windows)
P.O. Box 292
Lincoln, R.I. 02865

Nieco Products, Inc. (weather
  curtains and air screens)
887 Mitten Rd.
P.O. Box 4506
Burlingame, Calif. 94010

Park-A-Bike Systems
  (lockable bike racks)
Suite 111
180 Cook St.
Denver, Colo. 80206

G. W. Plossl & Co., Inc.
  (inventory control
  consultants)
P.O. Box 32490
Decatur, Ga. 30032

Porter Henry Knowledge
  Resources, Inc. (defensive
  driving course)
103 Park Ave.
New York, N.Y. 10017

Racor Industries, Inc.
  (waste-oil pump)
1137 Barium Rd.
Modesto, Calif. 95351

Radiant Products Co.
  (radiation curing equipment)
6224 S. Oakley St.
Chicago, Ill. 60636

Radiation Dynamics, Inc.
  (radiation-curing equipment)
1800 Shames Dr.
Westbury, L.I., N.Y. 11590

Revere Business Graphics, Inc.
  (business forms)
1123 Broadway
New York, N.Y. 10010

Robertshaw Controls Co.
  (range ignitors)
1701 Byrd Ave.
Richmond, Va. 23261

Rockford Clutch Div.
  Borg-Warner Corp.
  (energy-conserving fans)
1236 Windsor Rd.
Rockford, Ill. 61101

Rudkin-Wiley Corp.
  (drag-reducers)
760 Honeyspot Rd.
Stratford, Conn. 06497

Runzheimer & Co.
  (mileage rate compiler)
Runzheimer Park
Rochester, Wisc. 53167

Sangamo Electric Co.
  (tachographs)
Springfield, Ill. 62708

Sanstruction, Inc.
  (fiberglass windows)
Insulite Div.
6200 Vine St.
Cincinnati, Ohio 45216

Schrader Div., Scovill Mfg. Co.
  (master air gauge)
P.O. Box 586
Dickson, Tenn. 37055

Greg Schultz International
  (inventory control consultants)
New City, N.Y. 10956

Schwitzer Div., Wallace-Murray
  Corp. (energy-conserving fans)
1125 Brookside Ave.
Indianapolis, Ind. 46206

Shelter Shed (storage containers)
P.O. Box 149
San Mateo, Calif. 94401

Sprague Electric Co.
  (power-factor-correction
  capacitors)
481 Marshall St.
North Adams, Mass. 01247

Standard Packaging Corp.
  (heat-reflecting materials)
National Metallizing Div.
Cranbury, N.J. 08512

H. M. Surchin & Co., Inc.
  (used equipment)
11 Lucon Drive
Deer Park, N.Y. 11729

Systems Consultants, Inc.
  (conference call organizers)
2 Pennsylvania Plaza
New York, N.Y. 10001

Systems, Science and Software
  (drag-reducers)
P.O. Box 1620
La Jolla, Calif. 92037

3M Co.
St. Paul, Minn. 55133

Traveletter Corp.
  (travel expense checks)
143 South Beach Ave.
Old Greenwich, Conn. 06870

Truck & Tractor Components,
  Inc. (drag-reducers)
1201 South Mercury Dr.
Schamburg, Ill. 60172

Turner Co.
  (ether starting systems)
821 Park Ave.
Sycamore, Ill. 60178

Uniroyal, Engineered Systems
Dept. (rubberized fabric tanks)
Mishawaka, Ind. 46544

U.S. Flywheels, Inc.
(propulsion systems)
P.O. Box 185
San Juan Capistrano, Calif.
92675

VanDeMark Associates
(inventory control consultants)
P.O. Box 38069
Dallas, Texas 75238

Watkins System, Inc.
(supplier of chauffeurs)
2nd & Palmer Sts.
Chester, Pa. 19016

Westinghouse Electric Co.
(power-factor-correction
capacitors)
Distribution Apparatus Div.
Bloomington, Ind. 47401

Oliver Wight, Inc.
(inventory control consultant)
P.O. Box 435
Newbury, N.H. 03255

Yarway Steam Conservation
Service (energy conservation
consultants)
Blue Bell, Pa. 19422

Zephyr Wind Dynamics Co.
(windmills)
P.O. Box 241
Brunswick, Me. 04011

Index